The Race That Never Ended

The Race That Never Ended

The Making of Ben Hur

Geri Parlby

WHITE OWL
AN IMPRINT OF PEN & SWORD BOOKS LTD.
YORKSHIRE – PHILADELPHIA

First published in Great Britain in 2026 by
White Owl
An imprint of Pen & Sword Books Limited
Yorkshire – Philadelphia

ISBN 978 1 03611 790 0

A CIP catalogue record for this book is available from the British Library.

Typeset by Mac Style
Printed in the UK by CPI Group (UK) Ltd, Croydon, CR0 4YY.

MIX
Paper | Supporting responsible forestry
FSC® C013604

The Publisher's authorised representative in the EU for product safety is Authorised Rep Compliance Ltd., Ground Floor, 71 Lower Baggot Street, Dublin D02 P593, Ireland.
www.arccompliance.com

For a complete list of Pen & Sword titles please contact:

PEN & SWORD BOOKS LIMITED
47 Church Street, Barnsley, South Yorkshire, S70 2AS, England
E-mail: enquiries@pen-and-sword.co.uk
Website: www.pen-and-sword.co.uk
or
PEN AND SWORD BOOKS
1950 Lawrence Road, Havertown, PA 19083, USA
E-mail: uspen-and-sword@casematepublishers.com
Website: www.penandswordbooks.com

Contents

Acknowledgements

Researching the many diverse elements of this book would not have been possible without the help and support of numerous experts and organizations.

My particular thanks go to **Thomas R. Meeks Jr** of the **General Lew Wallace Study & Museum** in Crawfordsville, Indiana – sharing information and images with him has been a real pleasure. **Dr Alex Rich** from the **Ruth Gibson Barnett Museum of Art** at Florida Southern College was most generous with his time and insights regarding the museum's mysterious painting of *The Chariot Race*.

I am also deeply grateful to **Lisa Burton** and **Rebecca Milner** of **Manchester Art Gallery** for providing valuable background information and permission to reproduce Alexander von Wagner's *The Chariot Race*. **José Manuel Sancho** of the **Museo Ulpiano Checa** in Madrid kindly shared images, while **Manuel Carrera** of the **Accademia di Belle Arti di Carrara** provided helpful information. **Grace Hummel** of **Cleopatra's Boudoir** graciously allowed the use of images from her remarkable collection of vintage perfumes.

My thanks also go to **Jon Solomon**, whose research and writing in *Ben-Hur: The Original Blockbuster* remain the definitive guide to all things related to *Ben-Hur* – an invaluable resource for anyone seeking to understand the full scope of this cultural phenomenon.

Finally, I would like to thank **Pen & Sword Books** for agreeing to publish this work: **Olivia Camozzi** for her patience and **Tony Walton** for his encouragement and insightful copy editing.

Introduction

The Race Across Time

Long before Charlton Heston gripped the reins of a thundering quadriga in MGM's legendary 1959 epic, the spectacle of Ben-Hur had already galloped through the cultural imagination of the Western world. The tale's roots reach deep into the nineteenth century, not just with the publication of Lew Wallace's 1880 novel Ben-Hur: A Tale of the Christ, but with earlier visualizations that captured the visceral thrill of ancient Roman chariot racing. Artists painted the drama of wheels and dust, danger and glory, often inspired by classical sources and fed by a growing fascination with the ancient world.

From these early visual interpretations, Wallace's book emerged as both a religious epic and a gripping revenge saga. Its enormous popularity, second only to the Bible in American households for decades, sparked a chain reaction of reinterpretation. The story leapt from the printed page to church halls, theatres and living rooms in the form of readings and tableaux; it was animated in travelling magic lantern shows, then brought to life on the stage in audacious productions that featured real horses galloping on treadmills. Each new format added to the mythos, expanding the reach and resonance of the story.

The advent of cinema brought Ben-Hur to an even broader audience. The 1907 short unauthorized film version changed the face of copyright law. The 1925 silent film dazzled with groundbreaking stunts and vast sets, while the 1959 remake set a new gold standard for Hollywood epics, winning a record-setting eleven Academy Awards. Yet the journey didn't end there. Through television miniseries, animated adaptations, live arena spectacles and even a 2016 cinematic reboot, Ben-Hur has been continually reshaped to reflect the aesthetics, technology and moral questions of each era.

This book traces the remarkable transformation of Ben-Hur from painted fantasy to pop-cultural phenomenon. It follows the story's evolution through shifting artistic mediums, production triumphs and disasters, cultural reimagining and the enduring allure of its central spectacle: the chariot race. In doing so, it also explores what this long journey reveals about our changing relationship with faith, heroism, entertainment and historical reality.

Chapter 1

Before *Ben-Hur*: The Epic Vision Behind 'The Chariot Race'

Our story begins before the birth of Ben-Hur, with a single, breathtaking image: a monumental oil painting measuring 138cm by 347cm that sweeps you into the ancient world, right into the path of a chariot race. Horses thunder across the foreground, charioteers hunched low as reins snap taut, dust exploding in their wake. One driver, clad in red, leans forward with grim determination, while his rival fights to control a team on the verge of collapse. Behind them, wrecked chariots and fallen horses lie scattered as grim reminders of the race's danger. To the right, stands heave with cheering spectators, robes fluttering as they rise to their feet. At the centre of it all, high beneath a richly coloured canopy, the emperor surveys the chaos with imperial calm.

This is The Chariot Race, painted in 1873 by Hungarian artist Alexander von Wagner, a masterwork that distilled nineteenth-century Europe's fascination with classical antiquity. Originally titled The Chariot Race in the Circus Maximus, Rome, in the Presence of the Emperor Domitian, it was conceived on a scale as grand as its subject. The canvas doesn't simply depict a race; it evokes the pageantry, spectacle and power that defined both Roman public life and the era in which the painting was created.[1]

Although the scene is imagined, the painting draws heavily on historical detail. The Circus Maximus, Rome's largest chariot-racing stadium, could seat over 150,000 spectators. Originally built during the early Republic and later expanded by successive emperors, it stood as a powerful symbol of Roman ambition and grandeur. Chariot racing was the Empire's most popular spectacle, its rival factions inspiring fanatical devotion, much like the passion of modern sports fans. Wagner's details, from the vibrant crowd banners to the imperial box, anchor his imagined moment in historical reality.

Chariot racing in Rome was more than sport: it was politics, theatre and spectacle rolled into one. Emperors harnessed the games to project power, placate the masses and showcase Rome's wealth. Rival factions fought for prestige and influence, and the events themselves, fraught with danger and glory, mirrored the values of the Empire: speed, strength, endurance and domination. For ordinary Romans, these races were a chance to witness power in motion.

Wagner captured all of this with painterly precision, weaving together the athleticism of the racers with the wider drama of empire. The stands erupt with energy, the emperor's presence looms large and the architecture itself frames the story. At the centre of the background, a triumphal arch crowned with a bronze charioteer embodies the race's larger meaning: victory not just on the track, but for Rome itself.

Wagner's work stands apart for its sense of motion. Horses leap forward in a dramatic pose beloved by artists of the era, with all four hooves suspended mid-air. This convention, though visually thrilling, was anatomically inaccurate, a fact revealed in 1878 when photographer Eadweard Muybridge – using a pioneering sequence of high-speed photographs – proved that galloping horses gather their legs beneath them rather than stretch them outward.[2] Yet Wagner was less concerned with biological precision than with the rush of speed and danger, and in that, he succeeded. *The Chariot Race* feels almost cinematic, its energy anticipating the very medium that would one day bring ancient Rome and *Ben-Hur* to life.

Some scholars have suggested that Wagner's painting was inspired by Lew Wallace's 1880 novel *Ben-Hur: A Tale of the Christ*, given the iconic race scenes in both. Yet the timeline challenges this: Wagner's original painting dates to 1873, seven years before Wallace's novel appeared.

Wagner's work debuted at the 1873 Vienna World Fair, celebrating Emperor Franz Joseph I's twenty-fifth year on the throne of the Habsburg Empire and drawing millions of visitors. Its popularity led an English buyer to acquire the piece.[3] Later, a New York agency commissioned an expanded version for the 1876 American Centennial Exposition in Philadelphia. Although the expanded painting was twice the original's size and prominently displayed, critics found it 'crude and theatrical'.[4] The work reappeared at the

1893 Columbian Exposition in Chicago, but then faded from view until a damaged canvas surfaced in 2016 at Florida Southern College.[5]

Following *Ben-Hur*'s publication, other artists embraced the chariot race motif. Carlo Ademollo, an Italian painter, created a now-lost work titled *Chariot Race in the Circus at Antioch*, known through widely circulated engravings, one owned by Wallace himself. Spanish artist Ulpiano Checa painted multiple dramatic versions in the 1890s, winning acclaim in Paris and producing sculptures that immortalized the race in bronze.

These powerful nineteenth-century images would profoundly shape how *Ben-Hur*'s chariot race was visualized across media. The 1925 and 1959 film adaptations drew heavily from their dynamic compositions, crowd scenes and sweeping spectacle.

Wagner's original *Chariot Race* now hangs in Manchester Art Gallery, continuing to captivate audiences, while Checa's works are preserved in Madrid.[6] Though Ademollo's painting is lost, surviving etchings keep his dramatic vision alive.

So how did the chariot race paintings become so widely known and influential, especially when the original paintings themselves either ended up in private collections or were lost?

The clue lies with the black and white image of the Carlo Ademollo painting displayed on a shelf in Lew Wallace's office and preserved in a photograph.[7] The image was an etching, a form of printmaking using acid to incise designs on metal plates, the product of a revival of an ancient technique that had its origins in the sixteenth century.

Before widespread photography and modern mass printing techniques, etching allowed artworks – particularly large-scale historical or religious compositions – to reach audiences far beyond the walls of galleries and museums.

This etching revival was not simply nostalgic; it was driven by both aesthetic and practical impulses. Etching offered artists and publishers a means of reproducing highly detailed, expressive images that retained the hand-drawn quality of the original. These prints were typically sold individually or compiled into portfolios and art books, where they provided affordable yet sophisticated alternatives to oil paintings. For collectors, students and culturally engaged households, owning an etching of a celebrated artwork became a mark of both taste and education.[8]

This trend reached American shores just at a time when Lew Wallace had started to write his novels. In the 1870s, two Philadelphia-based portrait painters – Stephen James Ferris and his brother-in-law, Thomas Moran – recognized the untapped potential of etching for art dissemination. They set up their own engraving business, reproducing multiple copies of well-known works of art.

When they heard that Alexander von Wagner's painting *The Chariot Race* had been expanded for the Philadelphia Exposition, they were determined to produce a similarly ambitious etching of the original. Their enthusiasm, however, outstripped the available materials. Lacking a copper plate large enough for the task, they ingeniously fabricated one from the bottom of a copper boiler. The result was a triumph. Their etching of *The Chariot Race* was hailed as a landmark achievement in American printmaking, dubbed 'the most important etching yet produced in America'.[9]

However, etching was labour intensive and soon other more efficient and cost-effective printing methods started to be developed, bringing these famous artworks to an even wider market. This period marked a pivotal moment in cultural history, the beginning of mass art appreciation across all classes.

The new techniques that were beginning to be used included lithography, invented in the late eighteenth century by Alois Senefelder and refined for colour by the mid-nineteenth century, which enabled mass production of affordable art prints. Photogravure and collotype, emerging in the 1860s, used light-sensitive chemicals for greater image fidelity. Chromolithography, using multiple stones for different colours, revolutionized colour reproduction, bringing vibrant, painting-like prints into department stores, bookshops and classrooms.[10]

In Europe and the United States, chromolithographs were sold in mail-order catalogues and department stores like Le Bon Marché or Sears, Roebuck & Co, often marketed as 'art for the people'.[11]

The Victorian middle class eagerly embraced the domestic display of art prints, and hanging them in the home became a statement of taste, piety or emotional sensitivity.[12] Reproductions became a way for individuals to assert cultural literacy and moral identity within the home.[13]

While admired for their craftsmanship, prints of Wagner's *Chariot Race*, along with similar works by artists like Checa and Ademollo, became especially popular in the late nineteenth century thanks to a growing public fascination with action-packed imagery. These dramatic scenes, filled with galloping horses, swirling dust and the chaos of clashing chariots, brought historical spectacle vividly to life. For many, the ability to hang such images in their own homes offered not just decoration, but repeated access to a thrilling visual experience. These works gave viewers the sense of movement and excitement that would later become central to cinema long before film existed.

This growing appetite for dramatic storytelling through art created fertile ground for narratives that could capture the same intensity in words. Audiences were already enthralled by grand historical settings and scenes of peril and triumph, and soon, writers would rise to meet that demand. In the summer of 1876, as crowds marvelled at Wagner's *The Chariot Race* at the Centennial Exposition, a former Civil War general named Lew Wallace was quietly beginning a very different kind of race, one of imagination, scholarship and spiritual inquiry, that would lead to the creation of *Ben-Hur*.

Chapter 2

Ben-Hur: A Tale of Christ – The Book That Changed Everything

Underneath the quiet canopy of Midwestern trees, General Lew Wallace was sketching the outline of a book that would, against all odds, become one of the most influential novels in American history. He would name it *Ben-Hur: A Tale of the Christ.*[1]

Lewis 'Lew' Wallace was not a man easily categorized. Born in Brookville, Indiana, in 1827, he was the son of David Wallace, a prominent politician who served as governor of Indiana and briefly as a US congressman. Yet young Lew's path would take him far beyond the boundaries of conventional public service.[2]

Restless and intellectually curious, Wallace left formal education at the age of 16. He worked as a copyist in the county clerk's office and dabbled in journalism, briefly writing for the *Indianapolis Daily Journal.* After a short foray into newspaper editing, he turned to law, not out of passion but pragmatism. Still, adventure called. When war broke out between the US and Mexico in 1846, Wallace enlisted. The experience ignited his lifelong fascination with military service. Upon returning home, he resumed legal practice and entered state politics, serving in the Indiana Senate in the 1850s.[3]

Wallace's legal career resumed intermittently after the war, but law never truly captured his imagination. In his early 20s, he served as a prosecuting attorney in Covington, Indiana, but his greater passions – military affairs, history and literature – pulled at him persistently.[4]

When the Civil War erupted in 1861, Wallace was among the first to answer the call. He joined the Union Army and rose quickly through the ranks, becoming a major general at the age of 34, one of the youngest in the Union Army.[5] Under General Ulysses S. Grant, Wallace saw action at Fort Donelson and later at Shiloh, where his career took a blow.

Ordered to support Grant, Wallace's division arrived late, leading to questions about his competence and commitment. Grant and others accused him of disobedience, though Wallace always insisted he had followed his orders and had been misled by ambiguous instructions. He spent much of his life trying to clear his name. Historians have since re-evaluated Wallace's performance at Shiloh, suggesting that the confusion stemmed more from poor communication than negligence on his part.[6]

Later in the war, Wallace redeemed himself during the 1864 Battle of Monocacy in Maryland. Though his forces were defeated by General Jubal Early, Wallace delayed the Confederate advance long enough to allow Union reinforcements to arrive and protect Washington, DC. This earned him praise from military leaders and President Abraham Lincoln, who reportedly said, 'General Wallace, you saved the capital.'[7]

After the war, Wallace resumed his legal career but found the daily grind tedious. To distract himself, he took up writing. His first published work, *The Fair God* (1873),[8] a romanticized historical novel about the Spanish conquest of Mexico, demonstrated his flair for dramatic storytelling. Though not a bestseller, it earned respectable reviews and encouraged Wallace to keep writing.[9]

Wallace's true literary calling, however, would arise from a seed planted years earlier, a short story he had written about the Three Wise Men's journey to find the infant Jesus. The story of the arrival of the wise men, which appears only in the Gospel of Matthew, had fascinated him as a child. Matthew refers to them as Magi from the East bearing gifts of gold, frankincense and myrrh. Wallace had been inspired to write the story as a way of expanding on the vagueness of Matthew's account. In his tale, he elaborates on their number, names, origins, appearance, mode of transportation and religious backgrounds.[10]

That tale had sat quietly, unpublished, in his desk drawer. But everything changed one night in 1876 during a chance encounter on a train with Robert Green Ingersoll, the famed orator, Civil War veteran and self-proclaimed 'Great Agnostic'.

The two men debated fiercely. Ingersoll's eloquence and scepticism shook Wallace to his core. 'He vomited forth ideas and arguments like an intellectual volcano,' Wallace later wrote. Wallace, a Christian by culture if not by deep understanding, realized he couldn't defend his own faith. That night marked a turning point.[11]

Resolved to educate himself, Wallace became immersed in theological study. He began by studying the *Bible* intensively. He focused on both the Old and New Testaments, not only to understand the life of Christ but also to capture the mindset of the Jewish people under Roman occupation. He also consulted apocryphal and extra-biblical sources, as well as theological texts, to understand the culture, rituals and prophecies relevant to Judaism and early Christianity.[12]

He read the *Bible* with fresh eyes, not as dogma, but as narrative. He sought to understand the cultural, political and historical world in which Jesus of Nazareth had lived. He studied ancient Roman military practices, Jewish customs, Middle Eastern geography and even the agricultural cycles of first-century Palestine. Institutions like the Library of Congress in Washington, DC, became his intellectual sanctuaries.[13]

The work was exhaustive. He researched chariot designs and ancient sports in Greek and Roman cultures, along with ancient nautical practises relating to Roman galleys and trireme ships. He looked closely at Roman military customs and rankings, studied religious rites and Roman jurisprudence, and even analysed period-specific garments and food alongside Middle Eastern flora, fauna and geography.[14] With his research completed, Wallace then began to write, first beneath a beloved beech tree near his home in Crawfordsville, Indiana. His tools were simple: a wooden lap desk, pen and sheaves of paper.[15]

However, his book had to take second place to his public service duties. In 1878, President Rutherford B. Hayes appointed him governor of the New Mexico Territory, a role he held until 1881. Despite the demands of the job, Wallace kept working on his book, often writing late at night by oil lamp. He did this even while tackling the region's violence, including the Lincoln County War, a land dispute involving infamous outlaws such as Billy the Kid.

Billy the Kid, a 21-year-old outlaw whose real name was William H. Bonney, agreed to testify in exchange for a pardon from Wallace, but the pardon never came. After being sentenced to hang, Billy escaped jail, killing two deputies and threatening Wallace, before being shot dead by Sheriff

Pat Garrett. Wallace later had mixed feelings, but he believed his actions were justified.[16]

In one letter to his wife, Wallace summarized the chaos of his daily life: 'I am trying to do four things: First, manage a legislature of most jealous elements; second, take care of an Indian War; third, finish a book; fourth, sell some mines.'[17]

Despite the many demands on his time, Wallace remained dedicated to his writing. Without a typewriter or assistant, he painstakingly completed the manuscript by hand in purple ink, finishing it in 1883. When he delivered it by train to Harper & Brothers in New York, the publisher reportedly remarked: 'This is the most beautiful manuscript that has ever come into this house.'[18]

The finished novel, titled *Ben-Hur: A Tale of the Christ*, is a sweeping historical epic set in the early first century CE. Blending adventure, political intrigue, spiritual transformation and the story of Jesus Christ, it follows Judah Ben-Hur, a Jewish prince betrayed and cast into slavery. His journey from suffering to redemption unfolds alongside the rise of Christianity and the profound message of Jesus of Nazareth, creating a narrative that resonated deeply with readers.

Wallace structured the story into eight books, seven of which reveal a different phase in the life of Ben-Hur.

Part One: The Nativity

In the deserts of the East, three wise men – Balthasar, an Egyptian; Melchior, a Hindu; and Gaspar, a Greek – gather, drawn together by a shared vision. Each has seen a brilliant star in the sky, a divine sign guiding them westward toward Judaea. United by purpose, they embark on a journey across the desert in search of the prophesied Messiah.

Meanwhile, Mary and Joseph approach Jerusalem on their way from Nazareth to Bethlehem. Turned away at the inn due to overcrowding, Mary, in labour, finds refuge in a hillside cave, where she gives birth to Jesus. Nearby, shepherds tending their flocks witness a vision of angels announcing the Saviour's birth. They rush to the cave to worship the newborn child, later spreading the news throughout the region.

The three Magi arrive in Jerusalem, seeking the new king. Their inquiry disturbs Herod the Great – the Roman client king of Judea – who consults the Sanhedrin, the Jewish assembly. The priests point to the prophecy of Micah, identifying Bethlehem as the Messiah's birthplace. Alarmed, Herod orders his advisors to monitor the situation, while the Magi continue their journey to Bethlehem.

Part Two: Betrayal and Enslavement

Judah Ben-Hur, a Jewish prince of noble lineage, lives in Jerusalem. His childhood friend, Messala, returns from five years of education in Rome, now fully loyal to the Empire. The two clash. Ben-Hur remains devout and nationalistic, while Messala is arrogant and imperialistic. Their friendship ends in enmity.

Soon after, Roman governor Valerius Gratus visits Jerusalem. As he passes Ben-Hur's home, a loose tile falls from the rooftop and strikes him. Though the act is accidental, Messala seizes the opportunity to destroy Ben-Hur, accusing him of attempted assassination. Ben-Hur is arrested without trial, his family imprisoned and their property confiscated. As he is led away in chains, he vows revenge. On the way to a Roman galley, a young carpenter, Jesus, offers Ben-Hur water, leaving a profound impression.

Part Three: Redemption at Sea

Ben-Hur endures three years as a galley slave aboard Roman warships. Quintus Arrius, a Roman commander battling pirates, takes note of his resilience and intelligence. During a naval battle, Ben-Hur saves Arrius from drowning after their ship is destroyed. Grateful, Arrius adopts him, granting him freedom and Roman citizenship.

Part Four: Return to the East

Years later, now a respected Roman citizen, Ben-Hur journeys to Antioch, capital of Rome's province of Syria. There, he finds Simonides, a former servant of his father, who has safeguarded and grown the Hur family's wealth.

Though initially sceptical of Ben-Hur's identity, Simonides begins to believe him. His agent, Malluch, befriends Ben-Hur and confirms his story.

Ben-Hur learns that Messala is in Antioch, preparing for a prestigious chariot race there. Seeking revenge and justice, he partners with the wealthy Sheik Ilderim and offers to race his team of horses against Messala. Balthasar and his daughter, Iras, also in Antioch, encounter Ben-Hur. Balthasar shares the story of the Magi and speaks of a coming Messiah, whom he believes is now a man.

Part Five: The Chariot Race

As Ben-Hur prepares for the race, he learns that his mother and sister were imprisoned in the Antonia Fortress in Jerusalem. He also learns that they may still be alive but afflicted with leprosy. Meanwhile, Messala publicly denounces Ben-Hur, attempting to shame him as a criminal and traitor. Malluch arranges a large wager that will financially ruin Messala if he loses.

On race day in Antioch, Ben-Hur and Messala fiercely compete. Messala, attempting to sabotage Ben-Hur, is instead thrown from his chariot and trampled. Ben-Hur wins the race and earns public acclaim. Messala survives, broken in body and fortune.

Later, Ben-Hur is lured to the Roman palace under false pretences and ambushed by Thord, an assassin. He survives the attempt and retreats to the desert with Sheik Ilderim to plot a campaign against Rome.

Part Six: Reunion and Loss

With the help of Simonides and a bribe to the new Roman prefect, Pontius Pilate, Ben-Hur discovers that his mother and sister were hidden in a sealed prison cell and afflicted with leprosy. Released but shunned, they return secretly to their old home, where Amrah, a faithful servant, finds them and protects them in secret.

Ben-Hur becomes a local hero by killing a Roman soldier during a massacre of Jewish protesters. Galilean rebels begin to rally around him. Still searching for a greater purpose, he joins forces with Simonides and Ilderim to plan a resistance.

Part Seven: The Christ Revealed

Ben-Hur travels to Bethabara to hear John the Baptist preach. There, he recognizes Jesus, the man who once gave him water. Balthasar proclaims Jesus the Christ. Ben-Hur becomes a devoted follower, recognizing Jesus as a spiritual leader rather than a military one.

Back in Jerusalem, Ben-Hur reunites with his mother and sister, who are healed by Jesus during his triumphal entry into the city. Joy and faith fill the household. However, Iras reveals her love for Messala and her disillusionment with Jesus as a political saviour. She warns Ben-Hur that he has misplaced his hopes.

Part Eight: The Crucifixion and Aftermath

Ben-Hur witnesses Jesus' betrayal in Gethsemane. He tries to intervene but is too late. The next day, he watches in sorrow as Jesus is crucified. At the foot of the cross, Ben-Hur offers Jesus a final act of kindness, giving him vinegar in a gesture of remembrance. Through Jesus' death, Ben-Hur finds spiritual awakening and commits his life to the risen Christ.

Years later, Ben-Hur and Esther – the daughter of Simonides – are married and living in Misenum in Italy. They, along with Simonides and Malluch, have dedicated their wealth to supporting the early Christian Church. Learning of the persecution of Christians under Nero, they move to Rome and establish an underground church, the future Catacomb of Callixtus.[19]

In Wallace's story, Ben-Hur's journey from betrayal and revenge to faith and forgiveness reflects the novel's deeper spiritual message. Wallace contrasts the fleeting power of Rome with the eternal power of Christ's love: where Rome conquers through force, Christ redeems through grace.

It was a powerful work, but initially the novel was not a runaway success. It sold fewer than 3,000 copies in its first seven months, but momentum grew. By 1883, it had surpassed *Uncle Tom's Cabin* in sales, becoming the best-selling American novel of the nineteenth century, a record it held until *Gone with the Wind* appeared in 1936. It seemed that the novel's vivid depiction of the life of Christ and its morally uplifting story had resonated with a post-Civil War American public yearning for spiritual grounding and redemption.

Wallace was initially surprised by the book's success, having not anticipated that a historical novel steeped in religious themes would captivate the American public. He was even more amazed that in 1886, sales were averaging 50,000 copies a year.[20]

Influential endorsements helped. Ulysses S. Grant reportedly read it for thirty hours straight, and President James Garfield praised it in a glowing letter after reading it in stolen moments between meetings.[21] As a token of his appreciation, Garfield appointed Wallace as US Minister to the Ottoman Empire.[22]

Wallace served as US Minister to the Ottoman Empire until 1885, living in the heart of Constantinople – now Istanbul – during a pivotal moment in Middle Eastern history. The once-mighty Ottoman Empire was grappling with internal decline and mounting pressure from European powers, creating a complex and volatile diplomatic landscape.

Wallace returned to the United States in 1885 and settled in Crawfordsville, Indiana, where he had long maintained a residence. There, he constructed a lavish study, known today as the General Lew Wallace Study & Museum. The study became a sanctuary for his writing and intellectual pursuits. Wallace was deeply committed to education and often hosted writers, artists and intellectuals at his home.[23] Though now in semi-retirement, Wallace remained active in public life. He continued to write and speak, and his status as a national figure ensured he was consulted on political and military matters.

Wallace also took *Ben-Hur* on the road with a national lecture tour, while Harper & Brothers fuelled its momentum with an ambitious marketing blitz. The results were staggering: between December 1886 and December 1888, the novel sold nearly 200,000 copies. Harper capitalized on the craze with a stream of abridged, adapted and illustrated editions designed for audiences ranging from children to church groups. They even turned parts of the novel into stand-alone books. *The First Christmas* (1899) brought the Magi and Nativity scenes to readers as a holiday keepsake, while *The Chariot Race* (1912) celebrated the novel's most famous sequence, paired with striking illustrations by Sigismond Ivanowski. *Ben-Hur* had become more than a book; it was a cultural phenomenon.[24]

Harper published a 'Garfield Edition' of *Ben-Hur* in 1892, a luxurious two-volume set that included Garfield's letter praising the book. It was priced at an extravagant $30.[25]

When President Garfield appointed Lew Wallace as US Minister to Turkey, he encouraged him to research and write another novel during his time there. Confident in Wallace's talent, Harper & Brothers gave him a $500,000 advance. The result was *The Prince of India: or Why Constantinople Fell*, published in 1893.[26]

Despite the main title, the novel has little to do with India; the subtitle better reflects its story, which is set in the years leading up to the fall of Constantinople in 1453. The titular 'Prince of India' is actually the legendary Wandering Jew in disguise.

The Wandering Jew was a popular figure in nineteenth-century fiction, based on the myth of a man cursed with immortality after mocking Jesus on the way to Golgotha. According to legend, Jesus declared, 'Tarry thou until I come', condemning the Jew to wander the earth forever, witnessing countless deaths of loved ones over centuries.

In *The Prince of India*, the Wandering Jew is a vengeful character who arrives in Constantinople to propose a vision of a one-world religion to the emperor. When ignored, he instead became allies with Sultan Mehmed II, aiding in the capture of the city. Afterwards, the Wandering Jew is transformed into a younger version of himself and sets off on new, unrecognized adventures.

Though fictional, Wallace grounded the novel in historical events and figures, including the real siege of Constantinople in 1453. At the time of its publication, Wallace considered this his best work, even more so than *Ben-Hur*. Unfortunately, both critics and the public largely disagreed; one fan even boldly wrote to Wallace suggesting he should have stopped writing after *Ben-Hur*.[27]

Alongside writing novels, Wallace also published numerous essays, speeches and short stories. He continued to lecture around the country, often speaking on topics related to literature, the *Bible*, American history and the Civil War.

In 1893, Wallace published an article in *Youth's Companion* titled '*How I Came to Write Ben-Hur*'. Some details in this account did not fully align with official records or actual dates, but Wallace, ever the storyteller, had a flair for the dramatic. Like many nineteenth-century public figures, he was deeply conscious of his legacy and public image. His revisions and embellishments were likely attempts to shape how history would remember him.[28]

Meanwhile, *Ben-Hur* continued its extraordinary rise. By 1900, the novel had appeared in thirty-six English-language editions and had been translated into more than twenty languages, including Indonesian and Braille.[29] Although Wallace lived for twenty-five years after the book's debut, it was *Ben-Hur* that ultimately defined his legacy. More than a bestseller, it became a cultural touchstone, resonating deeply with America's spiritual consciousness and continually finding new life through numerous adaptations.

When Wallace died in February 1905 at the age of 77, he was celebrated as a national hero. Tributes poured in from across the country, honouring his service as a general, diplomat and author. He was laid to rest in Oak Hill Cemetery in Crawfordsville, Indiana.

His autobiography, *Lew Wallace: An Autobiography*, was published posthumously in 1906. Compiled from his own writings and edited with the help of his widow, Susan Arnold Elston Wallace – a noted writer and poet in her own right – the book included a revised version of '*How I Came to Write Ben-Hur*'.[30].

What accounted for *Ben-Hur*'s enduring appeal? Wallace's genius lay in his ability to weave together gripping adventure and profound religious themes. At a time when novels were often viewed with suspicion as morally questionable, *Ben-Hur* won widespread praise from the clergy, even receiving the personal approval of Pope Leo XIII.[31] Remarkably, Jewish readers also embraced the story; characters like Ben-Hur and Esther offered rare, respectful portrayals of Jewish identity during an era marked by growing antisemitism.[32]

But *Ben-Hur* soon became more than just a bestselling novel. Sears, Roebuck & Co reissued a million copies as part of the Wallace Memorial Edition, packaged in an ornate box featuring Ulpiano Checa's dramatic 1890 painting of the famous chariot race.[33] By the early twentieth century, *Ben-Hur* merchandise was everywhere, from coffee tins to bicycles. Entire fraternal organizations, such as the Tribe of Ben-Hur, were even formed in its name.[34] This was the dawn of mass advertising and the rise of visual culture. Paintings by artists such as Wagner and Checa were reused to sell everything from flour to sheet music.[35]

With trademark law still in its infancy, Wallace had little power to stop the commercial exploitation of his work. *Ben-Hur* had become a brand unto itself and America simply couldn't get enough.

Chapter 3

How the Birth of Christianity and the Roman Empire shaped Nineteenth-Century Storytelling

Lew Wallace wasn't alone in choosing to set his story in the early era of Christianity. In the nineteenth and early twentieth centuries, people in Britain and America became fascinated with the origins of Christianity. This was a time of religious revivals, social changes and growing interest in how faith could fit into a rapidly modernizing world. For many writers and readers, the Roman Empire – with all its drama, decadence and power – was the perfect setting to explore big questions about belief, morality and transformation.

Several novels from this period used the clash between pagan Rome and early Christianity to powerful effect. Alongside *Ben-Hur* (1880) were books like Edward Bulwer-Lytton's *The Last Days of Pompeii* (1834), Cardinal Nicholas Wiseman's *Fabiola* (1854) and Henryk Sienkiewicz's *Quo Vadis: A Narrative of the Time of Nero* (1896).

In Britain, movements such as Evangelical revivalism and the Oxford Movement encouraged people to look back at the early Church for inspiration and guidance.[1] In the United States, the 'Second Great Awakening' stirred up religious enthusiasm and a renewed focus on personal salvation.[2] These social and spiritual shifts helped create a receptive audience for stories set in ancient Rome, where faith was often tested in the face of persecution and empire.

Each of these novels brought something unique to the table. Bulwer-Lytton's *The Last Days of Pompeii* used the eruption of Mount Vesuvius to symbolize the end of paganism and the rise of a new spiritual age.[3] Wiseman's *Fabiola* focused on the courage of early Christians, showing them as heroic martyrs.[4] *Ben-Hur* mixed action and adventure with a heartfelt Christian message that appealed to a wide American readership.[5] And Sienkiewicz's *Quo Vadis* explored the tension between cruel Roman authority and Christian forgiveness, earning it global fame.[6]

The Last Days of Pompeii

First published in 1834, *The Last Days of Pompeii* quickly became one of the most influential historical novels of its time. It didn't just tell a gripping story; it also used the past to reflect on moral questions that were still relevant. By setting his novel just before the eruption of Mount Vesuvius in 79 CE, Edward Bulwer-Lytton gave readers a vivid and suspenseful picture of Roman life right before disaster struck. But the real drama isn't just in the ash and fire, it's in the spiritual awakening that comes from catastrophe.

Bulwer-Lytton was a hugely popular writer in his day. Though his dramatic prose style has sometimes been mocked (he is famous for coining the phrase 'It was a dark and stormy night'), his books were widely read and respected. He had a talent for combining sensational plots with big ideas – politics, philosophy and the occult were all fair game. With *Pompeii*, he found a way to blend archaeological fascination with moral storytelling.

Interest in ancient Rome was running high in the 1830s, thanks in part to new excavations at Pompeii and Herculaneum. Bulwer-Lytton saw a chance to turn this interest into something more than just historical curiosity. Inspired by his own trip to Naples and the powerful painting *The Last Day of Pompeii* by Russian artist Karl Bryullov, he set out to write a story that would entertain and provoke thought. He even dedicated the novel to Sir William Gell, a leading archaeologist on the Pompeii excavations, to underline its connection to real history.[7]

The novel follows Glaucus, a charming and idealistic Greek living in Pompeii. He's in love with Ione, a smart and noble Roman woman, but their happiness is threatened by the sinister Arbaces, an Egyptian priest who represents the darker side of pagan religion. Arbaces wants Ione for himself, and he'll go to terrible lengths, including framing Glaucus for murder, to get what he wants.

Another major character is Nydia, a blind slave girl who secretly loves Glaucus. Her love is unreturned, but her courage and loyalty shine through.

She plays a key role in rescuing Glaucus and Ione during the eruption, and her tragic fate adds emotional weight to the story.

There's also a Christian subplot, though it's not the main focus. Characters like Olinthus represent the quiet strength and moral clarity of early Christians, who live in stark contrast to the selfishness and cruelty of Roman high society. They don't have much power, but they are shown as spiritually rich, offering hope, compassion and a sense of purpose that the Roman world lacks.

When the volcano finally erupts, it's not just a natural disaster, it's a judgment. The world of Pompeii, with all its wealth and corruption, is literally buried under ash. Arbaces meets a fitting end, swallowed by the earth in a moment that feels almost biblical. Glaucus and Ione escape and later convert to Christianity, marking a personal transformation that mirrors the larger shift from paganism to Christian faith.

Although *The Last Days of Pompeii* isn't preachy, it's full of Christian symbolism. The eruption stands in for divine judgment. The Christians are small in number but strong in virtue. Arbaces, as a pagan priest, is the very picture of spiritual emptiness. And Nydia, blind yet wise, represents the idea that true vision comes from the heart.

The book's message is clear: even in a world that seems ruled by power and pleasure, truth and goodness can still survive and even triumph.

Fabiola: or The Church of the Catacombs

In 1854, Cardinal Nicholas Wiseman, a leading figure in Britain's Catholic revival, published *Fabiola: or The Church of the Catacombs*, a historical novel that blended early Church history with an impassioned defence of Catholic tradition. Far more than just an entertaining story, *Fabiola* was written with a clear mission: to show readers, especially British ones, that Catholicism was not a foreign relic, but the authentic expression of the Christian faith, stretching all the way back to the martyrs of ancient Rome.

Cardinal Wiseman was not your average novelist. Born in Seville in 1802 and educated in Rome, he was a theologian, scholar and, later, the first Archbishop of Westminster. His appointment came after the restoration of the Catholic hierarchy in England in 1850, a controversial move that triggered waves of anti-Catholic outrage. Dubbed 'Papal Aggression' by Protestant critics, the event became a flashpoint in British religious and political life.[8]

Wiseman's response was not a public tirade or theological treatise, but something quieter and arguably more powerful: a novel. In his own words, he hoped *Fabiola* would 'depict the Church of the Catacombs, as a living and suffering body, illustrating by example the doctrines and practices which she now maintains'.[9] It was, in short, a story designed to teach and inspire, a literary argument for the continuity, sanctity and heroism of the Catholic faith.[10]

Set during the final years of Roman persecution in the early fourth century, just before Emperor Constantine's conversion, *Fabiola* follows its namesake, a wealthy and proud Roman noblewoman. She lives in a society where Christianity is still illegal, yet quietly spreading among slaves, soldiers and intellectuals alike.

At first, Fabiola dismisses Christianity as a superstition. She is a product of her class and culture: elegant, intelligent and used to privilege. But her world begins to shift as she observes the lives of those around her, especially her cousin, Agnes, a gentle and devout Christian, and her servant, Syra, a secret believer whose quiet strength begins to open Fabiola's eyes.

The turning point in the novel is not just intellectual but deeply emotional. Fabiola witnesses the trials, suffering and ultimately the martyrdom of people she loves. Through their courage, she comes to see Christianity not as weakness, but as a source of astonishing inner strength. By the end of the novel, she has not only converted to the faith she once mocked, but has become one of its most steadfast defenders.

What sets *Fabiola* apart from other historical novels of its time is its deep reverence for Catholic tradition. Wiseman fills the story with vivid descriptions of early Christian worship. There are masses held in catacombs by candlelight, communities bound together by love and shared sacrifice, and saints who give their lives joyfully for a truth they believe eternal.[11]

The novel includes real historical figures such as St Agnes, St Sebastian and St Pancras, interwoven with fictional characters. Their stories, often ending in martyrdom, are not presented as tragedies but as triumphal proof of unshakable faith. The Roman catacombs themselves, only recently rediscovered under the streets and roads of Rome, become a symbol of the Church's resilience: humble, hidden but enduring.

In *Fabiola*, martyrdom is not something to be pitied. It's a sacred act, a final witness to truth and a challenge to the corruption and cruelty of Rome. Through this lens, the early Church is not a persecuted minority hiding in fear, but a bold and unified body of believers lighting the darkness with hope.

Fabiola was an immediate success. It was translated into many languages and became a fixture in Catholic homes and schools around the world. For English-speaking Catholics often living in predominantly Protestant countries, the novel served as both spiritual encouragement and historical validation. It reminded them that their faith had deep, ancient roots, and that the sacrifices of the past gave them strength to face the challenges of the present.

The book's popularity also reflected a broader trend. As Europe wrestled with modernity, industrialization and religious doubt, historical novels about the Roman Empire and the birth of Christianity provided both escapism and moral instruction. Readers were drawn to stories where courage, conviction and faith won out over tyranny and doubt.

Quo Vadis: A Narrative of the Time of Nero

By the late nineteenth century, Christian historical fiction had gained widespread popularity, reflecting growing concerns not just about modernity and secularism, but also political instability. Published in 1896, *Quo Vadis,* by Polish author Henryk Sienkiewicz, became an international success. Blending romance, politics and religion, the novel spoke to its contemporary audience while exploring themes of spiritual change that still resonate today.[12]

The title *Quo Vadis*, Latin for 'Where are you going?', refers to an early Christian legend. As St Peter fled Rome to avoid persecution, he met the risen Christ, who told him, 'I am going to Rome to be crucified again.' Peter, ashamed, returned to face martyrdom. This moment captures the central themes of *Quo Vadis:* the struggle between fear and faith, authority and conscience, excess and redemption.

Set in the decadence of Nero's Rome, *Quo Vadis* introduces readers to Marcus Vinicius, a Roman military officer of privilege, and Lygia, a young

Christian woman held as a political hostage. At first, Vinicius views Lygia through the lens of Roman entitlement, someone to be won, controlled, possessed. But Lygia's serene virtue, shaped by her hidden Christian faith, begins to unsettle and ultimately transform him.

As Marcus' infatuation grows into genuine love, he begins to question his own beliefs and those of Roman society, a culture built on power, entertainment and violence. His encounters with Peter and Paul, set against the backdrop of Christian persecution, reflect his gradual shift from Roman values to Christian faith.

At the centre of the story is Nero: vain, unpredictable and dangerous. His court is filled with figures like the philosopher Petronius, whose sharp wit highlights a society that values appearance over meaning.

When Rome burns in the Great Fire, historically blamed by Nero on the Christians, the persecution begins. Lygia is captured and sentenced to die in the arena, tied to a wild bull in a cruel public spectacle. In a dramatic climax, she is rescued by Ursus, her enormous, gentle protector, whose strength and loyalty symbolize the quiet power of the faith the Empire tries to crush.

The novel ends not with political victory, but with spiritual triumph. Nero may command armies, but it is the Christians – beaten, imprisoned and murdered – who claim the higher ground. Their endurance signals the coming fall of the old Rome and the quiet rise of a new, redemptive order.

When Henryk Sienkiewicz created *Quo Vadis*, he was not writing in peace or comfort. Born in 1846, he lived in a partitioned Poland under foreign rule, dominated by the Russian Empire. For Sienkiewicz and his readers, Rome's tyranny was not ancient history, but a metaphor for the political oppression they knew firsthand.[13]

Unable to write openly about Poland's struggle for freedom, Sienkiewicz turned to ancient history. In the Christians of *Quo Vadis*, he found moral heroes who defied empire with faith. In Nero's court, he offered a subtle yet searing critique of totalitarian power. The novel became, for Polish readers, a kind of coded prayer: a hymn to national survival through spiritual strength.[14]

Quo Vadis was an immediate international success. Translated into more than fifty languages, it captivated readers across Europe, America and beyond. Its grand scope and moral clarity made it ideal for stage adaptations and, eventually, film.

In the United States, the novel was promoted as a defence of Christian values amid increasing secularization. In Britain, it was seen as a companion to *Fabiola* and *Ben-Hur*, contributing to the growing genre of 'early Church fiction'. Its popularity extended even into missionary and educational circles.

When Sienkiewicz was awarded the Nobel Prize in Literature in 1905, it wasn't just for his storytelling. It was for his ability to inspire, to dignify the downtrodden and to elevate the past into a weapon of moral resistance. The Nobel committee praised him 'because of his outstanding merits as an epic writer', but to his fellow Poles, he was something more: a voice of faith under fire.[15]

Chapter 4

Readings, Tableaux and Pantomime

As the phenomenal success of *Ben-Hur* captivated readers nationwide, requests to transform the novel into a stage spectacle flooded in. Yet Lew Wallace and his publisher stood resolute, refusing every proposal. At the time, the theatre was viewed with disdain by the Church and the more refined segments of society. A play that featured the story of Christ would have been hugely controversial. Even Lawrence Barrett, America's most celebrated stage actor, eager to craft a theatrical extravaganza out of Wallace's epic, was turned away.[1]

But perhaps there was more to Wallace's refusal than mere religious caution. By this point, he had his own ambitions for the stage and was already working on a play about the scandalous Roman Emperor Commodus. Could it be that Wallace was saving *Ben-Hur* for his own grand vision, wanting to control how his cherished story leapt from page to stage?[2]

Whatever the reason, all requests to adapt *Ben-Hur* for the stage were ignored for the next several years. But the stage wasn't the only form of popular entertainment at the time. Another craze was sweeping the country: the art of recitation.

Recitation was more than simply reading aloud, it was the dramatic performance of written works, most often poetry or stirring prose. Practitioners combined literature with the techniques of public speaking, delivering their lines with carefully rehearsed rhythm, emotion and stage presence. A skilled reciter could captivate an audience as powerfully as a stage actor. By the late nineteenth century, this blend of art and oratory had become one of the most widely enjoyed and respected forms of entertainment across all levels of society.

The popularity of recitation reflected the period's deep appreciation for literature and moral instruction. It was seen as a way to shape character, improve speaking abilities and develop emotional awareness. Children learned to recite in school, often using pieces from Shakespeare, Tennyson or moral verse by poets such as Longfellow. Adults participated too, gathering in parlours for 'recitation evenings', where moving speeches or sentimental poems were often the highlight of the gathering.

By the late 1880s, public recitations and live readings of *Ben-Hur* were becoming increasingly popular. These performances took place in a wide variety of settings, from school assemblies and charity fundraisers to public halls and church services.[3]

One passage stood out above all others: Wallace's electrifying account of the chariot race. It became a staple in classrooms and on community stages, captivating audiences with its drama and energy. Churches also embraced the novel, with some even substituting Wallace's moving description of the Crucifixion for a traditional sermon.[4]

Alongside recitation, another captivating performance art was rising in popularity: the *tableau vivant*, or 'living picture'. In a *tableau vivant*, actors in elaborate costumes would pose in complete stillness, often within a frame, to recreate famous artworks, literary scenes or historical events. Each 'picture' lasted about thirty seconds before fading into the next, creating a striking illusion of paintings brought to life.[5]

Although the form peaked in the nineteenth century, its roots stretched back to ancient Greece and Rome, where performers portrayed gods or mythic heroes in ceremonial scenes.[6] During the Middle Ages, *tableaux* appeared in church plays and processions as frozen biblical scenes designed to teach and inspire largely illiterate audiences.[7] By the Renaissance, they had evolved into royal entertainments, with costumed actors and theatrical backdrops recreating historical or mythological moments.[8]

A pivotal figure in shaping the modern *tableau vivant* was Lady Emma Hamilton, wife of diplomat Sir William Hamilton and mistress to British naval hero Admiral Horatio Nelson. Her celebrated 'Attitudes', performed in Naples in the late eighteenth century, were a series of silent poses inspired by classical art. Using only a shawl and dramatic lighting, Hamilton transformed herself into figures like Cleopatra or Medea, captivating audiences with the sheer emotion of her gestures.[9]

Hamilton's performances fused neoclassical elegance with Romantic intensity, paving the way for the widespread popularity of *tableau vivant* as a Victorian-era art form.

In nineteenth-century England, *tableaux* became especially popular as domestic entertainment, particularly among women. Amateur performers would recreate scenes from Shakespeare, the *Bible* or famous novels or paintings, often as part of school exhibitions, charity events or holiday gatherings. These performances combined culture, morality and creativity.[10]

The trend crossed the Atlantic in 1831, when an English actress performed a *tableau* based on Ary Scheffer's painting 'The Soldier's Widow' at New York City's Park Theatre. It caused a sensation, and soon *tableaux* performances were appearing in American homes and church halls across the country. Women were the main performers, the focus on grace, poise and controlled expression reflecting nineteenth-century ideals of femininity and propriety.[11]

Ben-Hur would become a perfect vehicle for this new fashion of *tableaux* performances, the first versions starting to appear in the mid-1880s not long after the book was first published. They combined the essence of *tableau vivant* alongside recitation of passages from the book. These performances – often staged in schools, churches or reform societies – featured static representations of scenes such as the Nativity or the meeting of the Magi. Costumed amateurs posed in frozen compositions while a narrator read passages from Wallace's text.

One forward-thinking lady called Ellen Knight Bradford was so delighted by the reaction to her *Ben-Hur tableaux* charity event in 1887 in Washington, DC, that she decided to take it on the road. She even went so far as registering her performance with the Copyright Office, calling it *Selections from Ben-Hur Adapted for Readings with Tableaux*. She went on to tour multiple cities, but never once credited Lew Wallace or even asked his permission.[12]

Bradford, a natural at PR, would 'alert the media', placing adverts and newspaper articles in local newspapers well before her arrival in the town. The events were promoted as fundraisers for local charities. Her show became an instant sensation wherever it toured, largely due to her shrewd strategy of enlisting local performers from the city's elite. By rebranding the event as 'An Evening with Ben-Hur', she captivated audiences with a sophisticated allure. She provided exquisite costumes, and in each city, seventeen distinguished ladies and gentlemen elegantly posed in thirty distinct scenes from the novel. The two-hour spectacle mesmerized audiences, bridging the gap between regular theatregoers and devout churchgoers who typically shunned the stage as sinful. In Philadelphia alone, the production drew over 3,000 spectators, eager to witness the grandeur and artistry of this living storybook.[13]

Reviewers lavished praise on the production, commending the *tableaux* performers for their poised and remarkably steady poses, free from any noticeable trembling or involuntary movements. The recitationists were equally lauded for their skill and emotive power. In Detroit, Gertrude Marchand garnered particular acclaim, celebrated as a 'recitationist of power and discernment'. Apparently, her reading of Wallace's gripping description of the chariot race was so masterfully delivered that the audience leapt to its feet, clamouring for an encore. The elegance of the costumes and the striking presence of the actors themselves drew admiration, with the *Boston Globe* noting the 'tableau vivant, where beautiful girls, adorned in the splendor of oriental costumes and finery, played prominent roles', adding a vibrant allure to the performance.[14]

In 1888, a performance in Indianapolis marked the first step toward what would become a lucrative marketing ploy. A local clothing store used the name *Ben-Hur* to promote its clothing line, capitalizing on the popularity of 'An Evening with *Ben-Hur*'.[15] Everyone seemed to adore the production; everyone except Lew Wallace. He was understandably furious. Bradford had not asked his permission and had also failed to credit him as the author of the book. The show's success quickly attracted imitators, with other *tableaux* entrepreneurs launching their own versions, some seeking approval and others not.

Determined to see the spectacle for himself, Wallace slipped into the Indianapolis theatre unannounced and hid in the back row. What he witnessed left him outraged. In a scathing report to his publishers, he described the costumes as 'both absurd and beggarly cheap', and urged Harper & Brothers to investigate possible copyright infringement immediately.[16]

As upset as he was to see his story performed without credit, the experience gave him pause. Watching audiences so captivated by the visual dramatization of his novel made him reconsider his original decision to ban theatrical adaptations. It was the first step toward eventually allowing *Ben-Hur* to take the stage in a more official and authorized form.

Wallace returned home to Crawfordsville and began discussions with a local company about creating a more refined charitable production. This new performance would carry Wallace's personal seal of approval. He planned to oversee every aspect, from advising on costumes and scenery to shaping the script itself.

Once the arrangement was finalized, it developed into a full-scale travelling show, with Wallace granting the company a forty-year exclusive license. He claimed royalties of 5 per cent of the revenue from charitable shows and 6 per cent from commercial ones. He also included many conditions within the licence, including a restriction against portraying the figure of Jesus in any form.[17]

The company, which later became known as Clark and Cox, fiercely protected their rights, effectively keeping potential competitors at bay. As a result, Mrs Bradford's 'An Evening with Ben-Hur' gradually faded into obscurity.

The Clark and Cox production was titled *Ben-Hur in Tableaux and Pantomime*. The term '*Pantomime*' referred to a distinctive form of dramatic entertainment with roots in Roman mime, where performers used expressive gestures accompanied by music to tell the story. This was entirely different from the English tradition of Christmas Pantomime, which focused on children's fairy tales, cross-dressing and slapstick comedy.[18] Clark and Cox's version stood out because of its higher production values and closer collaboration with Wallace, which lent it an air of authenticity and prestige that Bradford's production lacked.

In 1889, *Ben-Hur in Tableaux and Pantomime* went on tour. Lafayette W. Seavey, a leading American scenic artist and theatrical designer, created the sets. Seavey had transformed theatrical production by developing a lightweight, portable system ideal for travelling shows. The costumes were designed to Wallace's exact specifications, and the production featured cutting-edge limelight technology for dramatic visual effects.

Although more than 250 people contributed to the show's creation, only ten members of the company travelled with it. The rest of the cast was recruited locally at each stop, often drawing from prominent members of the community. This strategy not only kept costs down but also boosted the show's popularity, as local audiences were eager to see familiar faces performing on stage.[19]

The show originally opened with fourteen distinct *tableaux*, culminating in a breathtaking depiction of the chariot race complete with live horses, an extraordinary addition to the *tableau vivant* tradition. Over time, the production expanded to include new sequences, featuring elaborate dance routines inspired by mythology and exotic scenarios with evocative titles such as *Arabian Girls' Frolic*, *Egyptian Fandango* and *Priestess Scarf Dance*. Additional scenes from the original novel were also incorporated, making the show even more dynamic and immersive.[20]

The production was a resounding success, touring the country for an impressive ten years. After a decade on the road, Wallace decided to conclude his business partnership with Clark and Cox, paving the way for the next chapter in the *Ben-Hur* story.

Chapter 5

Ben-Hur in Light and Shadow: The Magic Lantern Controversy

Despite Wallace's concerns about the integrity of his novel, adaptations in various forms continued to thrive, and the next challenge he had to face was the magic lantern.

Magic lantern shows had first emerged in the seventeenth century. Christiaan Huygens, a Dutch scientist, is often cited as the first person to describe and possibly build a working magic lantern in the 1650s. Though Huygens considered the lantern more a scientific curiosity than a form of entertainment, others quickly realized its potential as a tool for public spectacle. Around the same time, Athanasius Kircher, a German Jesuit scholar, published the first known illustration of a magic lantern in his 1671 book *Ars Magna Lucis et Umbrae* ('The Great Art of Light and Shadow'). Though it remains unclear whether Kircher built a working model, his book introduced the concept to a wider audience, and his description included a method for projecting demonic images to 'instill fear and wonder'.[1]

The lantern worked initially using a candle, a concave mirror to reflect and direct the light, a glass slide painted with an image and a lens to focus the projected picture onto a screen or wall. Over time, these components were refined, with candles replaced by oil lamps.

By the eighteenth century, the magic lantern had transitioned from a scientific tool into a popular medium for public entertainment and education. Travelling lanternists toured throughout Europe, staging elaborate performances that combined projected images with music, narration and occasionally live actors or sound effects. These shows captivated both elite and common audiences, signalling a broader democratization of visual culture.[2]

One of the most dramatic and theatrical uses of the magic lantern emerged in the phantasmagoria shows of the late eighteenth and early nineteenth centuries. Created by Belgian physicist and showman Étienne-Gaspard Robertson, phantasmagoria employed rear projection, movable lanterns and smoke screens to conjure ghostly apparitions and eerie illusions, thrilling audiences with the spectacle of seemingly supernatural visions.[3]

By the mid-nineteenth century, magic lanterns had become common fixtures in classrooms and lecture halls across Europe and North America. They were used to teach a wide range of subjects, from geography and biology to history and social reform. Churches adopted them to illustrate biblical stories and convey moral teachings. Their vivid imagery helped make complex or abstract ideas more accessible, especially for younger audiences. Missionaries used lanterns to visually communicate Christian doctrine in their efforts abroad.

Scientific and academic communities also embraced the lantern. Scholars, explorers and lecturers used lantern slides to present discoveries and research to the public, combining education with entertainment. Institutions like the Royal Institution in London regularly featured lantern projections in their public lectures and demonstrations.[4]

The introduction of photographic slides in the 1850s marked a significant advancement, enabling the projection of realistic, documentary images. This development greatly expanded the lantern's role in both education and visual communication, bridging the divide between art and scientific accuracy.

As the century progressed, the technology behind the magic lantern continued to evolve. A popular innovation featured dual-lantern systems with overlapping lenses, allowing for seamless transitions between images, such as a sunset fading into moonlight or a war-torn landscape giving way to peace. Ingenious slide mechanisms introduced motion through levers and rotating disks, simulating animation with scenes of rolling waves, moving trains or walking figures. Combined with narration and sound effects, these shows became early examples of multimedia storytelling. Later advancements included lanterns equipped with three optical systems and the widespread use of photographic glass slides, further enhancing their visual and narrative capabilities.[5]

While England had established a strong lantern-manufacturing industry, it was in the United States that the medium was more aggressively commercialized, beginning in the 1850s. American innovators developed the stereopticon, an advanced version of the magic lantern that incorporated limelight, superior lenses and dissolving views. This enhanced device quickly became central to a thriving national lecture circuit.[6]

Recognizing the growing potential of the American market, Riley Brothers, founded in the 1870s in Bradford, Yorkshire, strategically opened a branch office in New York. Renowned for their precision optical equipment and expansive slide libraries, the company produced series on a wide array of subjects, including religion, travel, science and social reform. Many of their slides were meticulously hand-coloured and paired with lecture scripts, allowing even non-experts to deliver compelling presentations.[7]

By this time, popular literary works such as *A Christmas Carol* by Charles Dickens and *The Pilgrim's Progress* by John Bunyan were being adapted into illustrated slide shows. These visual retellings offered audiences a new way to engage with literature, often experiencing these stories visually for the first time. In both Britain and America, magic lantern adaptations of *Uncle Tom's Cabin* by Harriet Beecher Stowe became fixtures of abolitionist lectures as well as religious and educational events, blending narrative power with social messaging.[8]

Ben-Hur was an ideal story to adapt into a lantern show, and by the 1890s, stereopticon slide presentations based on the novel had begun to appear across America. These shows were often independently produced by religious lecturers or educators, who used hand-painted or photographic slides to bring key scenes from the book to life. Many adopted a distinctly devotional tone, highlighting Ben-Hur's spiritual transformation and aligning the story with Christian evangelism.[9]

Such presentations were especially popular in churches and YMCAs, where vivid visual depictions of Christ's life and the Roman world were considered both morally uplifting and spiritually enriching.

Riley Brothers saw a far more commercial opportunity, and in 1896 they adapted the story using state-of-the-art three-lens lantern technology, enabling layered visuals and transitions, dissolving views, live music and sound effects such as thunder or hoof-beats. Their presentation lasted for two hours and included seventy-two hand-painted slides depicting various scenes from the novel, created by two different artists. The first twenty-five slides were made by Frank F. Weeks, who used his patented technique that involved photographing human models and then heavily reworking the image by painting.

A promotional item published in the *Optical Magic Lantern Journal* boasted that the slides were produced from 'living Jewish models' in Weeks' Leytonstone studio. Perhaps due to cost concerns, Weeks was replaced midway through the production and the remaining forty-seven slides were painted by illustrator Nancy 'Nannie' Preston. The slides were sold together with a forty-page printed 'reading' to accompany the presentation. The reading consisted of paragraphs of condensed versions of Wallace's descriptions of the scenes depicted.

Riley Brothers distributed this set across the United States, both directly and through a network of dealers, supported by a wide range of advertisements. Each show was carefully packaged as a special event, complete with printed programmes, souvenir booklets and, in some cases, lantern operators dressed in costume. These touches transformed every presentation into a fully immersive storytelling experience.[10] Riley Brothers also took the additional step of registering *The Stereopticon Illustrator of 'Ben-Hur': A Tale of the Christ* at the Library of Congress, further protecting and legitimizing their product.[11] This thoughtful marketing and branding strategy not only elevated the quality of the shows but also significantly boosted their popularity, making them a sought-after form of entertainment for communities across the country.

If Riley's promotional claims were accurate, their slide shows were being sold not only across the United States but also in Britain, Canada, Australia, New Zealand, South Africa and India.[12]

Wallace first became aware of the emerging threat posed by stereopticon slide shows when he began receiving unexpected requests from venues hosting these presentations. They were asking for a slide of him in uniform to include in their lantern shows. Outraged, Wallace turned to his publisher, Harper, demanding action. Harper, in turn, delegated the matter to Walter Clark of Clark and Cox. Clark enlisted the help of Augustus T. Gurlitz, a seasoned copyright attorney, who issued a stark warning: unless immediate action was taken to stop the Riley Brothers, 'the country will be overrun with these performances'. His concerns would soon prove valid.[13]

To Wallace, these unauthorized stereopticon adaptations were a clear violation of his literary copyright and any potential stage rights he might license. He also feared that the shows would 'cheapen the work'. For Clark, however, the concern was less about artistic integrity and more about profit. He saw the rising popularity of lantern shows as a serious threat to the lucrative *tableaux* market he relied on. Determined to protect his business interests, Clark became the driving force behind what would become a groundbreaking legal battle.

He did some undercover digging and even purchased a set of the Riley slides along with the script. When he asked the sellers about their popularity, they told him: 'The demand is so high, we just can't keep up.' It was disturbing news for Clark, Wallace and Harper.[14]

It then became clear that the only way to protect both Wallace's creative rights and Clark's commercial interests was to challenge the stereopticon shows through the courts, even if that meant pushing the limits of existing nineteenth-century copyright law. The resulting case, '*Wallace v Riley*', was unprecedented. At its core was a pivotal legal question: could a series of projected images based on copyrighted work, paired with a narrated text, be considered an unauthorized adaptation under the law?[15]

The case argued that Riley Brothers' *Ben-Hur* lantern show was a derivative work, infringing on Wallace's rights as the original author. Wallace contended that even a dramatized visual adaptation, even if presented through static images, transformed his literary creation into a new form of expression that required his explicit permission.[16]

Riley Brothers and their defenders argued that their *Ben-Hur* show was educational and religious in nature, designed for church groups and schools. They contended that the use of illustrations to support *Bible* lectures or Christian moral education fell within the 'fair use' tradition, particularly since many churches viewed such shows as spiritual enrichment, not commercial theatre.

Moreover, Riley Brothers claimed that they were not reproducing the text of the novel verbatim but merely interpreting scenes visually, with a lecturer providing narration. This, they argued, was akin to an illustrated lecture or religious sermon, not a theatrical adaptation requiring performance rights.[17]

At the time of the dispute, US copyright law was still evolving. The Copyright Act of 1870 protected literary works and dramatic compositions, but the definition of derivative works and the rights of authors over adaptations were not clearly delineated. The law did not yet fully anticipate multimedia adaptations, which combined images, narration and performance.

There was no established legal precedent to determine whether projecting visual scenes from a novel constituted a violation of an author's exclusive right to dramatize their work. This legal ambiguity made it difficult for Wallace to assert his claims in court, even though his moral and commercial arguments were compelling.[18]

The case was complex. After considerable debate, Harper and Wallace succeeded in securing an injunction against the unauthorized forty-page reading, but not against the lantern slides themselves. Nevertheless, the impact was significant. By 1902, Riley Brothers had begun quietly withdrawing *Ben-Hur* from their catalogues, and magic lantern companies that later offered similar material typically sought permission from Wallace's estate or publisher.[19]

Wallace's determined defence of his creative rights proved to be a resounding success. His steadfast insistence on authorial control, backed by the threat of legal action, prompted a significant shift in industry practices. By the time of his death in 1905, Wallace had firmly established himself as the guardian of *Ben-Hur*'s adaptations and ensured that his story was respected and carefully managed across print, stage and emerging visual media.[20]

The dispute with Riley Brothers stands as one of the earliest instances of an author asserting control over how their work was adapted into new media formats. While Wallace's legal victory was limited and somewhat informal, it set a vital precedent by demonstrating that writers could actively influence the interpretation and use of their creations across emerging multimedia platforms.

More than just a clash over lecture slides, the copyright battle between General Lew Wallace and the Riley Stereopticon Company signalled the need for intellectual property laws to evolve alongside new forms of visual storytelling. Wallace's determined stance anticipated the increasing importance of authorial control in the expanding world of mass media. This episode reveals that debates around adaptation, fair use and ownership were already taking shape well before the advent of cinema, occurring at the early intersection of literature, technology and the law. Importantly, it also laid the foundation for future copyright battles in the emerging film industry; battles that, fittingly, would once again involve *Ben-Hur*.[21]

Chapter 6

God, Glory and Galloping Horses: The Theatrical Rise of *Ben-Hur*

By the late nineteenth century, *Ben-Hur* had become a cultural sensation, inspiring *tableaux vivant* and magic lantern shows across the United States. As public appetite grew, requests for a full-scale stage adaptation multiplied. Still, Wallace resisted. He was deeply sceptical that *Ben-Hur* could succeed theatrically, not just artistically but morally. The theatre, he believed, still carried the stigma of being incompatible with religious themes, especially among 'God-fearing folk' who had long viewed it as immoral. Wallace feared that adapting a deeply Christian story for the stage might be seen as an insult to the Church.[1]

But why had the theatre earned such a poor reputation on both sides of the Atlantic?

In eighteenth-century England, the theatre was notoriously unruly, but it became increasingly regulated in the early 1800s. The Licensing Act of 1737, introduced under Prime Minister Robert Walpole, had restricted spoken drama to two 'patent theatres' in London: the Theatre Royal, Drury Lane, and the Theatre Royal, Covent Garden. Walpole's move was largely political; he saw satirical plays as a threat to his authority and the dignity of the monarchy. A particularly scandalous play, *The Golden Rump*, was said to depict the queen administering enemas to the king, and though its authorship remains unknown, it was enough to spark the crackdown.[2]

Theatres outside this duopoly were limited to illegitimate forms: melodramas, burlesques, pantomimes and musical entertainments. These genres became especially popular among the working classes, further cementing the theatre's low reputation among the middle and upper classes. It wasn't until the Theatres Act of 1843 that the performance of serious drama was legalized in a broader array of venues.[3]

Across the Atlantic, American theatre had fewer formal restrictions, but just as much controversy. In the early nineteenth century, its audiences were known for their unruly behaviour. While the elite occupied the pit and private boxes, the upper galleries were dominated by boisterous crowds. Audience members routinely heckled poor performances, booed actors and even hurled objects at the stage, especially when English actors were involved.[4]

In 1831 and 1832, New Yorkers rioted over rumours that English actor Joshua Anderson had insulted Americans during his voyage to the US. Just two years later, another incident erupted when English stage manager William Farren was overheard cursing the 'Damn Yankees'. The uproar was only quelled when Farren appeared onstage, waving an American flag and offering a public apology.[5]

The violence reached a tragic climax on 10 May 1849, when actor William Macready, half English and half Irish, chose to perform *Macbeth* at New York's Astor Place Opera House despite widespread protests. Chaos erupted. Clashes broke out inside and outside the theatre. Troops were eventually called in, and when they opened fire on the crowd, twenty-two people were killed and more than 100 injured.[6]

Beyond the violence, American theatres were also notorious for moral lapses. In the early nineteenth century, the upper balconies of New York theatres were known haunts for prostitutes, and these same sections were often the only seats affordable to young boys. This convergence of vice and youth fuelled fierce condemnation from both pulpits and the press.[7]

Religious institutions, especially the Catholic Church, played a major role in condemning theatre as a corrupting influence. Clergy warned that theatrical performances distracted from spiritual duties, labelling actors as 'instruments of Satan'. In the United States, the American Tract Society, a prominent evangelical organization, declared the theatre a 'school of vice and debauchery'. Theatres, often located near saloons, gambling houses and brothels, only reinforced this perception.[8]

Actors themselves held a complicated social status. To moralists like those in the Tract Society, they were the epitome of licentiousness. Yet by the mid-nineteenth century, actors were also beginning to achieve celebrity status, even among the upper classes.[9]

One of the loudest and most influential voices in theatre's rehabilitation was Charles Dickens. A lifelong lover of the stage, Dickens defended theatre as a morally enriching and intellectually engaging art form. Through his novels, performances and public readings, he championed a more dignified and respectable view of theatrical culture.[10]

Beginning in the 1850s, Dickens toured Britain and America giving dramatic readings of his work. These performances blurred the line between literature and theatre, helping elevate public perceptions of the stage.[11]

Still, suspicion of religious drama – particularly depictions of Jesus – remained deeply rooted in evangelical circles. Many Christians, especially Protestant evangelicals, considered it blasphemous for any actor to impersonate Jesus on stage. That controversy erupted in 1879 in San Francisco when dramatist Salmi Morse staged a Passion Play featuring a live crucifixion. The performance provoked riots, and the actor playing Jesus was arrested and carted off to jail still wearing a halo.[12]

This longstanding taboo made the figure of Jesus a major sticking point for anyone hoping to bring *Ben-Hur* to the stage, and on this point alone Wallace was immovable. Convincing him that there could be a solution would require not just tact, but true theatrical ingenuity. That challenge was taken up by two shrewd entrepreneurs: Marc Klaw and Abraham Lincoln Erlanger.

Klaw, a trained lawyer and former theatre critic, partnered with theatre manager Erlanger in 1888 to purchase a New York booking agency. By the early 1890s, Klaw & Erlanger had become major theatrical producers, but they needed a grand, ambitious production to really cement their reputation. The obvious choice for such a production was *Ben-Hur: A Tale of the Christ*, still an international bestseller.

Jesus was a central figure in *Ben-Hur* and omitting him from the stage adaptation was not an option. Yet portraying him onstage posed a serious dilemma: how could they depict him without inviting accusations of blasphemy?

The solution came through Joseph Brooks, a seasoned Broadway producer brought in by Klaw & Erlanger to help realize the production. In a later interview, Brooks recalled how the idea came to him one afternoon while sitting in his darkened study, smoking a cigar. As sunlight streamed through the shutters, the beam caught the drifting smoke, causing it to shimmer and dance in the air. In that moment, Brooks envisioned a solution: instead of using an actor, Jesus would appear as a glowing, abstract presence created with light and atmosphere rather than flesh and blood.[13]

Wallace was reportedly moved by the concept, finally convinced that the religious core of his novel would be handled with due reverence. He may also have been swayed by Klaw & Erlanger's more tangible incentive, which involved a generous share of the profits.[14]

With Wallace's blessing, production moved swiftly. The team enlisted William Young, a respected playwright, to adapt the novel. Young spent two days with Wallace at his home in Crawfordsville to outline his vision for the stage adaptation. Wallace was impressed, and Young completed a six-act script in just two months.[15]

Directing fell to Ben Teal, a veteran of the Broadway stage, known for his discipline and skill in managing large, complex productions. Teal was the ideal choice to oversee scenes like the naval battle and the legendary chariot race, which would go on to become one of the most iconic moments in stage history.[16]

The cast included a relatively unknown actor, Edward Morgan, as Ben-Hur, and William S. Hart as Messala, both delivering performances that resonated with audiences. Although Morgan portrayed Ben-Hur for just one season before fading into obscurity, Hart's stage success marked the beginning of a pioneering career in early American cinema. He went on to become a silent film actor, screenwriter and director, as well as one of the first major stars of the Western film genre.[17]

The next challenge Klaw & Erlanger faced was more practical: how could they possibly stage a full-scale, life-or-death chariot race, or even a no-holds-barred sea battle, on a theatre stage? The chariot race, being central to the plot, was essential and could not be omitted.[18]

Surprisingly, the practical obstacles were not insurmountable. By the late nineteenth century, theatrical production techniques had become remarkably sophisticated. Theatre has always been a medium rooted in illusion and spectacle. From ancient Greek amphitheatres – where mechanized devices like the *deus ex machina* allowed gods to descend dramatically onto the stage – to trapdoors and rolling platforms enabling sudden appearances and swift scene changes, ingenuity had long shaped theatrical storytelling.

By the seventeenth century, stage designers were employing machines and effects to simulate natural phenomena like waves, thunder and lighting transitions. Italian architect Nicola Sabbatini developed early lighting techniques, including dimming mechanisms and directed spotlights.[19]

The late eighteenth and nineteenth centuries saw a boom in immersive visual entertainments collectively known as the 'Orama craze'. These included panoramas, dioramas, cosmoramas, cycloramas and other large-scale spectacles. The craze began with the panorama, patented in 1787 by Robert Barker, who created vast, 360-degree paintings displayed inside circular buildings that completely surrounded viewers. Over time, panoramas evolved from static images to dynamic presentations, using long scrolls of painted canvas or paper unrolled between spools to create the illusion of motion and travel, often accompanied by narrators describing each unfolding scene.[20]

In 1822, French artists Louis Daguerre and Charles-Marie Bouton introduced the diorama, adding new sensory dimensions to the Orama format. These enormous translucent paintings were viewed in rotating auditoriums and dramatically lit from different angles using natural light manipulated through screens, shutters, curtains and coloured filters. This technique allowed for striking transformations, with sunsets fading to night or volcanoes erupting before the audience's eyes.[21]

The innovations of the Orama era transformed theatrical stagecraft. Daguerre's lighting effects, which convincingly shifted scenes from dawn to dusk, laid the foundation for gas lighting, limelight and eventually electric lighting in theatres. These technologies gave stage designers unprecedented control over mood and time-of-day effects.[22] Orama artists also pioneered new scenic painting techniques, including *trompe-l'œil* backdrops, angled flats and other visual tricks to create deeper, more realistic environments, which heavily influenced theatre design.

One of the most popular innovations was the moving panorama, a staple of nineteenth-century theatre. This device gave the illusion of motion long before the advent of cinema, carrying audiences past storm-tossed ships, bustling cities or rolling countryside. The moving panorama brought a sense of visual continuity and narrative flow that foreshadowed the immersive qualities of film.

As audiences grew accustomed to this level of spectacle and realism, their expectations pushed theatres to adopt ever more elaborate special effects. Smoke machines, thunder sheets, trapdoors and mechanical lifts were introduced to recreate the awe once inspired by panoramas and dioramas, raising the visual standard of theatre for generations to come.[23]

The moving panorama became a staple of nineteenth-century theatre, offering the illusion of motion long before the advent of cinema. With this device, audiences could witness ships crossing turbulent seas or carriages rolling through pastoral landscapes, introducing a seamless sense of narrative movement. It brought a new level of visual continuity to the stage that foreshadowed the immersive qualities of film.

One of the standout moments in *Ben-Hur* was the dramatic galley battle, a thrilling sequence that depicted a naval clash and Ben-Hur's heroic rescue of Arrius. While earlier nautical dramas like *The Tempest* or *Black-Eyed Susan* featured storm scenes and basic wave effects, *Ben-Hur* took things much further. Its battle scene was more technologically advanced, narratively integrated and visually immersive than anything that had come before.[24]

The production used movable ship interiors, synchronized sound and lighting, and detailed set pieces to fully immerse audiences in the chaos of naval combat. The stagecraft created the sensation of being at sea, not just watching a performance. Ships were mounted on spring-loaded platforms or pivoting bases to mimic the swaying of vessels on rough water. Actors playing chained galley slaves rowed in rhythm as the ship rocked with their motion. Painted cloth 'waves' were pulled back and forth by stagehands beneath the set, simulating the rolling sea. Blue lighting and steam enhanced the illusion, enveloping the stage in an eerie, oceanic atmosphere.[25]

A mechanical 'crash machine', hidden backstage, was used to mimic the sounds of ship collisions, including splintering wood, creaking hulls and clashing timbers, all produced through precisely timed metal impacts and percussion effects.

The entire sequence was meticulously choreographed. It began with Arrius standing above the rowing galley slaves on a raised platform at centre stage. As the battle escalated, the lights suddenly cut to black. The audience was plunged into darkness, surrounded by screams and the deafening chaos of battle. Then, as the lights returned, Ben-Hur and Arrius were revealed adrift at sea, perched on a rocking raft high above the stage, with a dramatic shipwreck scene unfolding behind them.[26]

This seamless transformation happened in full view without a curtain drop. It demanded extraordinary precision. The crash machine continued to rumble, masking the movement of actors and crew. As the lights went out, galley slaves dropped flat while their benches were swiftly removed. Ben-Hur and Arrius climbed to the central platform, which was then converted into a floating piece of wreckage.[27]

Simultaneously, one team lifted the painted backdrop of the galley to reveal the shipwreck behind it, while another crew dragged a large canvas to the front of the stage, covering the fallen slaves. Hidden beneath it, the actors used their oars, limbs and bodies to simulate the motion of rolling waves. The entire scene change, executed in near-total darkness with dozens of moving parts, was completed in roughly seven seconds, with no one missing a cue or colliding on stage.[28]

The sea battle in *Ben-Hur* was a triumph of stagecraft, but the *pièce de résistance* was undoubtedly the chariot race, one of the most remarkable theatrical spectacles ever staged. While elements such as moving panoramas, wind machines and mechanical platforms had been used in Victorian melodrama, no production prior to *Ben-Hur* had combined live animals, mechanized sets and realistic effects with such precision and scale. Even circuses and hippodrome shows, where live horses were common, had never attempted this level of integration into a narrative play. The chariot race was truly a theatrical first.

Each chariot was pulled by four live horses positioned on treadmills embedded in the stage. These treadmills allowed the horses to gallop in place while the set moved around them, generating the illusion of forward momentum. The chariots were mounted on rollers or electrically powered devices that spun their wheels, contributing to the kinetic energy of the scene without actual movement across the stage.[29] A rotating curved panoramic backdrop, featuring the tiers of seats at the Antioch Circus full of cheering crowds, moved in the opposite direction of the horses' motion, heightening the illusion of speed as the scenery appeared to whizz past.

To enhance the realism, blowers under the floor forced powder up through the treadmill to resemble dust. The roar of the crowd, the pounding of hooves and the clashing wheels were created using backstage machinery, metal sheets, rolling drums and custom-built crash boxes, all designed to intensify the action. Lighting was used strategically, both to dramatize key moments and simulate motion and danger.

The stage had to be reinforced with steel to support the live animals and machinery. Specialized crews trained the horses and managed the synchronization of the treadmills, while dozens of stagehands, mechanics, lighting technicians and animal handlers coordinated each performance.[30] Despite the immense complexity, the production ran almost faultlessly, even during Messala's dramatic wreck, achieved through a clever engineering trick. Only Ben-Hur's chariot wheels made contact with the treadmill, while Messala's rested on a spring-loaded yoke that kept his wheels slightly above the track. A motor spun his wheels, and at the climactic moment, a small electric motor blew off his wheels, allowing the chariot to drop onto the yoke. The treadmill and adjacent floor carrying Messala then jerked back 15 feet, permitting Ben-Hur to surge ahead and win.[31]

It was a breathtaking effect, providing the audience with five minutes of nail-biting action. William S. Hart, who played Messala in the original production, described the machinery as 'a gargantuan mass of wheels, boards and steel cables'. He recalled the atmosphere: 'The whirring of the treadmills, the machinelike cracking of our whips, the pounding of the horses' rubber-shod hoofs ... the noise was deafening – the applause was thunderous.' According to Hart, the mechanism worked perfectly in 399 of 400 performances. On the one occasion Messala accidentally won because the electric motor had failed, the actors simply carried on as though Ben-Hur had triumphed.[32]

The play was a phenomenal success, selling approximately 25,000 tickets per week. It ran on Broadway for twenty-one years and toured extensively across the country. The musical score by Edgar Stillman Kelley played a vital role in the show's emotional impact, underscoring dramatic and spiritual moments. Despite its significance, Kelley sold the rights for only $750, missing the financial windfall that followed.[33]

With a cast and crew numbering in the hundreds, only major venues in cities such as Boston, Philadelphia, Baltimore and Chicago could host the production. Audiences from nearby towns often took special trains to attend performances. Touring required two dedicated trains: one for personnel and another for animals, costumes, scenery, and equipment.[34]

Inevitably there were a few incidents with the animals. In Chicago, two of the horses dressed in race regalia bolted into the street at the entrance to the theatre and had to be rounded up by members of the public. In Baltimore, the girls from the chorus took to feeding Bluch the camel so many sweets that the poor beast eventually keeled over and died. The horses became so well trained that their handler insisted on shipping them over to England for the Drury Lane performance in 1902, believing that American horses could learn tricks faster than any other equine nationality.[35]

Some large theatres commissioned asbestos stage curtains painted with Alexander von Wagner's *Chariot Race* to promote the show. When *Ben-Hur* travelled internationally, key roles were cast locally. Among the most prominent was the English actress Constance Collier, who played the temptress Iras. She was so in demand that she performed in both *Ben-Hur* and *Ulysses*, dashing between Drury Lane and His Majesty's Theatre during performances. Collier later transitioned to film, becoming a screenwriter, script doctor and acting coach.[36]

The London production was even more ambitious than its American counterpart. At Drury Lane, the chariot race featured sixteen horses, double the usual eight, though, as we have seen, every animal and piece of equipment had to be shipped across the Atlantic from the United States.

Critical opinions were mixed, but the public and the Royal Family were captivated. King Edward VII and Queen Alexandra were so eager to experience the spectacle that a special box was built for them in the pit, allowing them to watch the chariot race at close range.[37]

As in the United States, *Ben-Hur* became a runaway success in London. Rival theatres struggled to compete, with many forced to close temporarily due to dwindling audiences. The producers capitalized on this popularity by limiting the number of touring cities each season and raising ticket prices, intentionally framing the show as a rarefied, elite event.[38]

A sophisticated marketing machine supported the production. Striking lithographs of the chariot race, the sea battle and the Star of Bethlehem appeared everywhere, alongside souvenir programmes, postcards and photographic editions of the novel. Touring companies were bolstered by advance agents who organized parades, secured church endorsements and staged public rehearsals, ensuring that *Ben-Hur* remained both a cultural event and a must-see theatrical phenomenon.[39]

Ben-Hur was more than just a spectacle. For the first time, opening-night audiences included clergymen, a rare sight in the early twentieth century, when theatre was often viewed with moral suspicion. This shift was the result of a bold marketing strategy by Klaw & Erlanger, who deliberately targeted Christian audiences. They secured endorsements from popular evangelist Billy Sunday and leaders across Protestant and Catholic communities, promoting the play as a moral and religious experience rather than mere entertainment. To reinforce this message, the book's full title, *Ben-Hur: A Tale of Christ*, was prominently displayed on all posters and promotional materials.[40]

The campaign went even further, framing the production as almost divine. Advertisements claimed its success stemmed from the presence of Christ's spirit during performances, likening the play to a sermon with the power to inspire spiritual conversion. At the same time, they reached out to Jewish audiences, gaining a public endorsement from Rabbi Samuel Hirshberg that was published in Yiddish newspapers.[41]

This inspired approach paid off. *Ben-Hur* became the most successful stage production of its era, seen by more than 20 million people and grossing over $10 million between 1899 and 1920, an unprecedented achievement at the time.[42]

The play's enormous profits propelled Klaw & Erlanger into the national theatre industry, where they joined forces with Charles Frohman, Al Hayman, Samuel Nixon and Fred Zimmerman to form the powerful Theatrical Syndicate. This group quickly gained control over American theatre, establishing an exclusive booking network that determined which shows could be performed, where and under what terms.[43] Klaw & Erlanger alone managed bookings for hundreds of venues, creating a centralized system that improved touring efficiency but severely limited creative freedom. Those unwilling to comply with the Syndicate's terms were effectively shut out of the country's major stages.

This monopolistic control soon provoked a backlash. The Shubert Brothers emerged as a formidable rival, offering an alternative circuit and opening doors for independent artists. Their competition gradually dismantled the Syndicate's dominance, paving the way for a more artist-driven theatre industry.[44]

The legacy of Klaw & Erlanger is therefore complex. On one hand, profits from *Ben-Hur* helped modernize American theatre, with nearly $1 million invested in upgrading venues across the country. On the other, their consolidation of power sparked a cultural rebellion that reshaped the future of theatrical freedom for generations to come.[45]

As *Ben-Hur*'s theatrical legacy reshaped the American stage, another revolution in storytelling was already underway. Audiences who had once marvelled at moving panoramas and mechanized chariot races would soon be introduced to a new form of spectacle, one that could capture motion itself. The invention of cinema promised to combine the immersive power of theatre with the portability and reach of emerging technologies. And as with every previous medium, *Ben-Hur* was destined to play a pivotal role in shaping this next great leap in popular entertainment.

Chapter 7

The Birth of Cinema

While the *Ben-Hur* theatrical extravaganza was reshaping the American stage, the moving image was undergoing its own turbulent evolution. This was not the result of a single, groundbreaking invention but rather a chain of experiments and cultural shifts unfolding across Europe and America. And just as *Ben-Hur* had dominated literature and theatre, Wallace's novel would soon leave its mark on this emerging medium, helping to shape the very future of cinema.

The roots of that future can be traced back to 1830, when a young Edward James Muggeridge left Kingston upon Thames in England to begin a new life in America as a bookseller. A devastating stagecoach accident left him with a severe head injury and a dramatically altered personality. Reinventing himself, he changed his name to Eadweard Muybridge, abandoned bookselling and devoted himself to photography. Working under the pseudonym 'Helios', Muybridge became renowned for his breathtaking panoramic landscapes, often risking his life to capture the perfect shot while experimenting with new photographic techniques.[1]

As we saw in Chapter 1, Muybridge's most famous experiment occurred in 1878 when Leland Stanford, a wealthy railroad magnate and former California governor, commissioned him to determine whether a galloping horse ever had all four hooves off the ground simultaneously. Stanford believed they did, but the motion was too fast for human eyes to detect.

Muybridge rose to the occasion and, after various earlier experiments in 1878, positioned twelve cameras around a track, controlled by trip wires triggered by the horse's legs. He took twenty-four photographs, shot in rapid succession, of a galloping horse called Sallie Gardner. The photographs not only showed for the first time how a horse ran, but also inspired Muybridge to become obsessed with the idea of using photography to study human and animal motion.[2]

He discovered that when a series of still images of a moving object were viewed at a certain speed, the illusion of motion is created. Muybridge later refined his techniques, producing hundreds of photographic sequences depicting human and animal locomotion.[3]

In order to prove the authenticity of his galloping horse pictures, he also invented a machine he called a Zoopraxiscope which projected painted silhouette images from rotating glass discs in rapid succession to give the impression of motion. Muybridge began using it in his public lectures around 1880, captivating audiences with animated silhouettes or painted versions of his chronophotographs, famously including a glass disc showing a horse skeleton in motion.[4]

While Muybridge was perfecting the Zoopraxiscope, a French physiologist called Étienne-Jules Marey was also studying the movement of humans and animals for medical and scientific purposes. In the 1870s, he developed a technique called chronophotography, recording a sequence of movements on a single photographic plate. In 1882, he refined this with the invention of the chronophotographic gun, which could take twelve frames per second. Though Marey's aim was not entertainment, his work influenced the visualization of motion and contributed key technical ideas to what would become cinema. Marey and Muybridge corresponded with each other and even met in Paris to discuss the use of 'instantaneous photography' to chronicle the movement of animals.[5]

Often overlooked in mainstream histories, Louis Le Prince, a French inventor working in Leeds, England, became inspired by the then fashionable moving panorama scenes. It led him to explore the possibility of creating moving pictures.

He created what is arguably the first true motion picture camera. In October 1888, using a single-lens device and paper film, he filmed members of his family for two seconds in the garden of their house in Roundhay Park, Leeds. This was followed by a film of people and traffic crossing Leeds Bridge.[6]

Tragically, Le Prince vanished mysteriously in 1890, just before he could patent or publicly demonstrate his camera. His disappearance has led to conspiracy theories that competitors were behind his death, leaving his contribution largely obscured by history.

Another British pioneer, William Friese-Greene, was a professional photographer and relentless experimenter. Collaborating with fellow inventor John Arthur Roebuck Rudge, he first created a device he called the Biophantic Lantern, which allowed multiple slides to be shown in rapid succession. Building on this success, Friese-Greene went on to develop a chronophotographic camera capable of capturing up to ten images per second on perforated celluloid film.

Unfortunately, the camera suffered from technical flaws and failed to achieve commercial success. He was not alone in the race to capture moving images – many other visionaries would also experiment with motion picture technology, only to fall short of lasting success.[7]

Across the Atlantic, American inventor Thomas Edison, who had already transformed the world of sound with his phonograph, turned his attention to visual motion. In February 1888, photographer and motion-study pioneer Eadweard Muybridge visited Edison's West Orange laboratory in New Jersey to demonstrate his Zoopraxiscope, a device that projected sequences of images from spinning discs. Muybridge proposed combining it with Edison's phonograph to create a synchronized sound-and-image machine.

Edison declined the partnership, but soon after he filed a patent caveat stating his intention to 'do for the eye what the phonograph does for the ear'. Though the device had yet to be built, he named it the Kinetoscope, derived from the Greek *kineto* (movement) and *scopos* (to watch).[8]

He tasked his assistant, William Kennedy Laurie Dickson, with developing the machine. The result was essentially a peep-show device. Unlike Muybridge's disc-based Zoopraxiscope, Dickson's design utilized the same principle William Friese-Greene had pioneered: flexible celluloid film. Inside a 4ft-tall cabinet, a continuous 50ft loop of 35mm film threaded around a series of spools was pulled along by a sprocket wheel. As the film advanced, an electric lamp illuminated each frame in sequence, creating the illusion of movement. Viewers peered through a peephole fitted with magnifying lenses, which enlarged the tiny images.[9]

The concept was an immediate success. Kinetoscope parlours began opening across the United States, where customers could watch short, eighteen-second loops of everyday scenes such as people sneezing, dancing or walking. Yet the novelty of these simple subjects quickly faded, pushing the Edison Company to experiment with more engaging and adventurous content.[10]

In 1893, Edison built the world's first movie studio in New Jersey. It was a black metal box dubbed the 'Black Maria' because of its cramped interior and black exterior. It had a roof that opened to allow in light to illuminate the action and was set on a turntable so it could follow the sun. It was here that Edison's team filmed some shocking treats for his peep shows.

They included *The Execution of Mary Queen of Scots*, produced in 1895, an eighteen-second film depicting the beheading of the unfortunate queen. It was the first film to use trained actors, as well as one of the first to use editing for the purposes of special effects.[11]

It shows a blindfolded Mary, inexplicably played by a man in Elizabethan drag, being led to the execution block. What the viewer did not realize was that although the executioner was first filmed raising his axe, filming then halted, the actor being replaced by a dummy. Filming then restarted as the dummy's head was chopped off. Viewers were said to have been totally shocked by this trick effect, some even believing that a woman had actually had her head chopped off during the making of the film. The film became a sensation, with people queuing up to see this dramatic and gory moment of history.[12]

Edison also turned his attention to filming boxing bouts for his Kinetoscopes, which became something of a money spinner, especially as prize fighting was outlawed at the time. His earliest attempt at selling boxing matches via Kinetoscope peep shows was a huge success. Prize fighters James J. Corbett and Peter Courtney were filmed fighting in the Black Maria studio in 1894. This short film became one of Edison's most popular Kinetoscope films, and he filmed many more.[13]

Edison remained devoted to the idea of viewing films in boxes, believing it would be far more profitable to earn a nickel every time his films were viewed rather than projecting them in a hall to a large audience. But he finally changed his mind and on 23 April 1896, at a music hall in New York, he demonstrated the Vitascope projector.[14]

These first Vitascope film screenings showed the stage darlings Edna and Stella Leigh dancing, followed by a short film featuring the breaking of waves on the seashore. The waves, dramatically projected on to a huge screen, are said to have been so realistic that people in the front row scrabbled back out of their seats to avoid getting wet.[15]

Another Edison film released at the same time featured dancer Annabelle Moore performing the serpentine dance. In the film, Annabelle is dressed in white veils that appear to change colour as she dances. This is the first and oldest-surviving tinted film. Each individual frame of film had to be hand painted using different coloured dyes.[16]

After Vitascope's successful launch in 1896, the Edison Company then produced the first film to ever provoke demands for censorship. Called *The Kiss*, the eighteen-second shocker showing Broadway stars John Rice and May Irwin kissing caused a scandalized uproar, with the police being called out to shut it down in many places where it was shown. One contemporary critic wrote: 'The spectacle of the prolonged pasturing on each other's lips magnified to gargantuan proportions and repeated three times over is absolutely disgusting.'[17]

By this point, the French were making giant strides towards developing their own version of moving pictures. In 1895, brothers Auguste and Louis Lumière had the first public exhibition of their moving pictures in Paris. Their invention was even more sophisticated than Edison's. Invented by Louis in a single night, when he had been unable to sleep, it was a portable hand-cranked camera capable of shooting, printing and projecting moving pictures. As it was hand-cranked, it could be moved and shoot films anywhere. It used the newly developed flexible celluloid film cut into 35mm-wide strips The film was moved around by an intermittent mechanism modelled on a treadle sewing machine.[18]

At their first public exhibition, the Lumière brothers showed ten films, each roughly fifty seconds long. The most well-known of these was *L'Arrivée d'un train engar de la Ciotat* (1895), or *The Arrival of a Train at La Ciotat Station*, in which they had filmed a train pulling into a station. Apparently, people in the audience really believed the train was about come out of the screen and ran from the theatre in terror.[19]

Another film was *L'Arroseur arrose* (1895), or *The Sprinkler Sprinkled* – the earliest slapstick comedy film ever made. The stars of the film were the Lumière gardener along with one of the young Lumière apprentices. The gardener is trying to water his plants but cannot work out why the water isn't coming through the hose, unaware that the young boy is standing on it. As he looks down the hose, the boy takes his foot away and the gardener is soaked. The boy runs off, pursued by the gardener, who catches him by the ear. *The Sprinkler Sprinkled* was the first film to have a poster designed that featured a scene from the film itself.[20]

Across the Channel in London, the first documented English projection of moving pictures took place in January 1896 at the Royal Photographic Society, presented by one of the society's Fellows, Birt Acres. The film was called *Rough Sea at Dover* and showed heavy waves crashing against Admiralty Pier in Dover. Despite its simple nature, *Rough Sea at Dover* became one of the most popular and widely screened early British films.[21]

Nevertheless, the French were leading the field at this point thanks to another hugely popular French movie pioneer of the time called Georges Méliès, a conjurer, cartoonist and inventor who experimented with trick photography to create magical effects. He was one of the first filmmakers to use multiple exposures, time-lapse photography, dissolves and hand-painted colour in his work. Because of his ability to seemingly manipulate and transform reality through cinematography, Méliès is sometimes referred to as the first 'Cinemagician'. Between 1896 and 1906, his Star Film Company made over 500 films.[22]

Perhaps his most fascinating film was *Le Voyage dans la Lune* (*A Trip to the Moon*), a fourteen-minute-long feature made in 1902 and released in both black and white and as a hand-painted version. It tells the story of a group of mad scientists who travel to the Moon in a cannon-propelled capsule spaceship.

The 'Man in the Moon' watches the ship as it approaches, and it hits him in the eye. The motley crew then get into all sorts of scrapes with various alien creatures before returning to Earth. Méliès revelled in the special effects and technical aspects of his film, but he also built in a storyline which really grabbed the attention of his audiences. It wasn't long before the Edison Company was once again jumping on the bandwagon. Edison managed to acquire a pirated copy of the film and released it across the US, with audiences flocking to see it.[23]

Because of the film's popularity, Edison decided that his company needed to look at making their own narrative films. In 1903, one of Edison's employees,

Edwin Porter, produced *The Great Train Robbery*. It was a primitive one-reeler action picture, about ten minutes long, with fourteen scenes. It is the story of a robbery, with a chase scene and the inevitable capture of the robbers. It was one of the first films to use cross-cutting, which is when the camera cuts from one action scene to the other, as well as the first to film on location.

The final scene was also a first: it ended with a close-up of the bandit chief, with his hat pushed back on his head. He points and shoots his revolver point-blank, directly into the camera and, of course, at the audience. The film and its unexpected ending caused a sensation.[24]

Porter had been highly influenced by the European film pioneers, particularly an English photographer called James Williamson, who became a key member of the loose association of early British film pioneers that would later be dubbed the Brighton School. A former chemist, Williamson's interest in filmmaking was sparked by meeting other members of the Brighton School who used his pharmacy to buy chemicals for developing their films. He took up photography, magic lanterns and cinematography as a sideline, but eventually wound up his business in Hove to concentrate entirely on filmmaking.[25]

He was one of the first filmmakers to ask actors to behave naturally so his films would be more realistic. Most of his early films were shot in the back garden of his house in Hove. One of his films, *Fire*, showed the occupants of a house in Hove being rescued by the local fire service.[26]

In 1903, Edwin Porter would go on to create a direct copy called *Life of an American Fireman* for the Edison Company, which borrowed Williamson's narrative model and developed it further by introducing close-ups.[27]

Porter was also influenced by the work of the Surrey-based filmmaker Cecil M. Hepworth, one of the founders of the British film industry. Hepworth had set up his own film company in a house in Walton-on-Thames, which he called the Hepworth Film Manufacturing Company, where he made around three films a week.[28]

One of his most famous films, made in 1905, was *Rescued by Rover*, in which a faithful family pet springs into action when a vengeful beggar woman kidnaps a baby to spite a 'respectable' family who had refused to give her alms. The film became such a global hit that Hepworth had to reshoot it twice, all existing prints having worn out from excessive use. It also popularized the name 'Rover' for dogs and turned Blair the collie, who had played Rover, into a canine superstar.[29]

Things were developing quickly in the movie industry, and over in America, with potential competitors springing up around him, Edison was struggling to control the rapidly expanding film industry which he claimed he had invented and for which he owned the patent rights. Initially his claims were challenged by his rivals.[30]

It took a brave man to challenge Edison, and in 1908 his two main rivals – Biograph and Vitagraph studios – decided it was safer to join forces with him. Together they formed a cartel called the Motion Picture Patents Company, more commonly known as the Edison Trust as it was clear who was in charge. It soon became officially illegal to distribute or show any films without permission of the Trust. They had the rights to every film and camera in the market.[31]

For the smaller independent production companies that refused – or were unable – to join Edison's Trust, there was only one option: leave town. Many packed up and made the 3,000-mile rail journey from New York to Southern California, a land of endless sunshine, sprawling orange groves, wide-open spaces and no Edison. Hollywood was about to be born.

With the early motion picture industry now firmly established, studios were desperate for compelling stories to bring to the screen. The stage was perfectly set for the first attempt to transform *Ben-Hur* into a true cinematic spectacle.

Chapter 8

From Screen to Supreme Court: The Kalem 'Ben-Hur' Case and the Birth of Film Copyright

By the early twentieth century, the name 'Ben-Hur' had exploded into a cultural sensation. From Ben-Hur coffee and flour to Ben-Hur insurance, rollercoasters, paddle steamers, mines, apartment blocks, sheet music, perfume and even cigars, this iconic name was stamped on every product imaginable, whatever its relevance to Roman history.[1]

It was a remarkable phenomenon that emerged just as another cultural sensation was revolutionizing the world – motion pictures. As we have seen, at the end of the nineteenth century, the Edison Company had led the way in developing the motion picture industry in the US with the first commercially screened moving pictures being viewed on Kinetoscope peep show boxes.[2] With the invention of the film projector, moving pictures then started to be viewed on screens before theatre-style audiences. With Edison's success, it didn't take long for other companies to jump on the bandwagon, eager to cash in on this hot new technology.

One of these was the Kalem Company, founded in 1907.[3] It was named after its founders – George Kleine, Samuel Long and Frank Marion. By using the first letters of their surnames, they created 'KaLeM'. The company began operations from a small office in a loft building at 131 West 24th Street in New York City. Unlike the Edison Company they had no studio, so all their films were shot on location. They were also able to lure the increasingly successful and charismatic actor/director Sidney Olcott away from rival production company Biograph to join them. Olcott was offered $10 per picture, and under the terms of his contract he had to direct a minimum of one, one-reel picture of about a thousand feet every week. By the autumn of 1907, his list of pictures was impressive. It was then that Frank Marion, who had seen how successful the stage production of *Ben-Hur* had been, decided that their next picture should be a retelling of that story. He believed Kalem could turn the book into the most exciting moving picture of the decade.[4]

They hired Gene Gauntier, a pioneering female screenwriter and actress, to craft the screenplay, which condensed Lew Wallace's expansive novel into a series of vivid *tableaux*. Gauntier was a trailblazer for women in film, handling both creative and logistical aspects of production at a time when few women had such authority.[5] The film's narrative focused on key moments: Ben-Hur's accidental injury of a Roman official, his subsequent enslavement and the climactic chariot race. Despite its brevity, the film aimed to capture the essence of the novel's dramatic scenes. With a modest budget of approximately $500, it was shot in locations such as Manhattan Beach and Sheepshead Bay in Brooklyn, New York.

The challenge was how to replicate the chariot race on the screen. The answer lay with the famous Pains fireworks spectaculars. Henry J. Pain's fireworks and pyrotechnics shows had been among the greatest attractions in New York's Coney Island for over thirty years. Between 1879 and 1910, each of Pain's elaborate performances recreating battle scenes and dramatic moments from history drew thousands of spectators to his massive outdoor stadium and lake at Manhattan Beach.[6]

Marion saw his solution when Pain's latest spectacular, held on the racetrack at Sheepshead Park, was closing for the season. This was a great opportunity to produce *Ben-Hur* using the Pain company's props, supers (extras) and standing scenery. Wasting no time, he sent Sidney Olcott and Gene Gauntier down to the track to inspect what was on offer.[7]

However, Pain's props and costumes, and even his extras, were not suitable for a moving picture, so Olcott and Gauntier had to start afresh. Gauntier, given just two days to create the scenario, would confess in a later magazine interview that at that point she hadn't read the book, yet within two days and nights she had planned out the scenes. The original idea was that Frank Oaks Rose, the stage manager for the Pain's Fireworks spectaculars, should direct, but moving pictures and pyrotechnic shows were vastly different, so after a few false starts Olcott had to step in.[8]

With a running time of just fifteen minutes and including only sixteen scenes, Kalem's 'Roman Spectacle' is very much a precis of the original book.

There is no reference to Ben-Hur meeting Jesus Christ or his presence at Christ's crucifixion. There is no galley scene; instead, a significant portion of the film is devoted to the chariot race. Just four chariots, including those driven by Ben-Hur and Messala, are depicted, with each being drawn by teams of four black horses. However, all that is shown on the film is the chariot passing by the static camera. Roman spectators on screen cheer as they pretend to watch the charioteers racing three laps around the track of the Hippodrome. The film then ends with spectators continuing to cheer, Ben-Hur being awarded a laurel wreath by the emperor and the injured Messala lying on a stretcher and gesturing toward his former friend.[9]

Advertisements for the film claimed that the chariots were driven using off-duty soldiers of the 3rd Battery of the National Guard in Brooklyn, with horses from the New York National Guard's artillery unit. However, it has also been suggested that the chariots were being driven by members of the local fire brigade, who regularly staged their own chariot race events. The adverts also claimed that the costumes were supplied by the Metropolitan Opera House. In fact, they came from Gus Elliott, a run-of-the-mill props and costume supplier in Manhattan.[10]

Another myth that grew up around the film was that actor William S. Hart, who had played Messala on stage, had reprised his role in the film. Although no-one is sure who played the key characters, it has been assumed that Herman Rottjer, an employee with Henry Pain's fireworks company and noted for his skill in driving chariots, took on the role of Ben-Hur.[11]

The film took just one week to complete and was soon being shown in Nickelodeon theatres across the country. It was especially successful when actors were employed in the theatres to perform sound effects and speak the dialogue in sync with the on-screen footage.[12]

Marion's vision had been realized, and after 500 showings the film was proving a huge success. Nevertheless, there was one fatal flaw in the planning: no-one had thought to ask the Lew Wallace estate for permission to turn the book into a film. Although Lew Wallace had died three years before the film's release, his son Henry Lane Wallace together with the book's publishers, Harper & Brothers, and stage producers Klaw & Erlanger were just as keen to ensure that *Ben-Hur*'s legacy and profitability remained tightly controlled.

On 20 March 1908, fourteen weeks after the release of Kalem's film version of *Ben-Hur*, Harper & Brothers, Klaw & Erlanger and the author's estate filed a joint copyright-infringement lawsuit against the Kalem Company as well as against the Kleine Optical Company, which had produced the copies of the film for Kalem's distributors.[13]

To counter the first salvo from the Ben-Hur estate, Kalem claimed that the film had served as good publicity for both the book and the play, an excuse that didn't wash with Wallace's heirs and business partners. They argued that it was not simply about the money; they felt that the motion-picture version was so poorly done it cheapened and degraded the original. However, what was really at stake was the very lucrative *Ben-Hur* franchise and the much larger issue of unauthorized film adaptations.[14]

The case went to court on 5 May 1908, and Kalem's initial defence was that their scenario writer, Gauntier, who was working from a first edition of the book, was unaware that a copyright had been granted in 1899 just prior to the development of the stage play. The Kalem lawyers then went on to argue that the film was made up of moving 'photographs' which were a form of artistic expression and therefore exempt from copyright protection. The judge disagreed and ruled Kalem had indeed violated the law by showing 'moving pictures' of ideas taken from a copyrighted book and play. Kalem appealed and the case would eventually end up in the Supreme Court.[15]

Taking on the *Ben-Hur* estate was an expensive exercise, but Kalem was supported by Edison and the Motion Picture Patents Company (MPPC). Because of the potential impact of the decision on the film industry, MPPC agreed to help finance the legal challenge to the Supreme Court.[16]

The Supreme Court hearing opened in 1911, with the highly respected Justice Oliver Wendell Holmes presiding, a man known for his clarity and brevity. Kalem's defence that they merely sold the films and bore no responsibility for how they were publicly screened quickly collapsed. The court found that Kalem not only knew their film would be used to stage *Ben-Hur*, but actively encouraged this.

The court firmly rejected the idea that filming scenes from a novel could sidestep copyright law. Holmes clarified that drama was not confined to spoken words: it also encompassed actions that conveyed a story and emotion.

By this standard, Kalem's moving pictures were a direct dramatization of *Ben-Hur*, even if the performance was captured on film rather than staged live.[17]

Holmes also dismissed concerns about copyright overreach. He explained that copyright protected the specific expression of a story, not its general ideas, a domain Congress was fully empowered to safeguard. He even noted that Congress had the authority to order all infringing film copies destroyed.

The verdict was decisive. Kalem and the MPPC were fined $25,000 each, and the ruling set a powerful precedent: from that point forward, every motion picture company was required to secure the film rights for any copyrighted work before adapting it to the screen.

The case, *Kalem Co v Harper Brothers*, established the landmark principle of 'rendering a copyrighted novel into a copyrighted moving picture play', a ruling later cited in nearly a dozen Supreme Court cases.[18]

Just two weeks after the decision, Henry Wallace issued a bold proclamation to the press: 'No motion picture company will be allowed to produce in films the story of *Ben-Hur*.'[19]

It was a statement of absolute certainty, an iron gate slammed shut on Hollywood's ambitions. Yet, as history would soon reveal, *Ben-Hur* was far too powerful a story to remain locked away. Despite Wallace's vow, the race to bring his epic to the silver screen had already begun…

Chapter 9

The Road to *Ben-Hur* – A Battle for the Big Screen

The copyright battle of Kalem Co v Harper Brothers did little to dampen the enthusiasm for turning Lew Wallace's *Ben-Hur* into a motion picture. The novel was perfectly suited to silent melodrama, full of intense emotion, spectacular set pieces and action scenes that could captivate audiences.

After Lew Wallace's death, his son Henry Wallace inherited the rights to *Ben-Hur* and proved to be even more protective of the novel's reputation. He had little regard for the fledgling motion picture industry, believing that films were a cheap, low-quality form of entertainment that would only diminish his father's legacy. Henry's concerns seemed justified when the Kalem Company had brazenly produced their unauthorized fifteen-minute version of the story.

In a letter to Harper & Brothers in 1912, Henry Wallace made his feelings clear:

> 'I will oppose in every way possible all attempts to produce any of General Wallace's work in moving pictures. The reason is because the average moving picture shows are wretched exhibitions utterly unworthy of dignified consideration.'[1]

Henry had a point. In the early 1900s, most films were short, cheaply made and often lacking in sophistication. But audiences were rapidly developing a taste for longer narratives with richer plots and subplots. Filmmakers and studios quickly adapted to meet this demand.

One such studio was Vitagraph, founded in 1897 by two Englishmen: J. Stuart Blackton, a former newspaper cartoonist, and Albert E. Smith, an ex-stage magician. Initially, they produced films under licence from

Thomas Edison, who held many early film patents. Before long, Vitagraph began producing its own content, including newsreels, comedies and magic trick films.

Recognizing growing criticism from religious groups toward cinema, Blackton and Smith made a bold move. In 1909, they embarked on *The Life of Moses*, which they marketed as 'the greatest scriptural narrative ever told'. To lend credibility, they hired Reverend Dr Madison Clinton Peters, a prominent clergyman, as a biblical consultant and writer.[2]

The film's visual style drew inspiration from renowned artists such as Briton Rivière, Gustave Doré, James Tissot and Lawrence Alma-Tadema. Their names even appeared on the film's intertitles.[3] Released as a five-part series between December 1909 and February 1910, each thirteen-minute instalment was a success and helped establish the biblical epic as a viable genre.[4]

As filmmaking evolved, so did the skill of its directors. One of the most influential was David Wark Griffith, better known as D.W. Griffith. Far from producing the 'wretched exhibitions' Henry Wallace decried, Griffith pioneered many of the storytelling techniques that define modern cinema.

At Biograph Studios, Griffith directed over 400 short films. With cameraman Billy Bitzer, he developed innovations in editing, close-ups, cross-cutting and visual composition.[5] By 1911, despite pushback from Biograph's executives, he began producing two-reel (twenty to thirty minute) films. In 1913, he secretly undertook *Judith of Bethulia*, a four-reel (one-hour) biblical epic based on the *Book of Judith*.[6]

The story followed Judith, a Jewish widow, who seduces and then beheads Assyrian general Holofernes to save her city. Starring Blanche Sweet, the film mixed religious spectacle with elements of sensuality.

Biograph executives were furious that Griffith made the film without their approval. They refused to let him produce more feature-length films and even delayed *Judith*'s release until Griffith had left the company, ensuring he received none of the profits.[7] Disillusioned, Griffith relocated to California, determined to make films on an even grander scale.

In 1915, Griffith released *The Birth of a Nation*, adapted from Thomas Dixon's novel *The Clansman*, a controversial, racist depiction of Reconstruction-era America that glorified the Ku Klux Klan.[8] While morally indefensible, the film was a technical masterpiece, introducing groundbreaking cinematic techniques like large-scale battle sequences, cross-cutting and colour tinting.[9]

Despite widespread protests and bans in several cities, *The Birth of a Nation* was a massive commercial success. Henry Wallace was among those impressed, not by the subject matter but by the technical achievement. He wrote to Joseph Brooks of Klaw & Erlanger, stating he would now consider a film version of *Ben-Hur*, provided it was produced on a comparable scale.[10] His asking price: $1 million.

Several major studios showed interest but balked at the cost. Adolph Zukor's Famous Players-Lasky (later Paramount) passed, as did the newly formed United Artists, whose proposed version would have starred Douglas Fairbanks as Ben-Hur and Mary Pickford as Esther, and been directed by Griffith.[11]

In August 1921, Henry Wallace finally agreed to sell the rights to Abraham Erlanger, who had dissolved his partnership with Marc Klaw, for $600,000. Erlanger formed the Classical Cinematograph Corporation with Florenz Ziegfeld and Charles Dillingham, intending to resell the rights for profit at the same $1 million figure. Once again, no buyers came forward.[12]

One determined contender was Goldwyn Pictures, founded in 1916 by Samuel Goldfish (who later changed his name to Goldwyn).[13] After Goldwyn himself was forced out of his own company in 1922, studio executives negotiated with Erlanger. Instead of paying $1 million upfront, they proposed splitting the profits fifty-fifty if the film matched the scale of *The Birth of a Nation*. Erlanger agreed, on the condition that he would have the final say over the director, cast and script.[14]

By this point, historical epics were in vogue, thanks largely to Italian cinema. Films like *Quo Vadis* (1912), *Spartaco* (1913) and *The Last Days of Pompeii* (1913) showcased vast sets, elaborate costumes and massive casts.[15]

The most famous of these was *Cabiria* (1914), directed by Giovanni Pastrone and filmed in Turin, then the heart of the Italian film industry. Set during the Second Punic War, *Cabiria* combined colossal sets, thousands of extras and innovative camera movements, including the famous 'Cabiria movement', an early form of the tracking shot.[16] *Cabiria* was so influential that it became the first motion picture screened at the White House in 1914, viewed by President Woodrow Wilson and his family.

Griffith openly borrowed from *Cabiria* when making *Intolerance* (1916), his response to the backlash over *The Birth of a Nation*. *Intolerance* featured four parallel stories from different eras, including an astonishing recreation of ancient Babylon.[17]

The Babylonian sets, designed by Walter L. Hall, were some of the largest ever built, employing hundreds of workers.[18] Set construction utilized wooden frames, plaster, canvas and forced perspective, where objects closer to the camera were built larger than those further away to create the illusion of depth. The steps of the Babylon set, for instance, tapered dramatically to create a sense of grandeur.[19]

If anything signalled that *Ben-Hur* would need to aim higher, it was Cecil B. DeMille's *The Ten Commandments* (1923). This was DeMille's first biblical epic, one of the most ambitious films of the silent era.[20]

DeMille hired French designer Paul Iribe to create vast Egyptian sets in the sand dunes of Guadalupe, California, including a full-scale city with 35ft statues of Pharaoh Ramses, twenty-one sphinxes and monumental gates.[21] Thousands of workers and extras, as well as animals such as camels and horses, populated the set.

The film's most famous sequence, the parting of the Red Sea, was a special effects triumph. Two water tanks were filmed pouring water inward; the footage was then reversed, making it appear as though the sea split apart. This was combined with miniatures, wind machines and smoke effects to complete the illusion.[22]

When filming concluded, DeMille had the entire set buried beneath the sand to prevent its reuse, giving rise to the legend of the 'Lost City of DeMille', which remained hidden for decades before its rediscovery.

The Ten Commandments became one of the highest-grossing films of the silent era and established a new standard for epic cinema. For Goldwyn Pictures and Erlanger, matching that level of spectacle posed a formidable challenge, but the era of the Hollywood biblical epic had truly begun – and *Ben-Hur* would surpass them all.

Chapter 10

Ben-Hur and the Silver Screen

With the deal finalized, work on getting *Ben-Hur* off the ground quickly began. June Mathis, head of Goldwyn's scenario department, immediately started lobbying Erlanger to secure her role as the screenwriter.

Interestingly, it was a woman, Jeanie MacPherson, who wrote the screenplay for Cecil B. DeMille's *The Ten Commandments*, as well as many of his early films. Another key figure was Gene Gauntier of Kalem Productions, one of the pioneering women screenwriters of the silent era. Back then, Hollywood was more welcoming to women in creative roles like writing and directing, long before the studio system of the 1930s made the industry more rigid and male-dominated. Many of these women came from journalism or literary backgrounds, bringing strong storytelling instincts to screenwriting, while others came from the stage, which gave them a solid grasp of performance and character.

Mathis had started her career as a stage actress but soon shifted to screenwriting, where she became known for her remarkable ability to craft compelling stories that worked visually and emotionally for the silent screen.

However, she wasn't just a writer, becoming the first female executive at Metro Pictures Corporation, a predecessor of MGM. In that role, she had authority over casting, production decisions and editing. By 1921, she was one of the highest-paid and most influential people in Hollywood – male or female.[1]

Probably her biggest success story was the film *The Four Horsemen of the Apocalypse*, where she collaborated closely with director Rex Ingram and was instrumental in casting Rudolph Valentino in the lead role. Ingram, one of the most influential directors of the silent era, helped shape the film into a critical and commercial success. For Valentino, it was a career-defining role: playing a passionate, brooding Argentinian hero who dances the tango in one of the film's most memorable scenes. That performance, especially the tango sequence, captivated female audiences and firmly established Valentino as the quintessential 'Latin lover', a Hollywood archetype defined by exoticism, dark looks and smouldering passion.[2]

Mathis started on the daunting task of adapting Wallace's novel and to some extent Young's play into a silent movie scenario, and finished it within two-and-a-half months.[3] Ever since securing the job of screenwriter, Mathis had been lobbying the studio to move the production to Italy. Mathis believed that filming in Italy would provide a more authentic backdrop for the ancient Roman setting of *Ben-Hur*. Italy's architecture, landscapes and ruins could lend a sense of realism and historical depth that studio sets in Hollywood simply could not match at the time.

In the early 1920s, Europe – particularly Italy and France – was still seen as the cultural heart of classical art and aesthetics. Shooting in Italy gave the production a degree of artistic credibility and association with high culture, aligning with Mathis' ambition to elevate *Ben-Hur* beyond just a spectacle into a prestigious cinematic event.[4]

Labour and production costs were considered lower in Italy than in the United States, which appealed to studio executives hoping to manage the film's massive budget. Italy also offered experienced craftspeople and extras, thanks to its own established film tradition.[5]

Several months passed as Goldwyn executives scouted Italian locations, then in late September 1923 came the announcement that the film would indeed be shot in Italy and the director would be Charles Brabin, a respected British director who also happened to be married to Theda Bara, Hollywood's original 'vamp'. Mathis had supported the decision to employ Brabin, although Hollywood gossip suggested he was a mediocre talent with a drinking problem, casting doubt on his suitability for such a monumental production.[6]

Rex Ingram, who had previously collaborated with June Mathis on *The Four Horsemen of the Apocalypse* and shared a close professional relationship with her, had long assumed he would be chosen to direct. He was devastated by the news that Brabin had been selected.

Despite deciding against Ingram as director, Mathis wanted Valentino to play Ben-Hur, but he was under contract to Famous Players. Studios tightly controlled their stars under exclusive contracts, and loaning talent between studios was rare, especially for a project as high-profile as *Ben-Hur*. Others were tested, and George Walsh was cast. Walsh was the brother of director Raoul Walsh and was relatively well-known as an actor and former Olympic-level athlete. He had the physicality and charisma for the role, but his acting skills were rated as little more than routine. However, he was rumoured to have had an especially close relationship with Mathis.[7]

Casting began for the role of Messala. The actor who really wanted the role was Francis X. Bushman, one of silent cinema's first major male matinee idols. Once dubbed 'The Handsomest Man in the World', he had starred in over 200 silent films and was adored by female audiences for his chiselled features and heroic roles, but also his availability as a bachelor. He was a top box office draw in the 1910s and early 1920s, earning up to $1,000 a week, an enormous sum at the time.[8]

Unfortunately, his popularity took a major hit when fans found out he wasn't the eligible bachelor he'd claimed to be, but was married with several children. To make matters worse, he was openly having an affair with his on-screen co-star, Beverly Bayne. At a time when movie stars, especially romantic leads, were expected to uphold a wholesome image, the news that Bushman had lied about his personal life and broken up his family outraged many fans, particularly among more conservative audiences. The scandal also marked the beginning of the end for him in Hollywood, where studio heads heavily depended on public image to sell their stars.[9]

Having not appeared in a movie for two years, Bushman was desperate to revive his career and lobbied hard for the role in the film, even though his name no longer carried the same clout.[10] The audition process wasn't typical. Rather than a formal screen test, Bushman arranged a private meeting with studio heads. To make his case, he arrived fully in costume, dressed in a toga and Roman sandals. He memorized and performed a dramatic monologue from the script, delivering lines with fiery intensity and measured poise. His theatrical background and experience with Shakespearean roles gave him an edge, and his commanding presence, even at the age of 40, won him the role.[11]

Having secured the part of Messala, Bushman was suddenly unsure about playing a villain, until actor William S. Hart, who had portrayed Messala on stage, gave him blunt advice: 'Take it, that's the best goddamned part in the picture!'[12]

Carmel Myers was cast as Iras without even a screen test, a testament to her established reputation for playing vamp roles. As a quintessential femme fatale, Myers brought a seductive intensity that aligned perfectly with the character. The term 'vamp', a shortened form of 'vampire', entered popular culture in the early twentieth century as a metaphor for a dangerously alluring woman. Gertrude Olmstead, one of the leading romantic stars of the silent era, was cast as Esther, the film's heroine and Ben-Hur's love interest.

Charles Brabin relocated to Rome in October 1923, with the rest of the cast and crew following soon after. The script was still unfinished when he arrived, but 3,000 costumes were on order. Brabin spent some time in Tunis filming the Three Wise Men scene with uncooperative camels. Apparently Brabin had to resort to building fires under the camels to get them to move, only to have them sit down on the fires and put them out.[13]

Meanwhile, significant changes were unfolding behind the scenes in Hollywood. In December, Samuel Goldwyn's company merged with Marcus Loew's Metro Pictures Corporation and Louis B. Mayer Productions, forming Metro-Goldwyn. As part of the new leadership structure, Loew appointed Louis B. Mayer as the new studio's first vice-president. Mayer had begun his career as a theatre owner and film exhibitor before setting up his own production company. He came with his 24-year-old protégé, Irving Thalberg, who was made second vice-president and head of production. Just a few months after the merger, the newly consolidated studio was officially renamed Metro-Goldwyn-Mayer, or MGM, a name that would soon come to dominate Hollywood's Golden Age.[14]

Unfortunately for MGM, Italy turned out to be a poor choice for filming. Benito Mussolini had seized power as prime minister just a year earlier, and the country was in political and social turmoil, with street battles between the socialist and fascist parties. Protest strikes disrupted production schedules, and construction on the sets stalled. With little progress being made, many of the cast found themselves with unexpected downtime. Francis X. Bushman, upon learning he wouldn't be needed for several months, embarked on a grand European tour with his sister, visiting twenty-five countries while awaiting his recall. Carmel Myers, meanwhile, took advantage of the delay by going on shopping trips around Europe with her mother. She even managed to shoot an entirely separate film during the production hiatus. George Walsh was left twiddling his thumbs in Italy, waiting for something to happen.[15]

When Mathis arrived in Italy, she found progress at a standstill and discovered Brabin had banned her from the set. Worse still, Brabin was drinking heavily and filming very little. He requested seventy full-sized galleys for the sea battle scene; twelve were prepared, but only two were fully functional and they capsized. Several hundred extras, each being paid $5–7 a day, sat around while the ships were repaired and anchored. When the galleys were finally fixed, port officials declared them unseaworthy, forcing Brabin to film a stationary sea battle.[16]

Back in Hollywood, new MGM executives Louis B Mayer and Irving Thalberg, and production manager Harry Rapf, viewed the footage and agreed that it was a disaster. Facing spiralling costs and with no usable material, they concluded that the entire Italian shoot was a costly failure. The decision was made to scrap nearly all the footage already shot and to replace the original cast and crew, including Charles Brabin and June Mathis. This move was bold, unprecedented and fraught with risk, but MGM was determined to salvage the film and restore its reputation.[17]

Thalberg and MGM realized that only a director with proven skill, discipline and experience working on large-scale films could salvage the project. The man they turned to was Fred Niblo, already a respected and successful director in Hollywood by the early 1920s. Niblo had directed several major features, including *The Mark of Zorro* (1920), a swashbuckling hit starring Douglas Fairbanks; *Blood and Sand* (1922), a lush Valentino vehicle and a commercial success; and *Thy Name Is Woman* (1924), a romantic drama starring an up-and-coming young Mexican actor called Ramon Novarro.

Niblo's ability to handle complex productions and work well with high-profile stars made him a trusted choice for studio heads. He was known for being organized, professional and good at delivering polished, audience-pleasing films on time. Perhaps more importantly, he was not a 'difficult' artist in the way some other directors of the silent era were.

Rex Ingram was devastated when he heard he had been passed over once again, but Thalberg knew that Ingram would not have kowtowed to the studio, and in particular to Louis B. Mayer, whom he loathed, regarding him as a meddling businessman with no real appreciation for art.[18]

Replacing the lead actor was perhaps the most dramatic aspect of the shake-up. Unbeknown to George Walsh, the studio had started to search for a new leading man. At the time, the rising young actor 25-year-old Ramon Novarro was under contract at Metro Pictures. He had appeared in several films, most recently working with Fred Niblo, and was gaining attention for his good looks, charisma and acting range.[19]

Irving Thalberg personally approved Ramon Novarro for the part. He believed Novarro had the physical presence, emotional depth and screen appeal to carry such a monumental film. Thalberg wanted to distinguish *Ben-Hur* not just with scale, but with quality, and Novarro's acting ability and growing fan base aligned with that vision.

Thalberg also understood the power of image. Like Valentino, Novarro's Mexican heritage gave him the 'foreign' mystique that studios marketed heavily in the 1920s, especially in romantic or biblical epics. Casting Novarro played directly into the 'Latin lover' archetype with which audiences were fascinated.[20]

Novarro was officially cast as Ben-Hur in 1924, and the entire production was retooled around him. Unfortunately for George Walsh, no-one told him he had been fired; he found out he'd been replaced through the press, not from the studio, a move that deeply embarrassed and angered him. His career never fully recovered from the dismissal. The incident became a classic example of how volatile and ruthless the studio system could be.[21]

Thalberg's choice was not universally praised. Many critics and fans disliked the casting of Novarro, who didn't have the height or athletic build of George Walsh. One fan wrote to movie magazine *Photoplay*: 'It will be a crime against filmdom ... if Ramon Novarro is allowed to play Ben-Hur ... I cannot visualise Novarro struggling to fit his small feet into the huge sandals of Ben-Hur.'[22]

Another casualty of the reorganization was Gertrude Olmstead. Although she had already filmed scenes as Esther, Thalberg dismissed her from the production. She was replaced by May McAvoy, a more prominent and bankable actress at the time, who had recently starred opposite Lon Chaney in *The Hunchback of Notre Dame*.

Thalberg did, however, approve of Francis X. Bushman's acting style, and he remained in his role as Messala. He and Novarro never saw eye to eye, partly because Novarro was only 5ft 6in tall, several inches shorter than Bushman, so to even things out he had lifts added to his sandals to give him extra height. Furthermore, Bushman and the axed Walsh had been friends.[23]

Carmel Myers also held onto her role as villainess Iras, although Niblo made her make up for the time she had spent doing nothing by insisting she found 'the most exciting headdress ever seen on the screen'. Myers and her mother ended up travelling to Vienna, where she purchased the striking white silk wig she wears in the film.

After the cast and crew reshuffle, filming resumed in Rome. Art director Horace Jackson and his team had been labouring away on a plateau outside Rome, building what was claimed to have been the largest set ever created for a motion picture: a reproduction of Jerusalem's Joppa Gate. It was 150ft high, even larger than the original. It was taking them months to finish the set due to Italian bureaucracy. Everything about the film was turning into a nightmare and Niblo's nerves were stretched to the limit, even before the near-disaster of the sea battle.[24]

The infamous sea battle between Roman and pirate forces was staged with plenty of ambition and chaos. The scene called for a pirate ship to ram a Roman galley, followed by hand-to-hand combat, culminating in one ship catching fire and crew members leaping into the water. Italian extras were hired to play the crews; eager to earn good money, some falsely claimed they could swim.

With Rome now firmly under fascist control, political tensions spilled onto the set. Fights frequently broke out between fascist and anti-fascist extras. In a misguided attempt at realism, someone had the bright idea to cast the crews along political lines, with fascists as Romans and anti-fascists as pirates. The situation escalated dangerously when it was discovered that both ships were stocked with real, sharpened swords. Director Fred Niblo intervened just in time to disarm them.[25]

Even after the weapons were removed, disaster struck. The Roman ship was supposed to catch fire during the scene, and extras were promised bonuses for staying aboard. However, a strong wind quickly turned the controlled blaze into a real inferno, sparking panic. Everyone jumped into the water at once, but many were unable to swim. Watching the chaos unfold, Francis X. Bushman reportedly cried, 'My God, Fred, they are drowning!', to which

Niblo shouted back, 'I can't help it, those ships cost me forty thousand dollars apiece!'

According to special effects expert Arnold Gillespie's 2012 memoir, fearing fatalities and a possible police investigation, the entire company fled to Rome. While the cast and crew lay low, wardrobe manager Adolph Siedel noticed that three costumes hadn't been returned. Worried about potential evidence, he burned the clothes of the missing extras, then loaded a rowboat with chains and weights to dispose of any bodies that might surface. After an hour of grim searching, he found nothing. To his great relief, a few days later, the three missing extras returned, still dressed in full Roman armour, asking for their clothes back.[26]

An early attempt to film the chariot race also resulted in tragedy, one stuntman being killed when his chariot wheel broke as he turned one of the set's corners. The hub hit the ground and the driver was catapulted through the air, landing on a pile of rubble. Even Novarro was injured when his chariot collided with Bushman's. According to Bushman, many horses were also killed during filming. Second-unit director B. Reeves Eason, who was charged with filming the race, had a ruthless reputation. 'The moment [a horse] limped, they shot it,' Bushman recalled. Eason would later become infamous for the same attitude in *Charge of the Light Brigade* (1936), after which the American Humane Society began overseeing film productions involving animals.[27]

For the galley interior shots, the crew dug a 30ft pool but accidentally destroyed a Roman catacomb, triggering a looting spree of ancient artefacts.[28]

Filming the raft scene off Livorno was brutal. In the film, Ben-Hur, whilst a galley slave, saves Quintus Arrius during a naval battle. Arrius, believing his fleet has been destroyed, tries to throw himself into the sea, but Ben-Hur prevents his suicide and rescues him. This act leads to Arrius adopting Ben-Hur as his son and heir, a major turning point in the story.

Normally, a scene this dangerous taking place on a burning ship, with water stunts, would have been performed using stunt doubles. But due to production issues in Italy, including poor planning, labour strikes and the general chaos of the early shoot, no doubles were available when the scene needed to be filmed.

Consequently, Novarro and the 69-year-old Frank Currier had to perform the action themselves in freezing water, wearing only loincloths. They were in the water for hours, and Novarro had to dose Currier with brandy and slap him between takes to keep him conscious. It made for a startlingly realistic scene.[29]

The constant battles between fascist and anti-fascist extras and crew members were turning *Ben-Hur* into a political bloodbath. Niblo said at the time: 'It's as though a crowd of Republicans and Democrats were to start hurling hammers, rivets, boards, or any other weapon at the other faction.'[30]

The ongoing turmoil in Rome and a steady stream of distressed letters from director Fred Niblo finally pushed Louis B. Mayer to travel to the set himself. He arrived with his family on 12 October 1924 to find the production in complete disarray. Carey Wilson, who had been assigned to rewrite the script, sent a blunt telegram to Irving Thalberg back at MGM in Culver City, Los Angeles, reporting that Mayer was a 'mental and physical wreck'. As if things could get no worse, Mayer was soon struck by a severe dental infection that led to the removal of all his teeth.[31]

Amid the chaos, there was at least one unexpected silver lining. Hoping to lift his spirits, Mayer took a brief trip to Berlin with his daughter. While there, he requested private screenings of the best new European films. One of them was *The Atonement of Gösta Berling*, a Swedish production directed by Mauritz Stiller and featuring a young actress named Greta Garbo. Mayer, immediately captivated by her on-screen presence, quickly arranged to sign her to a five-year contract with MGM. Garbo would go on to become one of the studio's most iconic stars, remaining with MGM until 1941.[32]

Back in Rome, however, things were going from bad to worse: the sets were taking forever to complete, and a warehouse fire destroyed essential props. The production was already haemorrhaging money and spiralling wildly over budget. With disaster mounting on all sides, MGM quietly activated its crisis PR machine, determined to keep word of the Rome debacle from reaching the press.

By the 1920s, Hollywood studios had already gained considerable experience in the art of crisis public relations, though most of it centered on managing the scandals and personal dramas of stars rather than production disasters. Much of this early PR work was managed by independent press agents, many of whom came from the theatre world. These agents were masters in the art of publicity stunts, scandal manipulation and media planting, cultivating close, mutually beneficial relationships with newspapers. Their tactics laid the foundation for what would become the methodological blueprint of early film publicity.[33]

While studios continued to rely on independent press agents, by the 1910s the major film companies had begun establishing in-house publicity departments. These teams included writers, photographers and publicists who not only promoted upcoming films but also shaped and maintained the public personas of their stars, often with fictionalized biographies and curated public appearances.[34]

These departments exercised tight control over actors' images, crafting elaborate backstories, arranging photo opportunities and managing all media access. But their most critical function was damage control, deflecting or covering up scandals and spinning negative stories to protect both the star and, more importantly, the studio's reputation.[35]

One of the most notorious examples of early crisis PR in action came just a year before production began on *Ben-Hur*. In 1921, comedian Roscoe 'Fatty' Arbuckle was accused of rape and manslaughter. Though he was ultimately acquitted, the sensational media coverage all but destroyed his career. Paramount Pictures responded by deploying press agents to issue carefully worded statements in an attempt to shield the studio from public backlash. The Arbuckle case revealed not only the immense power of the press but also the ruthless pragmatism of the studio system: despite his acquittal, Paramount swiftly terminated Arbuckle's contract to distance itself from the scandal.[36]

Of course, it wasn't the first time that Rome had presented MGM with a potential PR nightmare. When they took control of the film in April 1924, and the new executives made the daring decision to fire everyone, scrap everything and start again, had word got out it could have destroyed the reputation of the film and the new studio overnight.[37]

To control the narrative, the studio started to issue misleading press releases – Charles Brabin was ill and taking time to recover. Fred Niblo had been sent to Italy to scout exteriors for a different film. The releases kept the story of *Ben-Hur* alive in the trade publications, and if the editors chose to fill in the gaps with their own speculations, well that was fine as well. The announcement that Niblo had been appointed as the new director due to Brabin's illness was not unexpected. When Brabin attempted to sue MGM for breach of contract, he lost the case and no-one was surprised.[38]

Alongside spinning the news, it was also essential to occasionally contain it. When Thalberg offered Ramon Novarro the role of Ben-Hur, he did so with an added secrecy clause. Thalberg did the same for his new scenario writers, recruited in secret in readiness for Mathis' exit.

The changes were done so stealthy that as we have already seen, poor George Walsh was entirely unaware he had been fired until he heard about it from the press. MGM press releases presented the delays and reshoots not as failures, but as evidence of the studio's commitment to perfection.[39]

The man in charge of issuing the press releases from Rome was Lou Marangella, a former actor who had recast himself as a film publicist He arrived in Rome with a smattering of Italian, which was helpful, and he immediately set to work rewriting the narrative. His elaborately worded releases appeared regularly in *The Film Daily*, the first daily newspaper devoted to the movie industry, where he waxed lyrical on the impressive sets, such as the 150ft-high Joppa Gate and the extraordinary marvel of the Circus Maximus.[40]

Press releases framed the production as a marvel of ambition: thousands of extras, historically accurate sets and a chariot race so dangerous it was reportedly filmed without rehearsals to capture raw energy – another exaggeration, but effective PR.[41]

Trade papers were flooded with carefully controlled stories. *The Motion Picture News* and *Photoplay* published glowing previews of the epic scale. Behind the scenes, Marangella was fighting fires and clamping down on negative press. The death of a stuntman during the Roman shoot was minimized, and reports of spiralling budgets were buried under spectacle-focused press tours.[42]

With a background in the theatre, Louis B Mayer was a natural PR man. When he returned from his trip to Rome, despite the fact that he was toothless and still in shock at the total chaos he had witnessed, he was able to spontaneously spin a positive story, promising that *Ben-Hur* would be a 'mammoth picture … that will outlive this generation and future generations'.[43]

The truth of course was that Mayer wanted to pull out of Rome as soon as possible and bring the film back to California under the tight control of Irving Thalberg. Unfortunately, he was faced with a scenario that was almost impossible to spin without the press picking up the scent of failure.[44]

Then Benito Mussolini inadvertently saved the day. Rome itself had imploded following the assassination of socialist leader Giacomo Matteotti in late May, causing the Italian Parliament to fall into violent chaos with fist fights between politicians. Then in December 1924, Mussolini seized total power and fascist militia were filling the streets. Mayer announced to the press that for safety's sake he had ordered the *Ben Hur* company to return to the US immediately – Mussolini's violent takeover had given him the excuse he needed to leave the chaos of Rome without losing face.[45]

With the company back in Hollywood, Mayer breathed a sigh of relief and turned the project over to young whizz kid Thalberg to salvage. The stage was set for filming to begin in Hollywood.

Chapter 11

From Rome to Hollywood: Rebuilding *Ben-Hur*

The *Ben-Hur* company sailed on 17 January 1925. Most of the Italian sets had been demolished, but the circus was left standing in the vain hope that the unit could return in the spring to complete the chariot race. Thalberg had other ideas, and upon hearing the news Fred Niblo commented with a sense of irony: 'When archaeologists unearth Rome in years to come and chance upon the ruins of a great set, they will say "Ah, how great was the civilisation of those days".'[1]

Unsubstantiated rumours persist today that some of the remaining sets were dismantled and packed on board to bring them back to Hollywood, but when Thalberg heard how high the import duties would be he ordered them to be thrown overboard before the ship docked.[2]

Almost all evidence of the ill-fated Italian expedition appears to have been erased. All that survived was some of the crowd scenes at Joppa Gate, some of the chariot race shots and the dramatic and all-too-realistic sea battle sequence, filmed off the coast of Livorno. This footage would remain in the final cut, an elaborate set of miniature ships also being built on the MGM lot in Culver City to enhance the location filming.[3]

Once back in Hollywood, work had to start from scratch to build a new Antioch Circus set to shoot the chariot race. The design of the Rome version created by Horace Jackson was scrapped, so it was back to the drawing board for the art department. Preparations for the construction of the new circus had just begun on a large piece of land behind the MGM Studio when the Los Angeles City Council started work digging a huge storm drain on the site. Beginning to believe that the production was indeed jinxed, Thalberg's team had to frantically scout round for another site. One was eventually found on the corner of what is now Venice and La Cienega Boulevards.[4]

Meanwhile, Jackson and the team were redesigning the circus on a more massive scale, although much of the apparent size was achieved by a clever optical illusion, the brainchild of Cedric Gibbons. Gibbons had been head of Goldwyn Pictures' art department, and with the merger he became absorbed into MGM's art department, working under Jackson. He would go on to become MGM's art director and supervise the look of more than a thousand MGM films throughout his thirty-two-year career with the studio. He would also be responsible for the design the Academy Awards 'Oscar' statuette.[5]

Gibbons was tasked by Thalberg to design the Antioch Circus. It would be a challenging assignment, to create a set that looked enormous but was in reality an optical illusion. He designed the stands for the lower part of the audience, which would be filled with extras, while for the upper tiers he constructed a miniature model, complete with tiny wooden spectators that could be moved to mimic cheering crowds. With the geometry calculated to the inch, the model was hung in front of the camera to perfectly complete the illusion. Even today, it's all but impossible to see where the real set ends and the model begins.[6]

Despite the impressive effect of the new design, Thalberg thought the audience would not realize the scale of the circus so he commissioned German-born sculptor Eugene Maier-Krieg to build two colossal plaster statues of crouching giants for each end of the central barrier known as the *spina* that ran down the centre of the track. Maier-Krieg had recently emigrated to the US and spent time sculpting props for several Hollywood studios. Gibbons added the final touch by having the giants turn their heads sideways as if straining to see down the track and noting which chariots were in the lead. The statues worked so well that they would be duplicated in the 1959 version of the film.[7]

When built, the circus measured 1,500ft in length and was 80ft wide. The track surface was packed with tons of sand to ensure authenticity and to cushion it for the horses.

Decorating the track were classical Roman statues, Egyptian-style obelisks, victory columns and painted frescoes and sculptural elements made of plaster, wood and papier-mâché. Roman banners, shields and insignia adorned the arena walls. The entry gates, known as *carceres*, were constructed with enough scale and detail to appear imposing on film. Painted canvases and backdrops were used to extend the illusion of a full Roman city outside of the circus, The set used thousands of tons of timber, concrete and plaster, te construction process employing hundreds of carpenters, designers and labourers.[8]

Alongside the massive sets, an entirely new wardrobe of costumes had to be created. During the Rome shoot, one of Italy's leading artists, Camillo Innocenti, played a key role, not only as a costume and set designer, but also as a historical consultant, working alongside Professor Diego Angeli. Interestingly, some of Innocenti's early costume sketches were later used in pre-release publicity.[9]

It remains unclear whether any of the original costumes made it back from Italy. At the time, MGM was just beginning to establish its own costume department, and the only official credit for costume design on *Ben-Hur* is Hermann J. Kaufmann. Kaufmann was not based in Hollywood, but was the head of Theaterkunst, Germany's oldest and largest costume design house. With a staff of 350, Theaterkunst produced everything for the film from headgear and shoes to leatherwork, armour and swords. However, once production moved to Hollywood, Germany became a logistical challenge; when Ramon Novarro needed a fitting for his armour, he had to make a two-week journey by ship to Europe.[10]

In addition to the credited designers, several others contributed without formal acknowledgment. Surviving costume sketches show work by a young in-house designer named Harold Grieve, who was in his early twenties at the time. Grieve would go on to become a founding member of the Academy of Motion Picture Arts and Sciences, before eventually leaving the film industry to build a successful career as an interior designer to the stars. Among his many high-profile projects, he designed the interiors of Bing Crosby's home.[11]

Wherever the costumes came from, the ever-flowery press releases claimed that all the designs had been deeply inspired by classical Roman and Judaean art, mosaics and statuary. However, that wasn't always the case. When the production came back to Hollywood, Mayer had decided it was time to inject some Parisian glamour into MGM's films so he arranged to bring Paris' leading designer, Russian-born Romain de Tirtoff – better known as Erté – to work at MGM as art director.

Erté's extraordinarily extravagant Art Deco designs graced the covers of *Harper's Bazaar* and he was very much the man of the moment. Though primarily an artist, Erté had worked as assistant to the great couturier Paul Poiret and designed costumes for the stage, so on paper he seemed like a perfect match for Hollywood.

The MGM publicity machine went into high gear to trumpet the arrival of Erté in the spring of 1925. He was treated like a star, installed in a hilltop house on Beechwood Drive in Hollywood, given a chauffeured limousine and two bilingual secretaries, and was subjected to no fewer than 197 interviews with the press. Yet his costume designs that seemed so delightfully bizarre and elegantly eccentric on paper just didn't work in practice. Actresses needed to move and act, and Erté's costumes were just not practical.[12]

Most of the films he was scheduled to work on didn't materialize. He also managed to antagonize the actresses he dressed as ego met ego, especially the illustrious Lillian Gish, whom he dressed for the 1926 film *La Bohème*. After six months at MGM, he asked to be released from his contract and swore he would never work in films again. He declared that his only pleasant memory of Hollywood was working with Carmel Myers on *Ben-Hur*.[13]

Carmel's character, Iras, was supposed to be an Egyptian vamp, which allowed for some artistic licence in her dress and enabled Erté to go to town creating the most extraordinary outfit with a peacock headdress. He would go on to recreate the outfit sixty-five years later when, at the age of 97 and working alongside American sculptor Ira Bruce Reines, he produced a range of bronze sculptures of his designs, including the Iras costume.[14]

Make-up was a term that had only just been invented in 1920. The man who coined the phrase was also the man who not only revolutionized how screen make-up was created but also provided the opportunity for ordinary people to buy cosmetics. His name was Maksymilian Faktorowicz, better known as Max Factor. He had first started supplying cosmetics to Hollywood in 1914 when he created Flexible Greasepaint, the first make-up for film that made actors appear more human. *Ben-Hur* provided him with probably one of the greatest single make-up orders of all time, with more than 600 gallons of body make-up needed to be sprayed on the American extras to ensure they matched that of the darker-skinned Italian extras from the scenes filmed in Italy.[15]

Whilst Max Factor focussed on the body make-up, British-born George Westmore was the studio's in-house make-up artist. Silent film acting relied heavily on exaggerated facial expressions and body language. The heavy lighting used on film sets, combined with the limitations of early black-and-white film stock, tended to wash out facial features. To counteract this, actors wore heavy make-up, with dark eyeliner, thick brows and bold lip colours to enhance the visibility of their eyes and mouths, which were key to expressing emotion. Make-up also helped define a character's personality or status. Villains were often given sharper, more severe make-up to look sinister, while heroes had softer, more rounded features. Westmore went to town on Bushman, giving his character Messala black lips, character eyebrows and shadowed eye sockets, in contrast to Novarro's far more subtle features.[16]

While the new circus was being built, Niblo and his team set about choreographing the race itself. It would be a triumph of logistical planning, cinematographic innovation and sheer spectacle. Far from being a spontaneous creation, the race was the result of months of preparation and collaborative problem-solving on a massive scale.

Although it was a team effort, it would be the second unit director, Reeves (Breezy) Eason, who would do the filming.[17] However, Niblo had a clear vision for how it should be choreographed, and part of his inspiration is said to have come from Alexander von Wagner's painting. The painting's wide-aspect ratio and dramatic elements, such as the depiction of a wheel flying off intact, were mirrored in the film's cinematography, whereas this scenario did not appear in Lew Wallace's description of the race.

Niblo also wanted the race to look realistic. He insisted that the actors and stunt performers drove actual chariots at full speed, avoiding rear-projection or undercranking (the practice of filming at a slower frame rate to artificially speed up action). This approach required elaborate training for the cast, including Novarro and Bushman.

Eason had already spent several months filming detail work on the race in Rome, and some of that footage would be reused. However, it was a properly choreographed series of full-scale races that would provide the most dramatic footage, and this was filmed in one day. As it was the most important shoot, Hollywood declared it a holiday; alongside the 10,000 extras employed to take part, more than 4,000 sightseers turned up.[18]

To create the race, Niblo employed forty-two cameramen, hiding cameras in statues, behind shields, in trenches and on high cranes. Some panorama shots were filmed from a plane. Two Cadillacs fitted with balloon tyres and platform rigs raced at 40–50 miles per hour to capture close-up shots of the chariots. The ground was continually watered down and raked to maintain consistent conditions and reduce dust.[19]

The 3,000-strong crowd, divided into sections, was directed by assistant directors, one of whom was a young William Wyler, who would go on to direct the 1959 version of *Ben-Hur*. Wyler had been paid $10 and given a toga along with a set of signals to cue the audience. Niblo himself supervised from a podium, using a megaphone as large as he was, whilst Eason directed the details.[20]

When Thalberg decided that the 3,000-strong crowd was still not looking full enough, he had another 300 plucked from the curious bystanders and dressed them in makeshift costumes.

Stars and celebrities streamed onto the circus set and many of the Hollywood stars of the day had uncredited bit parts in this movie. Seated on the stands were silent movie legends such as John and Lionel Barrymore, Joan Crawford, Marion Davis, Douglas Fairbanks, John Gilbert, Dorothy and Lillian Gish, even theatre owner Sid Grauman. Gary Cooper is supposed to have played a Roman guard, as did Clark Gable, with Janet Gaynor and Myrna Loy playing slave girls. Before the race, fifty-four horsemen of the Roman Imperial Guard played a fanfare of trumpets. The horsemen were part of the cavalry troop of the Monterey Garrison.[21]

There were twelve chariots and forty-eight horses. Ben-Hur, as the hero, had a team of four whites, and Messala, the villain, drove four blacks. The stunt charioteers were rodeo riders, cowboys, circus performers and polo-pony breakers, with an offer of a substantial bonus to the man who won the race – the moment when Ben-Hur crossed the finish line would be filmed later.[22] Betting on which stunt man would win the race gave an added frisson to the day, meaning the film crew didn't need to whip up any forced enthusiasm with the crowd. The whole day was a riot, with the crowds responding like the audience at the original circus in Antioch.

The races produced a terrifyingly realistic piece of filming, including some horrific crash scenes. During one of the races, two chariots became tangled and caused a pile-up. Bushman alleged that at least five horses were said to have been killed, and assistant director Henry Hathaway had to run into the arena to try to stop oncoming drivers. Hathaway's unexpected appearance made it into the final cut, as did the crash itself, which became part of the final scene when Messala's chariot was wrecked. MGM always denied that any horses were killed, a claim backed up by the SPCA (Society for the Prevention of Cruelty to Animals) and an eyewitness account from the President of the American Animal Defensive League.[23]

However, Joe Cohn, one of the assistant directors, would later admit that the actual crash scene had been staged later in an empty stadium, when no-one could report what went on to the SPCA.[24]

It would take another two months to complete the chariot race scene with all the additional close ups of thundering hooves, spinning chariot wheels, flexing muscles and lashing whips. This extra filming included the frontal shots of Bushman and Novarro driving their chariots, pulled along not by horses but by specially designed camera cars. The circus and race sequence alone cost about $500,000, roughly an eighth of the film's total $4 million budget, an extraordinary figure at the time. Nevertheless, it was hailed as a technical and cinematic triumph, and the set became a benchmark for large-scale Hollywood set design. Its influence was felt decades later, especially in the 1959 remake directed by William Wyler, which modelled its race closely on this original.[25]

With shooting finally wrapped, Lloyd Nosler and the editing department faced the monumental task of trimming over 60,960 metres of footage down to just 228.6 metres for the iconic chariot race alone.[26]

A rough cut of the film was screened on 2 December 1925, but with the premiere only weeks away, Irving Thalberg – still recovering from a recent heart attack – ordered another round of cuts and retakes.[27]

The chariot race wasn't the only sequence to be trimmed from the original edit. In the early 1920s, Hollywood was under intense scrutiny following a series of high-profile scandals. Religious, civic and political groups widely condemned the film industry, claiming it undermined public morals. Various states introduced their own censorship laws, and political pressure on studios was mounting rapidly.[28]

In response, the studios decided that self-regulation was the only way to counteract growing opposition. They appointed Presbyterian elder Will H. Hays as president of the newly formed Motion Picture Producers and Distributors of America (MPPDA). In 1924, Hays, working alongside the studios, introduced a set of guidelines known as 'the Formula', which urged filmmakers to avoid certain content. By 1927, these recommendations were formalized as the 'Don'ts and Be Carefuls' list of eleven subjects to be avoided and twenty-six to be handled with caution, collectively called the Magna Charta.[29]

Among the strictest rules was number two on the 'Don'ts' list: 'Any licentious or suggestive nudity in fact or silhouette; and any lecherous or licentious notice thereof by other characters in the picture.' Ironically, the final footage of *Ben-Hur* contained a scene during Ben-Hur's triumphant procession in Rome featuring bare-breasted women in the background, and a naked man in the Roman warship galley scene; these were removed in the 1931 reissue.[30]

Another notable cut was a scene featuring Esther driving a chariot. In reality, the actress May McAvoy, standing just 4ft 11in tall, was physically unable to control the horses; the tension on the reins even caused dislocated wrists.[31]

The film also featured early use of colour technology. Several sequences, mainly those depicting Jesus, were shot using a two-tone Technicolor process with red and green filters. Although not the first film to include colour scenes, this early experimentation significantly boosted *Ben-Hur*'s production value and audience appeal.[32]

The finished film is mostly faithful to Wallace's epic story. It starts in Jerusalem under the reign of Herod. The birth of Christ introduces the historical period of the film, which then moves on to the story of Ben-Hur. He is arrested, along with his mother and sister, by ex-friend Messala, who now serves Valerius Gratus, the new Roman Prefect of Judea. Ben-Hur is forced into servitude as a slave in a Roman galley for three years, then saves the life of the ship's commander in a battle with pirates and is adopted by him. But his mind is on revenge and finding his family.

He goes to Antioch to find Simonides, a former slave of his father, who had been tasked with hiding the family's fortune, and falls in love with his daughter, Esther. Then he is enlisted by a sheik to drive his chariot in a race;

he accepts eagerly when he learns he must race against Messala and defeats him spectacularly by catching Messala's chariot wheel in his own. In the meantime, Esther goes to the Valley of the Lepers to bring Ben-Hur's mother and sister to Christ to be healed just as he is made to walk to his crucifixion. The film finishes at that point, whereas the novel continues beyond the death of Christ until the reign of the Roman Emperor Nero. In the book, Ben-Hur goes to Rome to help build the catacombs used by Christians escaping Nero's persecution. Another difference between the novel and the film is that in the novel, Messala survives the chariot race, although he is crippled for life. In the 1925 film, it is implied that he dies after the race.

With the picture finally finished MGM's publicity department started the hype. 'The Picture every Christian Ought to See!' was their pre-release tagline, although one quick-witted film critic suggested that it should be extended to include every Muslim, every Jew, every Buddhist and every sun worshipper in America, if the picture was ever going to recoup what it cost to make.[33]

Chapter 12

Ben-Hur and the Art of Ballyhoo: Publicity, Propaganda and Hollywood Spectacle

Publicity, or at least the right type of publicity, had become vital for promoting movies in an ever-growing competitive market. By the mid-1920s, the MGM publicity department was a well-oiled machine staffed by publicists, photographers, writers and graphic designers. By the end of the 1920s, the department would be ruled by Howard Strickling, the keeper of secrets, who along with MGM's general manager, Eddie Mannix, would become the fixer of all problems.[1]

Even before Strickling took over, the department was already taking control over nearly every aspect of a star's public image, including official biographies – often fabricated or sanitized – fan magazine stories, press announcements, scandal management and glamorous photo shoots. The glamour photos were always heavily retouched. In the era before Photoshop and CGI, retouching was a meticulous, manual process. Retouchers would physically alter the photographic negative, often using tools like pencils, to smooth skin, remove blemishes and enhance features.[2]

Scene stills were equally important. These shots were taken on-stage during filming, capturing key moments and scenes as they unfolded. The still photographer worked closely with the film crew to document the action, ensuring that each shot reflected the director's vision and the overall aesthetic of the production.

Stories, biographies and photographs of stars, scene stills and sets circulated through newspapers, magazines and promotional material played a vital role in shaping public perceptions of Hollywood.[3] Studios churned out hundreds of photos every week, storing them in archives that weren't just for creative use, but also a way to control how stars were seen. These archives helped make sure only approved images made it to the public. Studios often held exclusive rights to an actor's image, and photo shoots were carefully supervised by publicists to avoid anything unflattering or revealing being circulated.[4]

Everything about a star's look – hair, make-up, pose, even their gaze – was carefully planned to keep their public image consistent. For female stars in particular, photos were used to push certain ideas of femininity: innocence, glamour, elegance. Any unapproved images, like party candids or leaked snapshots, were quickly shut down. Studios would buy back negatives, threaten lawsuits or offer advertising money in exchange for media cooperation.[5]

The release of *Ben-Hur* marked one of the most elaborate photo campaigns of the silent film era. Under the direction of Ruth Harriet Louise, MGM's pioneering head of portrait photography, the studio's photographic department produced a striking array of images: heroic portraits of leading man Ramon Novarro in full Roman regalia, brooding shots of Francis X. Bushman as the villainous Messala and dramatic stills from the legendary chariot race, temple sets and grand Roman pageants.[6]

By the time *Ben-Hur* was ready for distribution, MGM had acquired a new and formidable publicity skill set courtesy of the man of the moment, Edward Bernays, nephew of Sigmund Freud. Often called the father of public relations, Bernays elevated the art of publicity into a calculated science. Drawing on his uncle's psychological theories and techniques developed during First World War propaganda efforts, Bernays did not merely respond to public opinion – he aimed to shape and direct it. In his groundbreaking 1923 book *Crystallizing Public Opinion*, he envisioned public relations as a powerful, almost cinematic force capable of molding mass consciousness.[7]

Bernays' strategies were innovative and influential: employ respected voices, use symbolism to mask messaging and target the public's emotions. Hollywood took notice. Studios eagerly adopted his methods, transforming movie stars into larger-than-life icons – representations of American ideals such as family values, patriotism and modern femininity.[8]

Films became more than just entertainment; they became national cultural events. Few campaigns would implement Bernays' vision with the scope and sophistication of *Ben-Hur*'s promotional rollout.[9]

Although press coverage had followed the film throughout its lengthy production, the official release was accompanied by a massive media blitz.

Serialized articles appeared in newspapers and magazines; production photos showcasing the epic scale of the sets and costumes were 'leaked' to generate buzz; and interviews with director Fred Niblo and the cast kept the public engaged.

Images from the chariot race became iconic, appearing on posters, billboards, in storefronts and throughout the press. The film's promotion extended beyond traditional media: churches and religious groups were enlisted to endorse the film, special screenings were held for clergy and marketing materials emphasized that the film was 'safe for families'. Cross-promotions with retailers encouraged themed window displays, while schools received educational guides connecting the movie to classical history and Christian ethics.[10]

The film premiere, first invented by Sid Grauman to promote his new Egyptian Theatre in Hollywood, was a must for *Ben-Hur*. Premieres had become orchestrated spectacles, complete with red carpets, camera flashes and carefully choreographed hype. However, MGM decided to buck the trend and hold the opening not in Hollywood but in New York City at the George M. Cohan Theatre on Broadway. The choice of venue was partly as a salute to the success of the play and the fact that Abraham Erlanger had shares in the film, but also because of New York's status as a major theatrical and cultural centre. The premiere was on 30 December, and was followed by a lavish reception. It was a huge success with critics and audiences alike.

The *Daily Variety* critic was overwhelmed, announcing in his review:

> 'There will be no further reason for a future production of "Ben-Hur" for the screen unless there is some tremendous change in the art of visualization of the dramatic, that is as yet unrealized. Then and only then, providing that there is some tremendous advancement in the art of direction and photography will another "Ben-Hur" be necessary. As the industry today stands, so does Ben-Hur stand: the greatest achievement that has been accomplished on the screen for not only the screen itself but for all motion picturedom ... It isn't a picture! It's the Bible!'

He carried on this way for six columns, certainly not needing the MGM publicists to prompt him.[11]

Alexander von Wagner – *The Chariot Race*, Manchester Art Gallery.

Reconstruction of the Circus Maximus (above) and a view of the site (below) (before 1704) by Jan Goeree, (Dutch, 1670–1731).

Eadweard Muybridge, *The Horse in Motion* ('Sallie Gardner', owned by Leland Stanford; running at a 1:40 gait over the Palo Alto track, 19 June 1878), 1878, albumen print. (*Library of Congress, Washington, DC*)

Chariot Race in the Circus at Antioch, engraving by Carlo Ademollo.

General Lew Wallace in a recliner with *Chariot Race* etching in background, courtesy of General Lew Wallace Study & Museum, Crawfordsville, Indiana.

Ulpiano Checa, *Carrera de Carros V.* Acuarela. Paris, 1900. Colmenar de Oreja, Museo Ulpiano Checa.

General Lew Wallace, photographed writing under his favourite beech tree, courtesy of General Lew Wallace Study & Museum, Crawfordsville, Indiana.

Lew Wallace, 1862, photograph by Charles DeForest Fredricks. National Portrait Gallery, Smithsonian Institution; gift of Mrs F.B. Wilde.

Reprint of Wallace Memorial Edition, courtesy of Colmenar de Oreja, Museo Ulpiano Checa.

Advertisement poster for Virginia Saffel Mercer's 'Ben-Hur's Show' (author unknown), Lilly Library, Indiana University, Bloomington, Indiana.

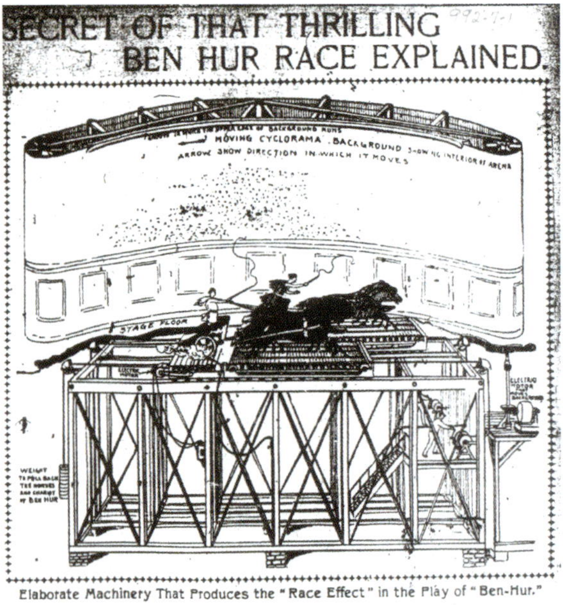

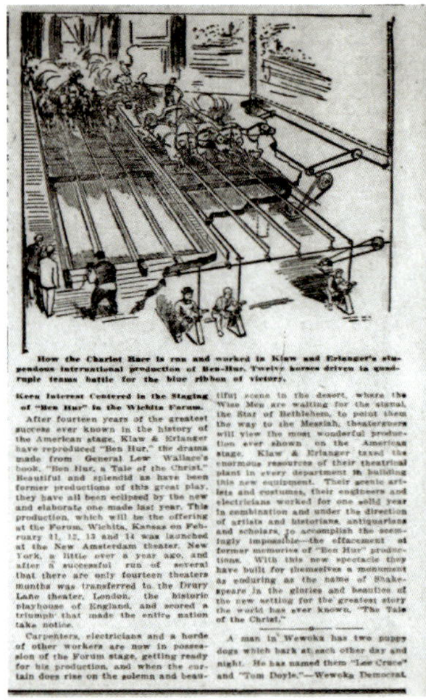

How the Chariot Race is run and worked in Klaw and Erlanger's stupendous international production of Ben-Hur. Twelve horses driven in quadruple teams battle for the blue ribbon of victory.

Keen Interest Centered in the Staging of "Ben Hur" in the Wichita Forum.

After fourteen years of the greatest success ever known in the history of the American stage, Klaw & Erlanger have reproduced "Ben Hur," the drama made from General Lew Wallace's book, "Ben Hur, a Tale of the Christ." Beautiful and splendid as have been former productions of this great play, they have all been eclipsed by the new and elaborate one made last year. This production, which will be the offering at the Forum, Wichita, Kansas on February 11, 12, 13 and 14 was launched at the New Amsterdam theater, New York, a little over a year ago, and after a successful run of several that there are only fourteen theaters months was transferred to the Drury Lane theater, London, the historic playhouse of England, and scored a triumph that made the entire nation take notice.

Carpenters, electricians and a horde of other workers are now in possession of the Forum stage, getting ready for his production, and when the curtain does rise on the solemn and beautiful scene in the desert, where the Wise Men are waiting for the signal, the Star of Bethlehem, to point them the way to the Messiah, theatergoers will view the most wonderful production ever shown on the American stage. Klaw & Erlanger taxed the enormous resources of their theatrical plant in every department in building this new equipment. Their scenic artists and costumes, their engineers and electricians worked for one solid year in combination and under the direction of artists and historians, antiquarians and scholars, to accomplish the seemingly impossible—the effacement of former memories of "Ben Hur" productions. With this new spectacle they have built for themselves a monument as enduring as the name of Shakespeare in the glories and beauties of the new setting for the greatest story the world has ever known, "The Tale of the Christ."

A man in Wewoka has two puppy dogs which bark at each other day and night. He has named them "Lee Cruce" and "Tom Doyle."—Wewoka Democrat.

Images of the horse race stage design, *Weekly Eagle*, Wichita, Kansas, courtesy of General Lew Wallace Study & Museum, Crawfordsville, Indiana.

Poster from the Brodway premiere of *Ben-Hur*. Produced by A.L. Erlanger and Marc Klaw, Manhattan Theatre, New York, NY, c. 1899; Strobridge & Co. Lith.

Illinois theatre poster of *Ben-Hur* using Alexander von Wagner Chariot Race painting. Strobridge & Co. Lith.

Stage curtain featuring Alexander von Wagner's *Chariot Race* from Wichita Forum, Kansas.

Advertisement for Thomas Edison's Vitascope.

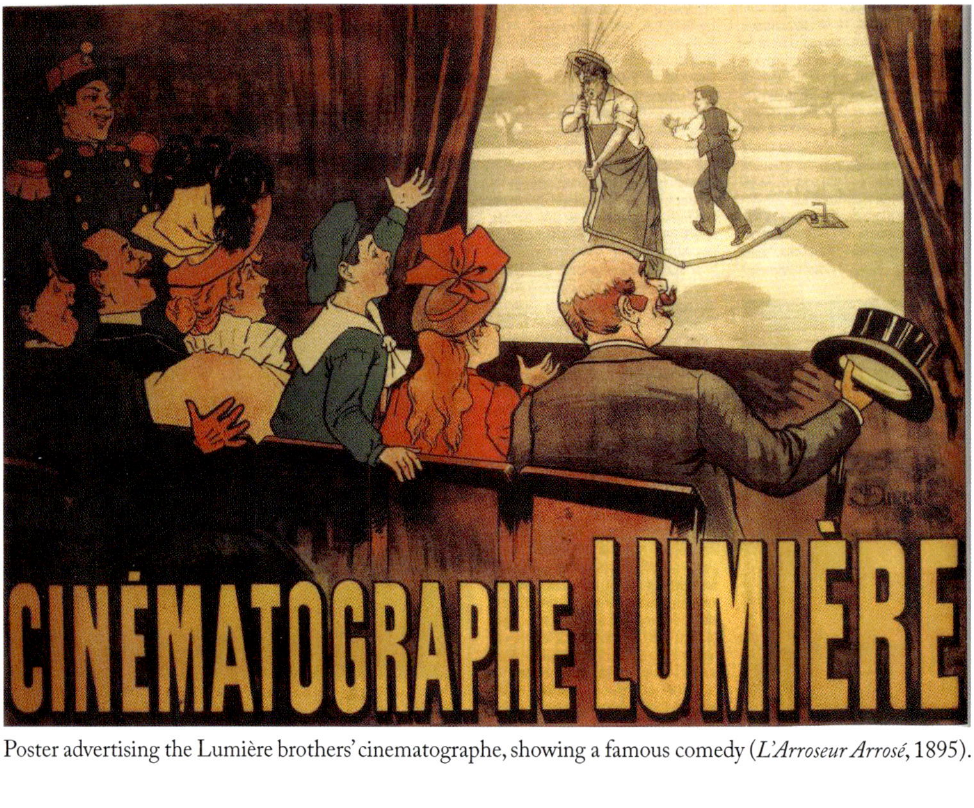

Poster advertising the Lumière brothers' cinematographe, showing a famous comedy (*L'Arroseur Arrosé*, 1895).

Frame from the hand-coloured print of Georges Méliès's 1902 film *Le voyage dans la lune*.

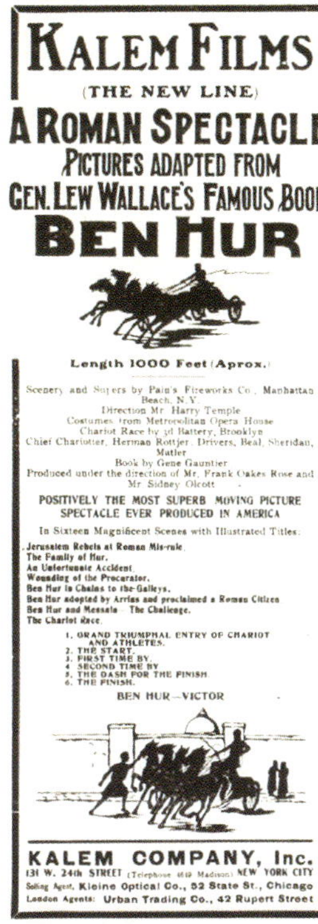

Advertisement for 1907 film *Ben-Hur* with heading 'KALEM FILMS'; published in the trade journal *The Moving Picture World* (New York, NY), 7 December 1907.

Films corrupting Young America (1910), Louis Glackens, Puck Illustrations.

Film cinema poster for *The Birth of a Nation*.

Ben-Hur (1925) cinema poster featuring Carmel Myers in white wig.

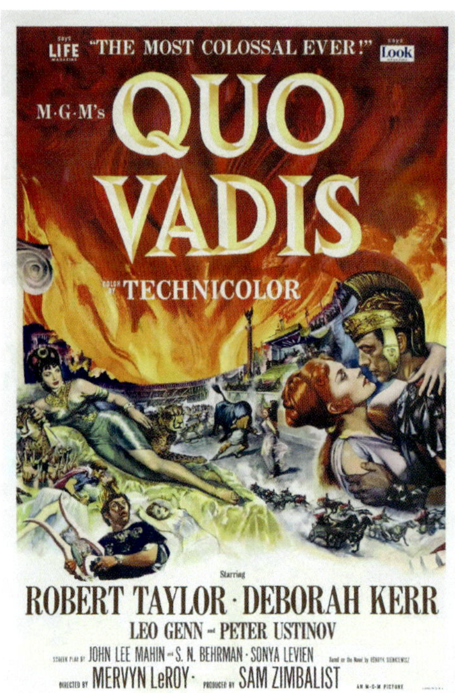

Quo Vadis (1951) cinema poster.

Poster for 1959 *Ben-Hur* film.

Advertising Poster, "Ben-Hur Flour is For Sale in This Town," circa 1910. (*The Henry Ford* (*thehenryford.org*))

Charlton Heston in chariot, 1959 *Ben-Hur* film – Touring Club Italiano.

Chariot race, 1959 *Ben-Hur* film – Touring Club Italiano.

Ben-Hur Cigars advert – courtesy of General Lew Wallace Study & Museum.

Wire-Fence Co. (c. 1890–1900), Boston Public Library.

Photoplay adverts with Jergens products.

Jergens Perfume, courtesy of Grace Hummel/Cleopatra's Boudoir.

Iras bronze statue by Erté, courtesy of Hickmet Fine Arts.

Journey of the Magi, mosaic, Basilica Sant'Apollinare Nuovo, Ravenna, *c.* sixth century. Names added at a later date.

The Monteleone chariot, sixth century BCE, Etruscan; Metropolitan Museum, New York.

Detail from *Ben-Hur*'s German Movie Poster, 1925.

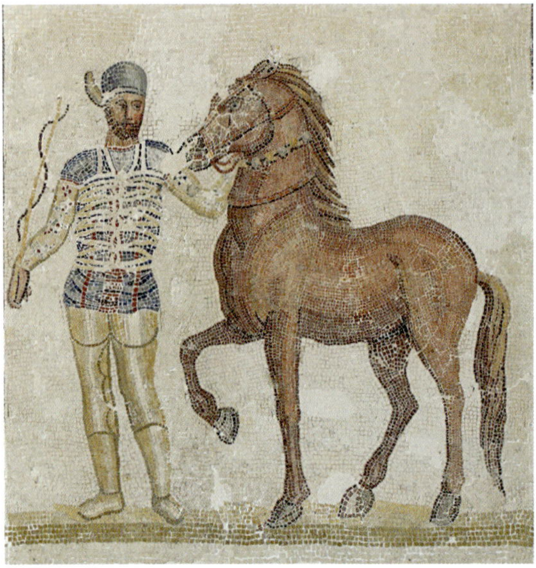

Pavement mosaic with a circus charioteer of the *veneta* (blue) faction. Roman artwork, first half of the third century CE. Palazzo Massimo alle Terme.

Ben-Hur costume with Star of David.

When all the ballyhoo around the film was finally over, one MGM executive remarked dryly: 'Nothing like it ever has been. Nothing like it ever will be. And nothing like it ever should have been.'[12]

Of course, the premiere was just the beginning. Indeed, 30 December marked not just the debut of a film, but the launch of one of the most ambitious and carefully orchestrated film release campaigns of the silent era. Following its premiere, *Ben-Hur* entered a meticulously planned roadshow release strategy that played a central role in both recouping its immense production costs and establishing MGM as a global cinematic powerhouse. The roadshow distribution model was reserved for high-prestige films and involved limited engagements in select first-run theatres, often accompanied by reserved seating, elevated ticket prices and elaborate promotional materials.[13]

MGM followed the precedent set by earlier epics such as *The Birth of a Nation* (1915) and *The Ten Commandments* (1923), but elevated the form with unprecedented scale. The studio prioritized cities with Loew's theatre holdings, taking advantage of its vertically integrated parent company, Loew's Inc, which allowed MGM to maintain strict control over both the exhibition quality and revenue streams.[14] In cities such as Chicago, Los Angeles, Boston and Philadelphia, *Ben-Hur* played for weeks or even months, often accompanied by live musical scores and printed souvenir programmes to emphasize its cultural significance.[15]

While MGM had initially feared that *Ben-Hur*'s staggering production cost – estimated at over $4 million, an unprecedented sum at the time – might never be recouped, its bold roadshow strategy proved remarkably effective. By the end of 1926, the film had earned more than $5 million in domestic rentals alone. Critical reception was equally enthusiastic, with contemporary reviewers hailing its visual splendour, spiritual gravitas and the now-legendary chariot race sequence.[16]

The financial model of the roadshow release, where theatres paid a flat fee or split profits under favourable terms, allowed MGM to recover its investment more quickly than a traditional general release would have permitted. The film's profitability also helped to solidify the studio's reputation for lavish, prestige filmmaking, a brand identity that would carry MGM through the 1930s as a powerhouse of Hollywood glamour and quality.[17]

Ever the showman, theatre impresario Sid Grauman recognized the film's box office potential early on. Having made a cameo as a crowd extra in the chariot race, Grauman secured a deal with Louis B. Mayer to host the film's Pacific Coast premiere and exclusive yearlong run at his iconic Egyptian Theatre in Los Angeles, turning the venue into a shrine for cinematic spectacle.[18]

Following its domestic triumph, *Ben-Hur* launched into international markets with equal grandeur. MGM expanded or reinforced overseas branches in cities like London, Paris and Berlin to manage localized promotion and distribution. In these cultural capitals, the film was treated not just as entertainment but as a high-profile artistic event, often accompanied by live orchestras, translated intertitles and custom-tailored advertising. In the UK, it premiered at London's Royal Albert Hall in 1926 with a full symphonic score, and by 1928 it had become one of the highest-grossing silent films ever released in Europe.[19]

The roadshow format proved equally effective abroad, with premieres in national theatres followed by gradual regional rollouts. Even after its initial runs concluded, the film continued to earn revenue through wider general release in smaller towns and second-run cinemas, keeping it in circulation well into the early sound era.

By 1931, *Ben-Hur* had grossed over $10 million worldwide, becoming the highest-grossing silent film of its time and one of the most financially successful films of the pre-sound era. It demonstrated not only the commercial viability of large-scale productions but also the power of roadshow distribution as a premium marketing strategy model that would shape the future of film promotion for decades.[20]

However, the film's global reach was not without resistance. It was banned in China, denounced as 'Christian propaganda decoying the people to superstition', and – more unexpectedly – in fascist Italy. Mussolini reportedly ordered the ban after learning that the noble-looking Roman character played by Bushman was, in fact, the villain, not the hero.[21]

By mid-1929, three-and-a-half years after its premiere, *Ben-Hur*'s popularity began to decline as audiences turned to the emerging novelty of sound films. Recognizing the cultural shift, MGM adapted. In June 1931, a synchronized sound version debuted in London, featuring a newly recorded score by original composers William Axt and David Mendoza, along with sound effects. The two-colour Technicolor scenes were replaced with alternate black-and-white takes, and the rerelease was a critical and commercial success.[22]

Ultimately, *Ben-Hur* not only proved that prestige cinema could be both spiritually resonant and commercially explosive, it redefined what a movie could be. With its monumental production, pioneering marketing and enduring impact, it became the definitive screen version of the story for more than three decades, setting the standard for epic filmmaking around the world.

Chapter 13

The Rise and Reign of Metro-Goldwyn-Mayer (1925–51) – The Golden Era of Hollywood

Ben-Hur had emerged not only as a cinematic triumph but as a cautionary tale etched into Hollywood's foundation. What had nearly bankrupted MGM before the studio had even found its footing ultimately solidified its place in film history. The astronomical budget, chaotic overseas shoots and unprecedented scope of the production pushed the studio to the brink, but also set a new standard for spectacle in American cinema. As the dust settled and audiences filled theatres, it became clear that the gamble – though nearly ruinous – had paid off. MGM had survived its trial by fire; *Ben-Hur* became the film that proved both the peril and promise of ambition in early Hollywood.

However, Mayer and Thalberg learned a hard lesson from their *Ben-Hur* ordeal: no matter how grand the film, it should always be shot within a day or two's reach of the MGM lot. It was a rule born of chaos, cost and near catastrophe, one they would break only once more in all their years working together.[1]

Although *Ben-Hur* had given MGM the public profile that Louis B. Mayer had always craved, it was actually the success of director King Vidor's Great War drama *The Big Parade*, released a month earlier and starring John Gilbert, that actually boosted MGM's prestige and provided the studio with a rock-solid financial footing that would last for more than twenty years.[2]

MGM certainly needed to boost its coffers, as the late 1920s witnessed a seismic shift in the history of movies with the advent of synchronized sound. Although experiments with sound in film date back to the early 1900s, the breakthrough came with Warner Bros' release of *The Jazz Singer* in 1927 featuring synchronized dialogue sequences.

The film's success demonstrated sound's commercial potential and triggered a rapid industry-wide conversion to talkies. By 1930, silent films had virtually disappeared from major Hollywood studios' production schedules.[3]

The transition to sound demanded enormous investment in new equipment and soundproof stages, and changes in acting and directing styles. Early sound films were technically limited, with static cameras and microphones restricting movement, but these limitations were quickly overcome as technology improved.[4]

MGM was slow to commit to sound. Mayer worked on the principle that it was better to let the other studios 'tussle with the technology and find out what worked and what didn't'. However, once he had decided the time was right, the studio was quick to equip itself with sound technology and to decide which of its stars could adapt best to the new format.[5]

Unfortunately, their star actor John Gilbert's transition to talkies was not a success. It has been suggested that Mayer's animosity to the star led to him sabotaging his performance by arranging for sound engineers to make his voice sound unnaturally high pitched, but it is more likely that it was Gilbert's old-fashioned theatrical diction that made his performances seem staged.[6]

In true Hollywood fashion, the much-publicized feud between studio mogul Louis B. Mayer and actor John Gilbert was said to have been sparked by a broken heart. According to legend, Gilbert had fallen deeply in love with Greta Garbo during the filming of the 1926 silent classic *Flesh and the Devil*. The two were reportedly set to marry in a lavish double wedding alongside director King Vidor and actress Eleanor Boardman. But on the big day, Garbo famously got cold feet, failing to appear at the ceremony and leaving Gilbert humiliated.

Mayer, never known for his tact, is said to have quipped that Gilbert would have been better off simply sleeping with Garbo rather than trying to marry her. Already reeling emotionally, Gilbert snapped. Enraged by the insult, he punched Mayer on the nose, breaking his glasses in the process. Mayer, bleeding and livid, allegedly swore revenge: 'I'll destroy him even if it costs me a million dollars.'

Whether myth or fact, the fallout was real and Gilbert's career soon began to unravel. He turned increasingly to alcohol, and despite a few brief comebacks, he never fully recovered his star status. He died of a heart attack in 1936 aged just 36, another tragic casualty of the golden age of Hollywood.[7]

Perhaps surprisingly, Garbo's transition to talkies was especially notable. MGM cast her as the lead in *Anna Christie*, the film adaptation of the 1921 play of the same name by Eugene O'Neill. The film was advertised with the catchline 'Garbo Talks'. Her opening line, 'Gimme a whisky, ginger ale on the side and don't be stingy baby', was a cultural moment in itself.[8]

As Gilbert's star faded, a new actor stepped in to take his place. Clark Gable was the son of an oil driller and a rough, tough, all-American boy, a very different actor for a different era, MGM's equivalent of Warner's James Cagney, except with sex appeal.[9]

The 1930s also saw the development of film genres: musicals, gangster films, screwball comedies, horror movies and spicy romances flourished, and Gable was able to adapt to them all.

The fun elements in the movies of the 1930s went some way to dissipate the misery of the Depression era. Unfortunately, in mid-1934, much of the fun was curtailed when Hollywood was forced to tone down its storylines. This was the time when The Motion Picture Production Code, commonly known as the Hays Code, became more strictly enforced by the Production Code Administration, better known as the PCA. After that, all scripts and films had to be submitted for approval, and movies without a PCA seal could not be released by major studios.[10]

With the new restrictions on sexuality, crime, profanity and other 'immoral' themes, studios began leaning more heavily on historical epics, costume dramas and literary adaptations as a 'safe' way to deliver spectacle, romance and drama without running afoul of the censors. Setting a film in the past provided a moral 'buffer'. Audiences and censors were more forgiving of risqué behaviour or controversial themes if they were presented as part of a bygone era. Big-budget historical dramas also allowed for lavish costumes and production values, which audience loved.[11]

Having cut its teeth on *Ben-Hur*, MGM was quick to embrace the idea of big-budget historical dramas, especially ones with a literary or theatrical background. *The Barretts of Wimpole Street* would be MGM's first foray into historical movies post-code. Set in the 1840s and taken from an original play by Rudolph Wilhelm Besier, the film tells the story of English poet

Elizabeth Barrett, played by Norma Shearer, who lives a reclusive and sickly life under the oppressive control of her domineering father, Edward Moulton-Barrett. When the poet Robert Browning begins corresponding with her, a romance blossoms. The story focused on Elizabeth's struggle to assert her independence, escape her father's tyranny and marry Browning.

Despite its period setting, the film contains deeply emotional and even incestuous overtones, especially in Charles Laughton's portrayal of the possessive father. For the screenplay, all overt suggestions of incest were removed, but Laughton assured producer Thalberg, 'They can't censor the gleam in my eye.' It was a phrase that went down in Hollywood history.[12]

Thalberg's methodical production system emphasized strong scripts and test screenings, making MGM films more polished than many of their contemporaries. It also expanded its stable of bankable stars, with Mayer declaring that the studio had 'more stars than there are in heaven'. Iconic names like Joan Crawford, Helen Hayes, Jean Harlow, Lon Chaney, Marie Dressler, Wallace Beery, Spencer Tracy, Mickey Rooney, Judy Garland and John and Lionel Barrymore were part of their stable, alongside Greta Garbo, Norma Shearer, Clark Gable and Ramon Novarro.

Thalberg continued to champion historical movies such as *Mutiny on the Bounty* with Clark Gable and Charles Laughton, which won Best Picture Award in 1935. He had started pre-production work on *Marie Antoinette,* once again starring his wife, Norma Shearer, when his health started to fail. Weakened by a congenital heart defect, he was unable to rally after a bout of pneumonia and died aged just 37 in September 1936.[13]

One of MGM's most significant contributions to film history came after his death and from outside the studio. The film version of *Gone with the Wind* was the brainchild of Mayer's son-in-law, David O. Selznick, who had worked at MGM alongside Thalberg but then left to set up his own studio.

Written by Margaret Mitchell, *Gone with the Wind* is set in the American South during the Civil War and Reconstruction era. Despite being a first novel, it was hugely successful and Mitchell won a Pulitzer Prize for her work. Several studios, including MGM, considered buying the film rights. However, MGM passed on the opportunity, reportedly because Mayer believed the story was too long, expensive and controversial to adapt effectively.[14]

Selznick, convinced it would be a success, shocked everyone by buying the rights to the novel for $50,000. Not only did he believe a film version of the book would be a blockbuster, but he also had just the man in mind to play the lead role of Rhett Butler.

Having committed himself to the project, he faced two problems. Firstly finance, as his studio didn't have the budget or the structure to finance and distribute such a massive epic; secondly, the actor he had in mind for Rhett Butler was Clark Gable, who was under contract to MGM. Never one to be beaten, he turned to his father-in-law and negotiated a crucial deal: MGM would finance part of the film and, in return, gain domestic distribution rights and the casting of Clark Gable, the studio's most bankable male star.[15]

Directed primarily by Victor Fleming, who was also brought in to complete *The Wizard of Oz*, another massive film that was under development by MGM, *Gone with the Wind* was an unprecedented cinematic undertaking. It employed Technicolor, massive sets and over fifty speaking roles. Released in December 1939, it became the highest-grossing film of all time when adjusted for inflation, a record it still holds.[16] It also launched the career of a new female star, Vivien Leigh, who would win a Best Actress Oscar for her role as Scarlett O'Hara, one of the eight Academy Awards the film would earn, including Best Supporting Actress for Hattie McDaniel, the first Black performer to win an Oscar.

Ironically, Mayer had once claimed that neither colour, widescreen nor television would ever revolutionize the movies as sound had. He believed colour distracted the audience from the story being told and was only good for short travelogues. After the phenomenal success of *Gone with the Wind*, he had to eat his words.[17]

Having ridden the storm of the Production Code, the next challenge to face MGM and Hollywood was unionization. The 1930s marked a turning point in Hollywood's labour history, as film industry workers began organizing for better wages, working conditions and creative rights. Studio executives strongly resisted these efforts, seeing unionization as a threat to their authority. In response, they used various tactics, ranging from promoting company-controlled unions to employing intimidation and blacklisting.

During this turbulent period, organized crime also became involved in Hollywood labour disputes. Criminal elements infiltrated key unions and used their influence to extract payments from studios in exchange for labour peace. Some industry figures opposed these dealings, but the influence of corruption was difficult to avoid.[18]

Despite these challenges, progress was made. New unions such as the Screen Actors Guild emerged, bolstered by public support and federal labour protections. By the end of the decade, the groundwork was laid for the modern system of Hollywood unions, though it came at a high cost. The conflicts of the 1930s reflected deeper tensions between labour, management and outside forces, issues that would resurface in later decades.[19]

The Second World War had a profound impact on Hollywood, with resources diverted to the war effort and many actors and filmmakers serving in the military. However, even if the war slowed down mainstream movie production, Hollywood was still able to play a significant role in propaganda and boosting morale. The US government collaborated closely with studios to produce patriotic movies, documentaries and training films. MGM focused on patriotic dramas, musicals and comedies that offered both support for the war effort and escapism for audiences. Films like *Mrs Miniver* (1942) demonstrated that MGM could handle serious themes with its characteristic elegance. It tells the story of a British family's resilience and quiet heroism during the Second World War as they face the trials of wartime life on the home front. It won the Best Picture Oscar and earned praise from President Roosevelt for bolstering morale on the home front.[20]

After the war, Hollywood experienced a boom period with record attendance and box office revenues. The return of servicemen and the baby boom generation fuelled demand for new entertainment, while technological innovations such as CinemaScope and improved colour processes enhanced the viewing experience.[21]

By 1947, MGM was still basking in its reputation for 'more stars than there are in heaven'. The studio continued to release glossy, high-budget films with big stars and high production values. MGM excelled in genres like musicals, melodramas and literary adaptations. During this era, the studio capitalized on the talents of stars such as Elizabeth Taylor, Judy Garland, Gene Kelly and Spencer Tracy.

Musicals, in particular, became MGM's signature product. *Easter Parade* (1948), starring Judy Garland and Fred Astaire, and *An American in Paris*

(1951), with Gene Kelly, were major box office successes and set the standard for musical filmmaking. The latter won six Academy Awards, including Best Picture, highlighting MGM's dominance in prestige productions.[22]

After the boom came problems. The post-war period also saw the rise of anti-communist sentiment, culminating in the Hollywood Blacklist and investigations by the House Un-American Activities Committee (HUAC). Many writers, directors and actors were accused of communist sympathies, resulting in career disruptions and heightened political censorship.[23]

In 1948, the Supreme Court made a big decision in a case called United States v Paramount Pictures, Inc, also known as the Paramount Decree. This ruling changed the way Hollywood did business. It forced major studios like MGM to sell off their movie theatre chains. Before that, studios could make a movie and control where it was shown, which gave them a big advantage. After the decision, that setup was no longer allowed. It was a devastating setback for the MGM. The studio had already experienced a 40 per cent decline in profits during 1947, which had led to cutbacks and the appointment of a new 'Thalberg' in the shape of former screenwriter and producer Dore Schary.[24]

Mayer and Schary rubbed along at first, but by 1950 they were arguing over films, assignments and everything. Then on 31 August 1951, twenty-seven years after he first joined MGM, Mayer resigned his position as its studio head. The resignation was not entirely of his choosing; relations had broken down with Schary so dramatically that Mayer told MGM's president, Nick Schenck, that 'It's either me or Schary'. Schenck chose Schary. The turmoil at MGM was symptomatic of what was going on across the whole of Hollywood. The studio system was disintegrating, while television was growing.[25]

By 1955, over half of American households owned a TV set, and movie attendance plummeted.[26] To lure audiences back into theatres, MGM embraced technological innovations such as Technicolor, widescreen formats and stereo sound. The most notable development was CinemaScope, which provided a wider and more immersive visual experience. These technological advances also encouraged epic storytelling and spectacle. What better place to find this sort of spectacle than with religious epics.

Chapter 14

Faith and Spectacle: The Rise of the Religious Epic in 1950s Hollywood

In 1950s Hollywood, epics reigned supreme and their dominant theme was religious. The explosion of large-scale biblical productions during this decade was no coincidence. A convergence of social, political and economic factors propelled Hollywood toward stories of faith, morality and divine intervention.

Post-Second World War America was a society in transition. After years of war and global uncertainty, many Americans turned to religion for comfort and identity. Church membership soared from 55 per cent in 1940 to 69 per cent by 1960, reflecting a renewed emphasis on spiritual values in everyday life. Religion became not just personal, but political, positioned as a bulwark against the perceived threat of 'godless communism'. In this climate, Hollywood aligned itself with the prevailing mood. Films that emphasized tradition, virtue and divine justice were not only culturally resonant but also commercially safe.[1]

Religious epics, with their clear moral frameworks and biblical roots, fitted neatly within the ideological landscape of the Cold War. These films often paralleled the era's dualistic worldview – good versus evil, freedom versus oppression – offering narratives that echoed the broader struggles of the time. In an age of McCarthyism and political paranoia, religious stories were beyond reproach. They were, in a sense, ideologically bulletproof.

There was also a more pragmatic reason for the rise of the religious epic: the growing threat of television. As more Americans stayed home, studios needed to lure audiences back to theatres. Biblical epics offered what TV could not: sheer spectacle. With expansive sets, exotic locations and casts of thousands, these films became showcases for emerging technologies like CinemaScope, VistaVision and Technicolor. They weren't just stories, they were events.[2]

Yet the religious epic was hardly a new invention. Hollywood had turned to the *Bible* before, most notably during the silent era. Pioneers like Cecil B. DeMille had used sacred stories to elevate cinema's cultural standing. His *The Ten Commandments* (1923) combined piety with grandeur, setting a template that 1950s filmmakers would follow, only their motivations were now less about artistic legitimacy and more about box office dominance.

The epics of the 1950s revived this tradition with renewed urgency. Studios saw them as commercial powerhouses, capable of drawing huge audiences while reinforcing shared values. And the public responded. The stories – grand, familiar, morally clear – offered both escapism and affirmation. Religious institutions also played a role. Churches often endorsed these films, even organizing group outings to view them. Some religious leaders dubbed them 'modern-day sermons in celluloid'.[3]

Understanding their value, studios courted religious approval. Clergy and biblical scholars were frequently consulted to ensure theological accuracy and avoid backlash. This not only safeguarded productions from controversy but also generated grassroots enthusiasm and word-of-mouth support.

Still, not everyone was convinced. Critics often accused these films of prioritizing spectacle over substance, lavishing attention on melodrama, opulence and even sensuality while glossing over theological depth or spiritual nuance. Yet for millions of viewers, the religious epic remained compelling: a fusion of faith and fantasy, reverence and entertainment, that defined a cinematic era.[4]

Perhaps inevitably it was Cecil B DeMille and Paramount Studios who started the ball rolling with religious epics in the late 1940s and early 1950s. In the uncertain glow of the postwar years, DeMille returned to a dream he had once shelved but never abandoned, the story of Samson and Delilah. The world had changed since he first imagined bringing the biblical tale to the screen in the 1930s. The Depression had passed, the war had ended and audiences had begun to seek not just escape, but grandeur, and DeMille was ready to deliver it.

At the centre of his new vision stood a curious and politically rich novel, *The Judge and the Fool*, written by Zionist author Vladimir Jabotinsky in 1930. It was this novel that helped shape the dramatic structure and psychological complexity of the final film. DeMille had already collected a mountain of research. A decade earlier, he had commissioned historian and screenwriter Harold Lamb to develop a script based on the biblical story from the Book of Judges, chapters 13 to 16. He had also brought in long-time collaborators Jeanie MacPherson and Sada Cowan to contribute. He even purchased the rights to Camille Saint-Saëns' opera *Samson et Dalila*, hoping to fuse sacred tradition with theatrical spectacle.[5]

Planning began in earnest in the spring of 1948. DeMille initially explored the possibility of filming in the Middle East, but with the formation of the new state of Israel and growing regional instability, Palestine was ruled out. Instead, a second unit was dispatched to North Africa. The team embarked on an ambitious journey across Morocco and Algeria, filming sweeping landscapes and historic ruins as a backdrop to the film.[6]

Casting brought its own challenges. Rumours swirled around the role of Delilah. Betty Hutton was said to be in contention, but it was Austrian actress Hedy Lamarr who would ultimately embody the biblical temptress. Her performance would leave an indelible mark on Hollywood's golden age. Matinee idol Victor Mature was cast as Samson.[7]

No DeMille production would be complete without monumental sets, and *Samson and Delilah* was no exception. The Temple of Dagon, where the story reaches its thunderous climax, was modelled on historical records from Pliny the Elder, the Roman naturalist. Reports suggested the temple would cost upwards of $250,000 to build; in truth, it was constructed for around $30,000, though it required five months to complete. When the planned detonation failed to bring down the set during the temple's collapse scene, DeMille ordered it rebuilt, complete with its 40ft statue of the god Dagon, at an added cost of $15,000. The final scene was reshot, this time successfully, and the resulting footage became one of the most iconic moments in the film.[8]

In total, the production cost approximately $3.2 million and premiered in New York on 21 December 1949, with a nationwide release following in early 1950. It was a massive success, becoming the highest-grossing movie of 1950 and winning Academy Awards for Best Art Direction and Costume Design.[9]

The biblical gauntlet had been thrown down and MGM were quick to follow up with a religious epic that had been in their pipeline since as early as 1925. The film was an adaptation of *Quo Vadis: A Narrative of the Time of Nero*, Henryk Sienkiewicz's sweeping tale of ancient Rome.

The story had in fact first appeared on film as early as 1912 with a silent Italian epic directed by Enrico Guazzoni. A landmark in early cinema, the film wowed audiences with elaborate sets, teeming crowd scenes and stunning historical reconstructions. For many viewers, it was their first exposure to a sympathetic, powerful vision of Christianity onscreen. Hugely successful in both Europe and America, it proved that the story's emotional and spiritual resonance translated beautifully to the silver screen.[10]

A troubled 1924 version followed, written and co-directed by Arturo D'Annunzio, son of poet Gabriele D'Annunzio. Despite big ambitions and an invitation to Rudolph Valentino to star, which fell through, the production collapsed under financial strain. German backers stepped in, bringing in a co-director, but the final film failed both critically and commercially. It effectively ended the career of producer Arturo Ambrosio, once a major figure in Italian cinema.[11]

MGM bought the talking-picture rights to the novel from author Henryk Sienkiewicz's heirs in the late 1930s. They had originally intended to make the film in Italy, but the outbreak of the Second World War caused it to be postponed.

After the war, production was restarted. Director Mervyn LeRoy was attached, actors were being tested and exotic locations like Mexico were floated for filming. But the war cast a long shadow. With global conflict tightening budgets and complicating logistics, *Quo Vadis* was shelved again, its elaborate vision choked by the real-life costs of war.[12]

The project was revived with fresh ambition in 1948. Announcements were made that the film would star Gregory Peck and Elizabeth Taylor, with Robert Morley as a flamboyant Nero and John Huston directing. MGM planned to shoot the picture in Rome, making use of $2.5 million in 'frozen' postwar funds stuck in Italy. But again, fate intervened. Peck developed a serious eye infection, and a rival production, *Fabiola*, threatened to steal *Quo Vadis'* thunder. Huston clashed with the studio and bowed out after producer Arthur Hornblow resigned. MGM's grand epic, now more than a decade in development, seemed cursed.[13]

The turnaround finally came in 1950. Director Mervyn LeRoy returned. Dore Schary, now head of production at MGM, gave the green light. A final script, credited to John Lee Mahin, S.N. Behrman and Sonya Levien, was finalized. Robert Taylor, who had long been associated with the project, was reinstalled as the lead. Deborah Kerr joined as Lygia, but Peter Ustinov, cast as Nero, would steal nearly every scene.[14]

Cameras rolled on 22 May 1950 at Cinecittà Studios in Rome. The facilities were in rough shape as they had been used by Nazi troops during the war and left partly in ruins, but MGM poured in resources to rebuild and modernize the studio. They were even given permission to refurbish a section of the Appian Way, the ancient road leading out of Rome. The production grew to a staggering scale: over 30,000 costumes, sixty-three lions and thousands of extras. Actress Sophia Loren and her mother, both unknown at the time, were among the crowd scenes in the Colosseum.[15]

The burning of Rome, one of the film's signature sequences, took three months to prepare and twenty-four nights to film. The technical team developed a system of piped flammable liquids and fireproof camera gear to capture the blaze from all angles. The crew also pioneered a technique of shooting simultaneously with four Technicolor cameras, a move that saved costs on retakes and gave the editors multiple angles on massive crowd scenes.[16]

True to form, incidents that happened on set have entered Hollywood mythology. Apparently, Elizabeth Taylor, who had originally been considered for the role of Lygia, was in an Italy during shooting. She had a row with husband Nicky Hilton and wanted somewhere to hide, so she asked if she could appear as an extra in the arena scene. There was also a problem with the fifty-plus lions that had been brought from circuses across Europe when they refused to attack the Christians; eventually the scene had to be shot as close-ups instead.[17]

After nearly six months of shooting, production wrapped on 1 November 1950; remarkably, ahead of schedule. More than half a million feet of footage were shipped to MGM's editors, who cut the film down to just under three hours.[18]

Quo Vadis previewed to test audiences in California in mid-1951. Reactions were enthusiastic, though split on whether the film needed an intermission.

MGM opted to include one for roadshow engagements. When the film premiered in late 1951, it was met with blockbuster box-office numbers and widespread critical acclaim for its spectacle, if not always for its storytelling. The *New York Times* called it 'a staggering combination of cinema brilliance and sheer banality'.[19]

The film was nominated for eight Academy Awards, including Best Picture and dual Best Supporting Actor nods for Leo Genn, who played Petronius, and Peter Ustinov, but took home none. Still, *Quo Vadis* was a massive commercial success, eventually grossing over $10 million in the US and Canada alone, rescuing MGM's finances in the process.[20]

What began as a passion project in the 1930s had finally – two decades later – become one of MGM's most ambitious and successful films, just not on the timeline anyone expected.

Quo Vadis was filmed in the 1950s, during a turning point in Hollywood history. American movies of the time were shaped by the intense political atmosphere of the Cold War and the rise of McCarthyism, as fears of communism gripped the nation. At the same time, filmmakers were still processing the trauma of the Second World War, especially the legacy of fascism. Themes of tyranny, resistance and moral struggle became common in popular cinema.[21]

Against this backdrop, a more subtle message was woven into many of the epic films set in the ancient world. These movies often carried a quiet but clear anti-imperialist message, reinforced through casting choices. British actors were frequently cast as emperors, generals or other tyrannical rulers, a nod to America's own revolutionary past and a way of distinguishing between foreign oppression and American ideals. This approach, sometimes called 'the aural paradigm', used accents and stereotypes to underline a deeper message: tyranny was external, while liberty was inherently American.[22]

The Roman Empire epics, in particular, became powerful vehicles for political commentary. On the surface, they promoted Christian virtue over pagan cruelty. But they also carried Cold War symbolism, drawing clear lines between oppressive regimes and the fight for freedom. The Romans often stood in for Soviet totalitarianism, while the suffering of early Christians paralleled the horrors of fascism, especially the persecution and genocide of the Holocaust.

Quo Vadis reflected these anxieties in vivid detail. Nero's Rome, with its sinister guards, grandiose rituals and authoritarian architecture, bore a striking resemblance to Nazi Germany. The black-robed Praetorian Guard, giving stiff-armed salutes, echoed fascist imagery. Scenes of Nero admiring scale models of his future city even recalled photos of Hitler studying plans for the Nuremberg rallies. Meanwhile, the portrayal of the Roman Empire as a brutal, controlling state also invited comparisons to Soviet Russia. In this way, *Quo Vadis* channelled the political fears of its time, using the ancient past to comment on the dangers of modern tyranny.[23]

Another passion project was *The Robe*. Written by Lloyd C. Douglas in 1942, the novel tells the story of a Roman tribune who presides over the crucifixion of Jesus and is profoundly transformed by his experiences, particularly after acquiring Jesus' robe.

Lloyd C. Douglas was a Lutheran minister and university professor who turned to novel-writing later in life. *The Robe* was his first major bestseller, combining his theological background with popular fiction to reach a wide audience.

Published during the Second World War, the novel tapped into contemporary anxieties about faith, sacrifice and moral courage. Set in the aftermath of Christ's crucifixion, it follows Marcellus Gallio, a Roman tribune and son of a wealthy senator, who is assigned to command the crucifixion of Jesus in Jerusalem. He wins Jesus' robe in a dice game and, after witnessing Christ's death, begins to suffer from overwhelming guilt and confusion.

Returning to Rome, Marcellus finds himself tormented by nightmares and inexplicable psychological anguish. Eventually, he travels back to Palestine with his slave and companion, Demetrius, seeking answers. There, he encounters early Christians and learns of Jesus' teachings, miracles and resurrection. Marcellus undergoes a slow, transformative conversion, not through miracles, but through moral realization. He gives up his Roman privileges and publicly professes his faith. His reward is martyrdom at the hands of Emperor Caligula, who demands he renounce Christianity.[24]

The Robe sold millions of copies and became a staple of Christian fiction. Unlike the earlier religious novels of the nineteenth century, such as *Fabiola* or *Ben-Hur*, Douglas' narrative is less interested in early Church politics or supernatural drama and more in the inner moral revolution that faith produces.[25]

Marcellus' story reflects the challenges faced by modern believers living morally in a flawed world, dealing with guilt and holding onto faith without clear answers. The robe isn't portrayed as a magical object but as a symbol that helps Marcellus wrestle with both the presence and absence of Jesus.

Douglas also crafts a narrative that is non-denominational, appealing to Protestants and Catholics alike. This was part of its wide appeal, especially in mid-century America, where ecumenical spirituality was gaining traction.[26]

Producer Frank Ross had bought the rights to the novel in 1942 before author Lloyd C. Douglas had even finished writing it. For ten years, *The Robe* had languished in development hell. It had survived war shortages, a rotating carousel of directors and stars, blacklisting, strikes and moral scrutiny.[27]

Then in the spring of 1952, spurred on by the success of *Samson & Delilah* and *Quo Vadis*, Darryl F. Zanuck, head of production at Twentieth-Century Fox, negotiated a quiet but significant coup: the rights to *The Robe* would transfer from RKO to Fox. It was not just a business deal; it was a bet on the future. Zanuck didn't just see a spiritual epic, he saw a stage for a revolution. Fox was developing a secret weapon, a widescreen format called CinemaScope that would dwarf anything audiences had ever seen. If *The Robe* could be the first to use the format, it wouldn't just be a film, it would be an event.[28]

Invented by French astronomer Henri Chrétien in the 1920s and long ignored, the CinemaScope lens compressed a wide-angle image onto standard 35mm film. When projected through a companion lens, the image stretched back out, filling screens more than twice as wide as the norm. Unlike bulky three-strip systems such as Cinerama, CinemaScope needed only one camera, one projector. It was simple. It was elegant. It was the future.[29]

Fox bought the patent, rebuilt Chrétien's war-ravaged lab and ordered thousands of lenses. Then they made the boldest move yet: they offered CinemaScope not just to themselves but to rival studios. Hollywood, weary of declining ticket sales and the rise of television, listened.

But the debut had to be perfect. The first CinemaScope film needed grandeur. It needed spectacle. It needed spiritual resonance. Fox spared no expense for *The Robe*. The cast included Richard Burton as Marcellus, Jean Simmons as Diana and Victor Mature as Demetrius. Rome was reborn on the studio lot, and the panoramic Jerusalem backdrop – painted for the crucifixion scene – was the largest ever created. The chase sequence was filmed in Calabasas, California; the rest on massive soundstages, with special lighting systems developed for the new Eastman colour film stock.[30]

Yet CinemaScope brought its own complications. Focus issues plagued production, as the lenses had to be calibrated with extreme precision. Actors couldn't move too far forward or backward. Scenes had to be blocked like stage plays. And the camera, so used to close-ups, had to pull back – wide and sweeping – to fit the format. Still, the results were astonishing.

The Robe premiered on 16 September 1953, at the Roxy Theatre in New York. Audiences gasped. The image was vast, the sound immersive. For the first time, cinema felt like it had torn through the borders of the screen. Jean Simmons pressed her hands into cement outside Grauman's Chinese Theatre in Los Angeles, alongside a plaque commemorating *The Robe* as the first CinemaScope release.[31]

By the end of 1953, *The Robe* had grossed over $16.5 million domestically, playing in only a small number of theatres equipped for the format. Fox had reshaped the industry, and they knew it. They offered exhibitors loans to retrofit their theatres. They produced short films, newsreels, even travelogues; anything to build a CinemaScope ecosystem. And in a move both generous and strategic, they opened the technology to competitors. Warner Bros dropped WarnerScope, while MGM also signed on. Paramount held out, pushing their own system called VistaVision, but the tide had turned.[32]

The Robe won Oscars for Art Direction and Costume Design and earned a nomination for Best Picture. Burton was nominated for Best Actor. Fox received an honorary Academy Award for its introduction of CinemaScope. French inventor Chrétien, along with Fox's technical team, was honoured for developing the lenses and process.[33]

Religious leaders across denominations praised the film and the book as effective evangelistic tools, particularly for presenting Christianity as a moral way of life rather than an abstract theology. Schools, churches and Sunday schools used the book as a teaching aid.[34]

While largely faithful to the novel's structure, the film condensed several plotlines and added emotional tension between Marcellus and Diana. Victor Mature's character of Demetrius was expanded.

Just three weeks after *The Robe* wrapped, production began on its sequel, *Demetrius and the Gladiators*, with Mature reprising his role as the slave servant in *The Robe*. He was joined by Susan Hayward as Messalina, Michael Rennie reprising Peter and Jay Robinson as Caligula, with supporting performances by Anne Bancroft, Ernest Borgnine, Debra Paget and others.[35]

It continues the story from *The Robe*, following Demetrius, a Christian slave and former servant of Marcellus. After losing faith and becoming a gladiator, he struggles with violence, temptation and loyalty. Ultimately, he regains his faith and helps protect the robe from Emperor Caligula's obsession. The film mingled theological conflict with roaring spectacle: tigers, swords, crowds and inner turmoil, all embraced by CinemaScope. Released in June 1954, *Demetrius and the Gladiators* earned approximately $26 million, making it one of Fox's biggest hits and the fourth highest-grossing film of 1954.[36]

The success of *Demetrius and the Gladiators* showed that spectacle and a sequel strategy could sustain Fox's widescreen momentum. From here, biblical and historical epics in CinemaScope would follow, leaning even harder into the grandeur that only widescreen could deliver, setting a trend throughout the industry.

In 1952, Cecil B. DeMille had announced plans to return to *The Ten Commandments*, this time with the full force of sound, colour and VistaVision behind him. He planned to focus the new version entirely on the life of Moses, omitting the modern storyline of the 1923 film. The new script took three years to write. The film would take two more to shoot.[37]

Chief among his collaborators was Henry Noerdlinger, his head researcher. In preparation for the film, Noerdlinger and his team consulted nearly a thousand books, combed through just as many periodicals and assembled over 2,900 photographs from thirty libraries and museums across three continents. The research culminated in Noerdlinger's book *Moses and Egypt*, published in 1956, which documented not only the film's historical basis but its commitment to accuracy. It was used to promote the film, particularly in Europe, where interest in biblical epics was especially high.[38]

Though DeMille was rumoured to have considered other actors such as William Boyd, James Griffith and Cornel Wilde for the role of Moses, he ultimately had no doubts. Charlton Heston, with his chiselled features and bearing, was his choice from the beginning. There was even a mystical touch to the casting: Heston's resemblance to Michelangelo's statue of Moses was widely noted, and promotional photos were taken of the actor alongside the sculpture in Rome. Heston's commitment to the role ran deep. He remained in character between takes, even during rest periods, at DeMille's insistence.[39]

The casting of other principal roles followed similar paths. Yul Brynner was offered the part of Rameses II during an intermission of *The King and I* on Broadway. Yvonne De Carlo, cast as Sephora, caught DeMille's eye in a film screening for a different actress. Edward G. Robinson, blacklisted and struggling, found a rebirth in the role of Dathan. 'DeMille returned me to films,' he wrote, 'and restored my self-respect.'[40]

Filming began in Egypt in October 1954. It was a massive undertaking. A city was built at Beni Youseff near Cairo, complete with gates 107ft high, flanked by statues of Rameses with the face of Brynner. Some 7,000–10,000 extras were used, along with 5,000 head of livestock. DeMille brought four VistaVision cameras to Egypt and had the film negatives packed in ice due to the desert heat.[41]

DeMille suffered a heart attack during filming but returned to the set days later. Portions of the exodus and chariot chase were filmed in Abu Ruwash, and the burning bush sequence was staged near St Catherine's Monastery on Mount Sinai. Heston, Brynner and Henry Wilcoxon were the only major actors to appear on location; the rest were doubled in long shots.[42]

Back in Hollywood, the production's scale grew no less daunting. John P. Fulton, the special effects master behind the 1923 version, returned to part the Red Sea once more. Using massive tanks and hydraulic pumps, his team created a deluge that could pour 360,000 gallons of water in two minutes. The parting itself was once again filmed in reverse and composited using a complex blend of miniatures, live-action and matte paintings. Sound designers used thirty-five separate tracks, including a recording of an atomic bomb test, to create the thunderous sonic landscape. Musical duties eventually fell to Elmer Bernstein after Victor Young, the original composer, fell ill. Bernstein's score was later released on vinyl and has been widely lauded as one of the great epic film soundtracks. Several chants and background songs, written by Bernstein and others, accompany the priests and rituals seen throughout the film.[43]

The Ten Commandments premiered not with a general release but as a roadshow event, with reserved seats, advanced pricing and limited screenings. At seventy weeks, its run at New York's Criterion Theatre became legendary. The film earned mixed critical reviews. *Time* magazine called it 'the most vulgar movie ever made', while others praised its scale and sincerity. The *New York Times* declared it a 'moving story of the spirit of freedom riding in a man', especially relevant amid the political turmoil of the day.[44]

Awards followed. The film won the Academy Award for Best Special Effects and was nominated in six other categories, including Best Picture. Heston received a Golden Globe nomination, while Brynner was named Best Actor by the National Board of Review.

It would be Cecil B DeMille's last picture; he was planning one last biblical epic based on the Book of Revelation when he died of a heart attack in 1959.

Chapter 15

A Studio on the Brink: How the 1959 *Ben-Hur* Resurrected MGM

By the mid-1950s, despite the success of *Quo Vadis*, MGM was in trouble. The studio that once reigned supreme was now struggling to compete. Rivals like Paramount and 20th Century Fox were dominating the box office with lavish biblical epics, and MGM desperately needed a triumph of its own. Something grand; something spectacular. They needed more than just a story; they needed a true cinematic spectacle. *Ben-Hur* offered exactly that.

At the heart of *Ben-Hur* lay a sequence that could outshine anything Hollywood had so far produced: the legendary chariot race. MGM recognized it as their ace in the hole, an action set piece that, if executed correctly, could stun audiences and anchor the entire film. It had captivated viewers in the silent 1925 version. Now, with the advent of Technicolor, improved special effects and modern filmmaking techniques, it had the potential to be even more breathtaking.

There was another advantage: MGM still owned the rights to Lew Wallace's 1880 novel *Ben-Hur: A Tale of the Christ*. They didn't have to fight for the property, as it was already theirs.

In December 1952, MGM officially announced its plan to remake *Ben-Hur*. What followed would become one of the most ambitious and storied productions in Hollywood history.

In an attempt to stabilize the Italian economy after the Second World War, the Italian government had banned the movement of lira out of the country. As the studio had substantial assets in Italy that needed using up, it was decided very early that the shoot would happen in the newly constructed Cinecittà Studios 8 miles outside Rome. This would free up resources elsewhere for the studio. Foreign labour was also cheaper to hire, American unions having started to drive up the production costs.[1]

From the first announcement that MGM intended to remake the 1925 original, speculation was rife as to who might be selected to play Ben-Hur. Names like Stewart Granger and Robert Taylor were first suggested, even Marlon Brando, but he along with Rock Hudson and Burt Lancaster turned the role down. Lancaster stated he refused the role because he found the script boring and belittling to Christianity. Paul Newman turned it down because he was still recovering from his role in the 1954 historical epic drama *The Silver Chalice*, which he described as the 'the worst motion picture produced during the 1950s'. He claimed that he couldn't cope with another film where he had to wear a 'cocktail dress' because he didn't have the legs for it.[2]

The stars may not have been decided, but producer Sam Zimbalist was assigned to the project in November 1953. Zimbalist had an impressive pedigree and had produced MGM's *Quo Vadis* in 1951. He had even worked on the 1925 *Ben-Hur* as one of the editors cutting the film.[3]

Zimbalist's first challenge was getting the script right. He brought on board seasoned screenwriter Karl Tunberg, regarded as a safe pair of hands. The studio then announced in July 1954 that production would start the following March. One of their leading directors, Sidney Franklin, who had won acclaim for *Random Harvest* and *Mrs Miniver*, would direct. Shooting would occur in Rome and Spain, and it was said that Marlon Brando was up for the lead. Then it all went quiet until September 1955, when Zimbalist announced that a $7 million, six-to-seven-month production would begin in April 1956 in either Israel or Egypt, using MGM's new 65mm widescreen process.[4]

In early 1956, before shooting could begin, MGM called a halt. At this point, their annual losses were approaching $5 million and faction fighting was splitting the studio, which eventually ended in a boardroom coup.[5]

With a new executive hierarchy in place, Zimbalist finally convinced the studio that rather than driving MGM further into debt, the *Ben-Hur* project could be their saviour. The hunt was then on to find a new director, Sidney Franklin having fallen ill and being reluctant to work overseas.[6]

In 1957, William Wyler was approached by Zimbalist. Wyler had built up a career directing a wide variety of films, but epic movies were not his forte. However, like Zimbalist, he had been involved in the 1925 *Ben-Hur*, working as an assistant director on the chariot race shoot. When Zimbalist approached him, Wyler assumed it was to direct the chariot race, as he regarded the film itself as too much of a spectacle, more in keeping with Cecil B. DeMille's directorial style. However, Zimbalist was insistent and eventually Wyler was persuaded, in part because as a Jew, he was inspired by the idea of making a film about the freeing of Jewish people from oppression and tyranny.[7]

Not all the film had been scheduled to be shot in Italy; some background scenes were to have been filmed in North Africa. MGM announced that shooting would begin in Libya on 1 March 1958, with 200 camels and a staggering 2,500 horses already secured. Then, just days before filming in Libya was to commence, disaster struck. On 11 March, the Libyan government revoked the film permit on religious grounds, forcing the production to find a new location. Then Israel also pulled its permit for religious reasons. Not a frame from those locations made it into the final cut. Consequently, Italy became the main location.[8]

Casting the film was continuing to cause complications. After working through a variety of possible leading men, it was Charlton Heston who ended up being cast as Ben-Hur, but his appointment was officially announced only a few months before principal photography began. Heston was already identified as an epic hero for his performance as Moses in DeMille's *The Ten Commandments*.

Aged 35 and well over 6ft (1.8m) tall, Heston brought a ruggedly mature masculinity to the role. However, in the novel, Ben-Hur had only been 17 when he was sent to the galleys. By selecting the muscular athletic Heston to play Ben Hur, Wyler made the tale of the charioteer much more than the coming-of-age saga of the novel.[9]

Another actor who could have captured the more mature style of Ben-Hur was Kirk Douglas. He had lobbied Wyler for the title role, but Wyler had already decided on Heston. Instead, he offered Douglas the role of Messala, which the actor rejected, going on to produce and star in the box office smash *Spartacus*.[10]

English actor Stewart Granger was also offered the part of Messala, but he turned it down, reluctant to play second fiddle to Heston. Irish actor Stephen Boyd was finally selected to play Messala. Just a few years earlier, Boyd had been a starving out-of-work actor eking a living as a cinema doorman in London. Whilst an usher during the British Academy Awards in the early 1950s, he was noticed by actor Sir Michael Redgrave, who used his connections to introduce Boyd to the director of the Windsor Repertory Group. His stage career flourished, leading to a contract with 20th Century Fox. It was after Brigitte Bardot chose him as her leading man in *The Night Heaven Fell*, directed by Roger Vadim, that Hollywood began to take notice. So when he auditioned for the role of Messala, he was pushing at an open door. His screen test convinced director William Wyler that he had found the perfect villain for his epic.[11]

Rather like Ramon Novarro, Boyd had to wear lifts in his shoes to bring him up to the same height as Heston, also needing brown contact lenses to ensure his eyes were a different colour from the hero.

Veteran English actor Jack Hawkins was persuaded to play Quintus Arrius, although he was initially unwilling to act in another epic movie so soon after 1957's *The Bridge on the River Kwai*. An unknown Israeli actress, Haya Harareet, was signed to play Esther after Wyler met her at the Cannes Film Festival. Welsh actor Hugh Griffith, sporting heavy make-up, was cast as Sheik Ilderim. British actress Marie Nye was originally cast as Ben-Hur's mother, Miriam, but was fired after two days of work because she couldn't cry on cue. Heston suggested Wyler cast Martha Scott, who had played his mother in *The Ten Commandments*. Cathy O'Donnell was Wyler's sister-in-law, and although her career was in decline, he still decided to cast her as Ben-Hur's sister, Tirzah.[12]

The one key cast member whose name never appeared on the credits and whose face was never fully shown on screen was Claude Heater, who played Jesus Christ. At this time it was deemed unacceptable to show or indeed credit an actor playing the role of Christ. Heater was an American opera singer who was performing in Rome when the *Ben-Hur* crew first arrived. Production manager Henry Henigson saw him on stage and was struck by the singer's 'magnificent' voice and 'beautiful spiritual face'.[13]

The rest of the cast were assembled and Wyler decided to have all the Roman characters played by British actors. Stephen Boyd was a Roman brought up in Judea, so his Irish burr was OK. The Hebrews would be played by Americans.[14]

At this point, Wyler felt that the script needed some editing, particularly objecting to its 'modernist' dialogue. He wanted dialogue that sounded slightly archaic, which he thought would evoke a distant period in the past. Tunberg didn't agree, believing that because the language people spoke 2,000 years earlier sounded contemporary to them, the modern audience should relate to it as contemporaries would have done. However, by this time Tunberg was already embarking on another film project, so Wyler was able to bring in so-called 'script doctors' to start rewriting some of the scenes without any interference.

The first team of 'script doctors' were the American playwrights and authors S.N. Behrman and Maxwell Anderson. Nevertheless, Wyler was still unhappy with the script and invited novelist Gore Vidal to become involved, a decision which would lead to a huge amount of controversy after the film was finished. Vidal was only involved with the film for a few months, but he would later claim that he restructured key scenes and rewrote much of the dialogue to better reflect the historical context, as well as introducing a controversial homoerotic subtext to the relationship between Ben-Hur and Messala. He also suggested that Messala's betrayal stemmed from a spurned romantic interest. This was a change he claimed was approved of by Wyler and Stephen Boyd, but it was agreed to not share this information with Heston, who would not have agreed. This interpretation was later disputed by both Wyler and Heston.[15]

British playwright Christopher Fry was the final writer to work on the script. Arriving in Rome in May 1958, Fry was tasked with elevating the dialogue to a more formal and archaic tone suitable for the film's biblical setting. He worked closely with Wyler throughout the production, often rewriting scenes on set to align with the director's vision. Wyler later credited Fry as being more responsible than any other writer for the final screenplay.

Wyler wanted Christiopher Fry to receive the screenwriting credit, but the Writers' Guild insisted that the credit should be given to Tunberg. An extremely unpleasant battle in the media ensued, and eventually Tunberg won the day.[16]

Whilst the script was being rewritten, work had begun recruiting the huge cast of extras. MGM opened a casting office in Rome in mid-1957, people travelling to the city from all over the world in the hope of being selected as one of the 50,000 persons needed for the film. Even members of Europe's aristocracy lined up for work. There were counts, duchesses and baronesses, and even princes and princesses, hailing from Italian, Spanish, Hungarian and Russian nobility, who were selected by Wyler to play upper-class Roman patricians in the party scenes.[17]

A notice in Rome's newspapers calling for bearded men to report to the studio nearly caused a riot. Anticipating the opportunity, many Romans had begun growing beards months in advance. The day after the announcement, over 5,000 men showed up, sporting everything from mere stubble to a luxurious beard nearly three feet long.[18]

Countless Italian women contributed their hair to bring authenticity to the epic film. Over 181 kilos of these donated tresses were crafted into intricate wigs and beards. Much of this hair came from the peasant women of Upper Piedmont, a region renowned for generations for its exceptionally fine locks.[19]

To feed the huge cast of extras and bit players, the studio built and maintained a 'high-speed' restaurant which at its peak fed 5,000 extras in twenty minutes. Even on location, the cast of extras was vast. During the week the company filmed in the nearby mountains, the entire village of Arcinazzo, with its 300 inhabitants, was transformed into a bustling community of actors. Located 100 miles from Rome, the mountain village became the town of Nazareth, with every resident cast in a role.[20]

MGM's Art Department produced more than 15,000 detailed sketches – 8,000 just for costumes – mapping out every set, prop and scene. Each was meticulously catalogued and cross-referenced. By the time cameras rolled, over a million props had been fabricated.[21]

Vast sums were spent on the manufacture of costumes. From Thailand came silks, from England the embroidered woollens and tooled leather, while the knee-high boots were made in Italy and the armour came from Germany. From South America came more woollens, Switzerland provided pieces of rare costume jewellery and France bolts of lace. Seamstresses, leather workers, armourers and dry-cleaning experts all took up residence in three dedicated studio buildings, watched over by British costumer designer Elizabeth Haffenden and colour co-ordinator Joan Bridge.[22]

Even the musical score took two years of research. Written and conducted by Dr Miklós Rózsa, it incorporated homophonous chants of the early Greeks and Romans in which everything is played or sung in unison, but written in a way that although sounding archaic did not become grating to the ear.[23]

For research purposes, the production department reached out to a leading Protestant, a Catholic and a Jewish authority. When a parchment was needed for a scene with visible Hebrew text, a professor at the University of Jerusalem, who had been studying the Dead Sea Scrolls, copied a section directly from the ancient Jewish manuscripts.[24]

Although several sets still standing from *Quo Vadis* were refurbished, 300 different sets scattered over 148 acres and nine sound stages were built. Covering twenty blocks on the set was a recreation of the streets of Jerusalem, large enough to accommodate thousands of extras and featuring the huge Gate of Joppa, reaching 75ft into the sky. One of the most lavish sets was the villa of Quintus Arrius, which included forty-five working fountains and almost 9 miles of pipes.[25]

To capture the grandeur of ancient Rome and the emotional power of its story, Wyler turned to one of Hollywood's most seasoned cinematographers, Robert L. Surtees, who had already worked on several major epics of the era. Surtees had previously won Academy Awards for *King Solomon's Mines* (1950) and *The Bad and the Beautiful* (1952), establishing his reputation for handling large-scale productions.[26]

To maximize the epic scale of *Ben-Hur*, MGM used a special widescreen process called MGM Camera 65. This system used 65mm film, which was much larger than the standard 35mm, allowing for incredibly sharp and detailed images. It also employed a special anamorphic lens that compressed the image during filming and then expanded it during projection, creating a breathtakingly wide and immersive view on the big screen. Developed in response to the rise of television, MGM Camera 65 was designed to give audiences a grand cinematic experience that couldn't be replicated at home.[27]

Importantly, this setup would allow *Ben-Hur* to be projected in a variety of theatres, including those without expensive new 70mm equipment, making distribution easier and more profitable for MGM. As part of the production, six Panavision 65mm lenses, each worth around $100,000, were shipped to Rome for use during the shoot.[28] The stage was finally set for filming to start

Chapter 16

Racing Through Time: The Legacy of the 1925 *Ben-Hur* in the 1959 Epic

Principal photography finally began in Rome on 18 May 1958, even though the script was still unfinished. Director William Wyler had read only the first dozen pages. The shooting schedule was relentless: twelve to fourteen-hour days, six days a week. Sundays were no rest either, reserved for intense story meetings with the screenwriters and producer Sam Zimbalist.[1]

To keep the momentum going, a doctor was stationed on set to give vitamin B complex injections to anyone who needed a boost, though Wyler later suspected the shots might have contained amphetamines.[2] Actors were kept in costume and on standby, ready to jump into pick-up scenes at a moment's notice. For nearly all of November 1958, actresses Martha Scott and Cathy O'Donnell – who played Ben-Hur's mother and sister – wore full leprosy make-up, waiting in the wings for their scenes.[3]

The gruelling shoot lasted nine months. Three of those were spent filming the legendary chariot race, a cinematic milestone in its own right. Because of the length of the shoot and the extraordinary sets, Cinecittà Studios and the *Ben-Hur* sets became a regular stop for Rome's sightseeing buses, which arrived hourly for guided tours. Over 25,500 tourists from around the world visited the production.[4]

The sea battle was one of the first action sequences created for the film. Developed entirely without modern digital technology, this sequence showcases the remarkable ingenuity of mid-twentieth-century filmmakers. Through a combination of full-scale galleys, intricately crafted miniatures, dynamic special effects and groundbreaking production techniques, the sea battle remains a towering example of practical effects in epic pre-CGI era filmmaking.

Wyler and his team wanted to show how brutal Roman naval warfare could be, and they used the battle to change the course of Ben-Hur's journey. Art director Edward Carfagno and special effects expert A. Arnold 'Buddy' Gillespie led the effort. Their team pored over historical texts, museum records and archaeological data to create accurate depictions of Roman and Macedonian galleys. They knew they couldn't film the entire scene with only real ships or just models, so they decided to use both. They built giant water tanks for filming, one at Cinecittà Studios in Rome and another miniature version at MGM Studios in California.[5]

The team built two full-size Roman galleys, each about 175ft (53m) long. These ships were large enough to float and be filmed on water. They were placed on mechanical platforms (called gimbals) that could move the ships to simulate waves and rough seas. These were mainly used for scenes inside the ships and close-ups of the actors. Charlton Heston even trained to row like a real galley slave so his performance would look realistic.[6]

At Cinecittà Studios, they created a massive outdoor tank filled with water to make it look like the open sea. They added wave and wind machines to stir up the water and make scenes appear stormy. To hide the modern buildings nearby, they used a giant painted background showing the ocean and sky. While full-scale ships delivered immersive close-ups, the heart of the sea battle was filmed using more than forty highly detailed miniatures, ranging from 1:12 to 1:24 scale. These handcrafted models featured intricate details such as rigging, sails, breakaway hulls and concealed pyrotechnic devices. Special effects artists designed internal mechanisms that allowed ships to splinter, burn or sink on cue.[7]

To make the models look like huge ships, they were pulled slowly through a water tank while being filmed at a high speed – seventy-two frames per second instead of the normal twenty-four. When played back, the footage looked slow and heavy, just like real ships would move. One clever trick was pulling a ship model into a hidden pit in the tank using wires and pulleys, which made it look like the ship was sinking after being hit. Fire and smoke effects were also added to create the chaos of battle. One of the hardest parts was making it appear that the actors were really in the middle of the battle. The film crew used a mix of painting, projection and editing to blend the different parts together. Matte paintings extended the battle beyond the set and helped join the real and miniature scenes.[8]

Rear projection let filmmakers show background footage of the model battles behind the actors. For example, Heston was filmed on a real ship set, but the background showing other ships came from model footage. Editor Ralph E. Winters made sure the cuts between shots were smooth, keeping the action exciting and easy to follow.

The filmmakers wanted the battle to feel real. They hired Italian extras who had amputations to play injured slaves and soldiers. With prosthetic limbs and realistic makeup, they showed the brutality of naval combat. These shots were used carefully so the violence felt real without being too overwhelming. Costume and make-up teams worked hard to make everyone look authentic. Galley slaves looked tired and bruised, and soldiers wore Roman-style armour. The rowing scenes were carefully choreographed to show both the harshness of slavery and the strict control on the ship. Sound and music brought the whole scene to life. Sound editors added realistic noises such as wood breaking, waves crashing and people shouting.[9]

One amusing incident recounted by A. Arnold Gillespie in his memoirs occurred during the galley miniature shooting. All activity aboard – moving oars, miniature people etc – was triggered by a radio signal. At 2.00 am one dark night, the dozing watchman was awakened by strange noises coming from inside the huge, covered hangar where the galleys were kept overnight. Cautiously entering the hangar, the watchman got the fright of his life when he saw the ships' oars in full motion and a crew of miniature sailors moving backwards and forwards on deck. Some wayward electronic signal had triggered all the switches.[10]

Though William Wyler was a master of character-driven storytelling, he delegated much of the sea battle's execution to second-unit directors Andrew Marton and Yakima Canutt, the latter a stunt coordinator renowned for his ingenuity. Wyler focused on the emotional elements of the story such as Ben-Hur's transformation and survival whilst a galley slave, while Marton and Canutt engineered the battle's physicality and flow.

Marton and Canutt each had an assistant director, who shot additional footage. A young Sergio Leone – who shot to fame in the following decade directing Spaghetti Westerns – was senior assistant director in the second unit and responsible for retakes. Wyler shot the 'pageantry' sequence that occurs before the race, scenes of the jubilant crowd and the victory scenes after the race concludes. The pageantry sequence is a shot-by-shot remake of the same sequence from the 1925 silent film version. Knowing that the chariot race would be primarily composed of close-up and medium shots, Wyler added the parade in formation (even though it was not historically accurate) to impress the audience with the grandeur of the arena.

The chariot scene took five weeks (spread over three months) to film at a total cost of $1 million, and required more than 200 miles (320km) of racing to complete. Dynamite charges were used to show the chariot wheels and axles splintering from the effects of Messala's barbed-wheel attacks. Three lifelike dummies were placed at key points in the race to give the appearance of men being run over by chariots.[11]

The 1925 film had set a high bar for the chariot race spectacle, with its massive arena modelled after ancient Roman circuses. The production team studied the original's set closely, using it as a blueprint to capture the same grandeur and historical authenticity. They expanded on its scale and detail, constructing a massive arena at Cinecittà Studios that was both a tribute to the 1925 design and a technological leap forward. The set was modelled after the ancient circus in Jerusalem; its construction kept more than a thousand workmen occupied for a year carving its oval shape out of a rock quarry.

The racetrack featured 1,500ft (460m) straights and five-storey-high grandstands. Over 250 miles (400km) of metal tubing were used to erect the grandstands. Matte paintings created the illusion of upper storeys of the grandstands and the background mountains.[12]

Other elements of the circus were also historically accurate. Imperial Roman racecourses featured a raised 10ft (3.0m) high *spina* (the centre section), *metae* (columnar goalposts at each end of the *spina*), dolphin-shaped lap counters and *carceres* (the columned building in the rear which housed the cells where horses waited prior to the race. The four statues atop the *spina* were 30ft (9.1m) high.[13]

To support the chariots and horses but provide drainage and a soft top that wouldn't lame the animals, the track comprised steamrolled ground rock debris covered with a layer of ground lava and topped with 40,000 tons of white sand imported from nearby Mediterranean beaches. The track cost $1 million. [14]

Planning for the chariot race took nearly a year to complete. Seventy-eight horses were bought and imported from Yugoslavia and Sicily in November 1957, and trained by Hollywood animal handler Glenn Randall to pull the *quadriga* chariots. Andalusian horses were used for Ben-Hur's Arabians, while the others in the chariot race were primarily Lipizzans, originating in Lipica in Slovenia. Messala's horses were dyed black for effect.

Over the years, Randall had trained literally hundreds of animals to do his bidding, but getting the horses ready for *Ben-Hur* was a huge undertaking. Two sets of teams for each chariot had to be trained to not only pull chariots but also perform stunts. Four Arabian steeds had to be taught to kiss and nudge their master affectionately. Others had to learn to walk through a tent at a signal and stop at a call, and to fall and rise on command. In a magazine interview in 1960, Randall explained that he had to deliver four horses who could fall, four who could jump, four who could raise their front legs high in the air and four who could nudge on cue. Then, of course, all of them had to be trained to pull a chariot in a race. According to Randall, the animals were conditioned and trained as if they were being prepared to run the Kentucky Derby, the Preakness, the Belmont Stakes and participate in a fox hunt all in one day.[15]

A training track, the same dimensions as the track in the huge stadium where the race was to be filmed, was built near the stables. It was here that the horses learned the difference between pulling a chariot and a wagon. It was here too that Heston, Boyd and seven Hollywood stuntmen learned to drive the chariots and execute the spills and tricks they later performed in front of the cameras.[16]

Randall's team included a vet, a harness maker and twenty stable boys employed to care for the horses. When a blacksmith could not be found to make the horseshoes, an 18-year-old Italian boy was trained in the art of blacksmithing to take on the job.[17]

Upon arriving in Italy, Heston had started training for the more athletic elements of his role straight away, spending three hours a day on chariot driving practice and one hour on javelin practice. Because the chariot race was considered so dangerous, a twenty-bed infirmary staffed by two doctors and two nurses was built next to the set to care for anyone injured during shooting. None of the drivers needed medical help, but the staff were kept busy administering to the 15,000 extras, treating heatstroke and minor illnesses.

The race action scene directed by Marton and Canutt – filmmakers who often acted as second-unit directors on other people's films – and took three months to complete. Each man had an assistant director, who shot additional footage. In a deviation from the novel, the race is not run at Antioch but at Jerusalem, with Pontius Pilate presiding.[18]

Seven thousand extras were hired to cheer in the stands. Economic conditions in Italy were poor at the time, and as shooting for the chariot scene wound down only 1,500 extras were needed on any given day.[19] On 6 June, more than 3,000 people seeking work were turned away. The crowd rioted, throwing stones and assaulting the set's gates until police arrived and dispersed them.[20]

Filming the chariot race came with its fair share of challenges, especially when it came to the cameras. The 70mm lenses used had a minimum focal length of 50ft (15m), which meant the camera had to be far from the action. To keep ahead of the racing chariots, the crew mounted the camera on a small Italian-made car. But there was a problem: the horses were simply too fast. They accelerated down the straight much quicker than the car could manage, leaving Marton and Canutt with very little time to capture usable shots.

The crew tried upgrading to a more powerful American car, but even that couldn't keep up for long. At best, it gave them only a few extra seconds of filming time, even with a head start. To capture the intensity of the race, the horses needed to be running at full speed, so Marton made two bold decisions: switch to a lens with a much shorter minimum focal length and have the camera car stay just a few feet in front of the charging horses.[21]

This was a risky move. If the car slowed down or missed a turn, it could have resulted in a deadly collision. But the gamble paid off, the new setup solving their filming problems. As the shoot went on, they recorded an enormous amount of footage. The ratio of footage shot to footage used was a staggering 263:1, one of the highest in film history.[22]

Eighteen chariots were built for the race by the firm Danesi Brothers, and Heston and Boyd had to spend many hours learning how to drive them.

Heston was a quick learner; he already had some experience with horses, whereas Boyd was a complete novice and his hands were almost permanently blistered and bloody. Both actors decided that they would do all the driving themselves, leaving only the most hazardous scenes to their stunt doubles.[23]

Boyd chose to stay for the close-ups in the scene where Messala is dragged under the chariot, as using a dummy would have looked too false. He was protected with some steel coverings but still ended up with some very authentic cuts and bruises.

As well as directing and co-ordinating the race, Canutt was also responsible for the training of Boyd and Heston. Canutt was a renowned stuntman, rodeo rider and horse trainer. He had also had a short career as an actor and became good friends with John Wayne, whom he taught how to fall off a horse.[24]

His son, Joe, was working with his father on this film as a stunt man. It was his stunt while driving Heston's chariot which is still to this day hailed as one of the most spectacular in Hollywood history. In the scene where Messala forces Ben-Hur's chariot against the wall and into the path of the wreck of two other chariots, Joe Canutt – doubling for Heston – was supposed to avoid the wreck by jumping his entire team and chariot over it. However, he misjudged his speed and as his team flew over the debris, he landed too hard and catapulted himself into a headstand and was thrown out of the front of the chariot between the horses. He managed to seize the cross bar and was dragged along the ground, but somehow managed to climb back on the careering chariot. The stunt was inadvertently so dramatic that it was kept in the film, with Heston filming it as a rather more carefully choreographed close-up.[25]

Canutt Senior couldn't have been more different in his attitude to horses than Reeves 'Breezy' Eason in the 1925 *Ben-Hur*. Horse welfare was paramount to Canutt. He and his team selected and tamed seventy-two horses and allowed them to run around the track eight times a day, so they got used to running as a unit. Whilst a few actors and extras ended up with minor injuries, not a single horse was injured during the making of the movie.[26]

Wyler had agonized over how to portray Jesus in the film, and particularly the crucifixion scene. Unlike the film's big action sequences, this moment was quiet, emotional and deeply spiritual. Wyler wanted the audience to feel the power of the moment without showing it in a graphic or sensational way, and it would take four full days to capture. One of his most important decisions was never to show Jesus' face. Instead, Jesus is seen only from behind, in shadows or with his face turned away. This gave the character a sense of mystery and holiness, letting viewers imagine him in their own way.[27]

The crucifixion scene was filmed on a simple outdoor location near Rome, which added to its natural and realistic look. Dark skies, wind machines and special lighting created an eerie atmosphere that matched the mood of the crucifixion story. These effects helped show that this was not just a personal tragedy, but a world-changing event. Rather than focusing on the crucifixion itself, Wyler directed attention to how other characters reacted, especially Ben-Hur. As he watches Jesus die, his hatred and anger begin to fade. This moment is a turning point in his journey, showing how forgiveness and compassion can heal deep wounds.

To enhance the emotion, Wyler worked closely with the music and sound teams. Composer Miklós Rózsa created a quiet, powerful score that added to the solemn mood. The scene avoided dramatic action and instead focused on silence, sorrow and inner change.

Wyler directed this sequence himself, unlike the sea battle or chariot race, which were partly handled by second-unit directors. He believed the crucifixion was too important and personal to leave to anyone else. His careful direction helped turn this scene into a moment of spiritual awakening, both for the characters and the audience.[28]

With the final scene completed, the production finally wrapped on 7 January 1959. The crew returned to the US to start editing one million feet of film, closely supervised by Wyler. The first cut of the film was four-and-a-half hours long, but Wyler's goal was to bring it down to three-and-a-half hours. When the editing was finished it ran for 213 minutes, making it the third-longest picture ever made at the time. Not all the cut footage was wasted; Charlton Heston went on to use the leftover scenes from the sea battle in his 1972 film *Antony and Cleopatra*.[29]

One notable change in the film was in the opening titles. Wyler was concerned that the traditional roaring MGM lion would clash with the sensitive and sacred nativity scene that opens the film. He received permission to use a quiet version of the lion logo instead, marking the first time in MGM's history that the lion did not roar.[30]

Before returning to the States, the rest of the production crew began the long process of dismantling the sets. It cost MGM $150,000 to complete this work, but unlike the 1925 production, this time they were able to transport almost everything back to the US duty free.

The studio then starting to sell whatever it could in a bid to recoup their costs – everything from 10 miles of steel tubing used to erect the stands for the chariot race to the horses themselves. Whilst some of the horses were adopted by the men who trained them, many of the camels, donkeys and other exotic animals were sold to circuses and zoos in Europe.[31]

Interestingly, the studio had a second sell-off in 1970 as part of a massive auction of its studio impedimenta, including props and costumes from both *Ben-Hur* movies. A Sacramento restaurateur paid $4,000 for a chariot from the 1959 production and was arrested in 1973 for driving it on a freeway to conserve petrol. Three days later it was stolen.[32]

Whilst the behind-the-scenes practicalities were taking place, MGM's marketing division swung into action. They pioneered the kind of product tie-in campaigns that accompany the marketing of today's blockbuster action films. The studio licensed hundreds of companies to manufacture products for every room in the house. They included Oriental designs for clothing, household goods and jewellery, food products, paint-by-number art sets and an amazing array of charioteer action figures.[33]

Publicity was key to guarantee the box office success of the movie, and MGM set up an international press office in New York City more than a year before the film's premiere on 14 November 1959. The press office issued hundreds of releases intended to create and sustain interest in the film. The releases were full of faux legends and human-interest anecdotes surrounding what could, by 1959, be called a Ben-Hur tradition.[34]

Wyler and Heston both knew what the film meant for MGM, which had massive investments in its outcome, the budget having gone from $7 million to $15 million. They were aware that if it failed at the box office, MGM might go bankrupt, so they were happy to do interviews and press tours to promote it.

However, Heston was brutally honest about his experiences whilst making the movie. When asked in an interview what part of the movie he most enjoyed making, he replied: 'I didn't enjoy any of it. It was hard work.' To be fair, Wyler was a director who demanded perfection, and he was especially tough on Heston. Initially, he was unconvinced by Heston's portrayal of Ben-Hur, making him reshoot the line 'I'm a Jew' no fewer than sixteen times. Boyd, meanwhile, described the filming of *Ben-Hur* as the most exciting experience of his life.[35]

The picture was released in 1959 with top ticket prices an unprecedented $3.50. It may have cost $15 million to produce, but it would make a staggering $74,442,231 worldwide, making it the highest grossing movie of the year. Audiences mobbed movie theatres in the months after it opened.

The 1960 Academy Awards presented *Ben-Hur* with eleven of twelve awards for which it had been nominated. The major categories – Best Picture, Best Director and Best Actor – were all won. Sadly, producer Sam Zimbalist didn't make it to the end of the film's shoot, dying of a heart attack on set. However, he received a posthumous Oscar for the film and remains the only person to ever posthumously receive a Best Picture award.[36]

Curiously, the only category for which it was nominated but not awarded was Best Screenplay. This faux pas was largely the result of confusion and controversy over who had written the script. Although Karl Tunberg received credit for the screenplay, both Wyler and Heston would credit Christoper Fry as the writer who deserved that accolade. As Heston delivered his acceptance speech for Best Actor, he made certain to thank Fry for the screenplay.[37]

Chapter 17

Ben-Hur Across Media: From Epic Films to Bold Reimagining

The runaway success of the 1959 *Ben-Hur* didn't just dominate the box office; it sparked a wave of larger-than-life spectacles that spilled far beyond the cinema. In 1961, the legendary French Gruss-Jeannet circus troupe rolled out *Ben-Hur Vivant* at the Palais des Sports in Paris, a jaw-dropping live reinterpretation of Wallace's epic complete with the chariot races, thunder of hooves and sea battles all performed live under a massive circus dome. Merging high-stakes circus artistry with the dramatic scope of the film, this wildly ambitious production toured across France, Spain and Belgium until 1965, captivating thousands with its sheer scale and ingenuity.[1]

Around the same time, another showman took up the reins. In 1962 and 1963, charismatic French animal trainer Sacha Houcke brought his own dramatic version of *Ben-Hur* to the iconic Blackpool Tower Circus in England. His live show, centred on daring equestrian stunts and chariot displays, presented another breath-taking version of the Ben-Hur legend.[2]

But even the thrill of live horses thundering around a ring couldn't quite match the cinematic spectacle burned into audiences' memories. By 1971, the power of Charlton Heston's portrayal had come full circle, this time into American living rooms. CBS aired the 1959 film on network television for the first time and an astonishing 60 million viewers tuned in, making it one of the biggest TV audiences of the era. A few years later, in 1978, the UK's ITV paid a record sum to secure the broadcast rights. Decades after its debut, *Ben-Hur* was still proving its blockbuster worth on screen, under the big top and now on primetime TV.[3]

Whilst the 1959 film continued to be celebrated, like many silent films, the 1925 version of *Ben-Hur* faced the harsh fate of neglect and deterioration. The nitrate film stock used in the 1920s was highly flammable and prone to decomposition, and to add insult to injury, studios often discarded or neglected older films to make room for new releases. As a result, many silent films were lost entirely or survived only in incomplete or damaged forms.[4]

Over the decades, prints and negatives of *Ben-Hur* had become scattered worldwide across various archives and private collections. While some prints survived, many were incomplete or suffered from severe deterioration. Unfortunately, the original negative was lost and the existing American prints varied widely in quality and completeness.

In the 1980s, a nitrate print containing the original Technicolor sequences of *Ben-Hur* was discovered in the Czech Film Archive.[5] Then in 1987, film historians Kevin Brownlow and David Gill, working with Thames Television in the UK, the Czechoslovak Film Archive and Turner Entertainment, completed a 35mm restoration of the film. This version featured the original colour tints and two-strip Technicolor scenes. The team were also able to include a previously censored shot of Christ's hand on the cross, recovered from a private collector in Germany.[6] The restored *Ben-Hur* was shown at the London Film Festival in 1987, with a full orchestra conducted by Carl Davis.

The most ambitious and comprehensive restoration of *Ben-Hur* began in the late 1990s and culminated in the early 2000s. This project involved collaboration between the Library of Congress in the United States and the Gosfilmofond archive in Russia.[7] The restored *Ben-Hur* premiered at the National Gallery of Art in Washington, DC, in 2000 and was subsequently released on DVD and laserdisc, making it accessible to film scholars and enthusiasts.[8]

Since the early 2000s restoration, *Ben-Hur* has been rereleased several times in restored formats. Film festivals and silent film events often screen the restored print, accompanied by live orchestral music, offering audiences an immersive experience of the silent epic.

Yet as *Ben-Hur* was continually reborn through cinematic restoration, its story also began to evolve in an entirely new direction: the stage. By the mid-1980s, the idea of a musical adaptation had begun to take shape. In 1986, *The Adventures of Ben-Hur: A Musical Spectacle* was copyrighted in the United States as a two-act production. By 1999, this vision expanded into *Ben-Hur: The Musical*, an ambitious, multi-million-dollar show based in Orlando, Florida. Despite its scale and investment, the production struggled to attract audiences and ultimately closed in 2000, marking the first major setback in *Ben-Hur*'s otherwise triumphant cultural journey.[9]

But the story didn't end there.

In 2002, a new musical vision emerged. *Judah Ben-Hur: The Epic Musical* premiered at the University of Singapore's Cultural Centre, launching with a cast and crew of over 120 and playing an impressive fifty-six performances. This vibrant and faith-focused adaptation remains available for licensing today, keeping Wallace's tale alive on stages across the world.[10]

The advent of home media brought new opportunities for *Ben-Hur*. In 2001, a special edition DVD was released, featuring extras like commentary by Charlton Heston and a documentary on the film's production. A 2002 deluxe edition included reprints of film posters, photographs, autographs, a 35mm film frame and a reproduction of the original poster.

In 2003, *Ben-Hur* galloped into a new era with a direct-to-video animated adaptation produced by GoodTimes Entertainment, a company known for its budget-friendly animated reimagining of classic stories. Specializing in family-oriented titles during the 1990s and early 2000s, GoodTimes carved a niche in the home video market by offering simplified, accessible versions of beloved tales. This adaptation of *Ben-Hur* was developed in collaboration with Charlton Heston's production company, Agamemnon Films. The film aimed to deliver a faith-centred retelling that could resonate with younger audiences and families alike. It was inspired by a separate, earlier venture Heston had undertaken, a 1998 live-action television special titled *Charlton Heston Presents the Bible*, in which he recited passages from scripture.

At the helm of this new animated *Ben-Hur* was executive producer Fraser Heston, son of Charlton Heston, working alongside Bill Kowalchuk, an experienced director and animator whose work often emphasized moral storytelling and educational content. Kowalchuk had previously directed animated versions of *The Ten Commandments* and *The Prince of Egypt*, establishing a reputation for handling biblical epics with care and clarity for younger viewers.

What truly set this version apart, however, was the voice of Charlton Heston, returning to the world of *Ben-Hur* more than four decades after his legendary, Oscar-winning performance in the 1959 film. Heston served as the narrator of the animated feature, lending it a powerful sense of continuity and gravitas. It would be his last film role before his death in 2008.[11]

In September 2006, French director Robert Hossein brought *Ben-Hur* to life in a grand theatrical spectacle at the Stade de France in Paris. Hossein had become famous for directing large-scale stage productions, often staged in unconventional venues such as sports arenas or historic sites. Collaborating with historian Alain Decaux, he adapted Lew Wallace's 1880 novel into a series of vivid *tableaux* depicting Ben-Hur's journey from Roman captivity to spiritual redemption.

The production featured a cast of 300 actors and 100 animals, including thirty-two horses trained by renowned equestrian Mario Luraschi. A highlight was the twelve-minute chariot race, involving seven chariots and requiring nine months of rehearsal. The show also included a naval battle, Roman Army parades and gladiatorial combat.[12]

Over five performances, the spectacle attracted 300,000 spectators, including notable figures such as leading French politician Nicolas Sarkozy and singer Lionel Richie. With a budget of €10 million, it was one of France's most ambitious theatrical productions. At the time, the production stood out as one of the most ambitious stage adaptations of *Ben-Hur* ever attempted, reaffirming Hossein's reputation for staging massive historical dramas in unconventional venues, following earlier successes like *Les Misérables* and *Notre-Dame de Paris*.[13]

Two years later, a German concert impresario named Franz Abraham set out to outdo Hollywood. His vision was to transform *Ben-Hur* into a live spectacle, an epic arena show that fused the visual impact of a rock concert with the dramatic gravitas of classical theatre. The price tag was a staggering £19 million, which Abraham boldly self-financed. But against the odds, his dream materialized. *Ben-Hur Live* premiered at London's O2 Arena, launching a production unlike anything the venue or any theatre had ever seen.

On stage, more than 400 performers formed a kinetic army of actors, dancers, tumblers, stuntmen and technicians. The animal cast was no less extravagant: forty-six thoroughbred horses, flocks of doves (including twenty understudies), eagles, falcons and vultures. There were even twenty lorry-loads of sand to recreate the Roman arena floor.

The show featured breath-taking sequences: wheeled galleys rowed by human muscle, pirates attacking in motorized beach buggies and a climactic chariot race with five *quadrigas* thundering through the arena at breakneck speed. Adding to the historical authenticity, dialogue was delivered in Latin and Aramaic, with narration in English by Stewart Copeland, drummer for The Police, who also composed the show's original score.[14] In a symbolic gesture of unity and reverence, Abraham arranged for a rabbi, an Anglican priest, a Russian Orthodox priest and a Catholic priest to consecrate the O2 Arena on the eve of opening night.[15]

The show sold over 12,000 tickets and Abraham planned a global tour using 360-degree stages and massive projection screens. Sadly, the grand vision soon faltered, and despite its scale and ambition, the production was plagued by financial difficulties. Ticket sales underperformed, and by early 2010, Abraham's production company, Art Concerts, had declared bankruptcy. The collapse led to the cancellation of scheduled performances, leaving many ticketholders without refunds. Abraham blamed the failure on financial backers pulling out, disappointing ticket revenue and a critical article in *Focus* magazine that damaged the show's reputation.[16]

Still undeterred, Abraham wasn't finished. As of 2025, his official website proclaimed a new project in the works: *The Untold Story of Ben-Hur*, a feature film chronicling the chaos, ambition and behind-the-scenes drama of *Ben-Hur Live*, as well as the rich legacy of the original novel and its many screen adaptations.[17]

After lying dormant for half a century, the saga of Ben-Hur returned to the screen in 2010, this time reimagined as a two-part television miniseries. Departing from the Technicolour splendour and religious solemnity of its 1959 predecessor, this latest adaptation sought not to replicate but to reinterpret. Developed by the Alchemy Television Group in collaboration with Drimtim Entertainment and Muse Entertainment, and with David Wyler – son of *Ben-Hur*'s 1959 director William Wyler – on board as an executive producer. Whilst the project carried a sense of legacy, it also set out to do its own thing. Directed by Steve Shill, best known for his work on the TV series *Dexter* and *The Tudors*, the miniseries first aired on CBC in Canada and ABC in the United States.[18]

Screenwriter Alan Sharp, a seasoned Scottish writer with a penchant for complex narratives, was given the task of adapting Lew Wallace's 1880 novel. Rather than keeping to Wallace's devoutly Christian framework, Sharp offered a more grounded and contemporary take, transforming the story into an intimate political drama, where themes of power, loyalty and personal identity took precedence over religious beliefs.[19]

One of the most noticeable changes in the miniseries is the way Messala is portrayed. Played by British actor Stephen Campbell Moore, he is no longer just a clear-cut villain like in the original novel, where he was shown as an arrogant and scheming Roman. Instead, this version of Messala is more emotionally complex. His betrayal of Ben-Hur still happens, but it's shown as something he struggles with. He's torn between his duty to Rome and his friendship with Ben-Hur, which makes his actions feel more tragic than evil.

Esther's character is also updated. Played by Canadian actress Emily VanCamp, she is no longer just a quiet, supportive figure in Ben-Hur's life. In the miniseries, she is stronger, more independent and plays an active role in shaping Ben-Hur's path, rather than simply standing by and watching.

British actor Joseph Morgan takes on the role of Ben-Hur and really grounds the series with a performance that feels more modern and relatable. This version of Ben-Hur isn't some chosen figure on a spiritual mission; he's just a man dealing with betrayal, loss and love. His journey is less about finding faith and more about working through the pain in a way that feels honest and human.

The supporting cast reads like a 'Who's Who' of British character actors: Ray Winstone delivers a gruff and paternal Quintus Arrius, the Roman commander who adopts Ben-Hur, while Hugh Bonneville lends a cool authority to Pontius Pilate.

Visually, the miniseries reflects the evolving capabilities of early twenty-first-century television. Notably, it employs computer-generated imagery (CGI), a technology that didn't exist in the era of the 1959 epic. Although CGI had been developing in film since the 1970s, it reached a new milestone with *Toy Story* in 1995, the first fully CGI-animated feature. In the 2010 *Ben-Hur*, CGI was used selectively. The sea battle, for instance, combined practical sets and matte backgrounds with fully computer-generated wide shots, blending digital spectacle with traditional filmmaking. Interestingly, the famous chariot race was made smaller in scale, reflecting Judea's status as a minor province on the edge of the Roman Empire.[20]

When the miniseries came out, reactions were mixed. Some critics liked its emotional depth and focus on the characters, especially Morgan's take on Ben-Hur. But others missed the big, epic feel of the older versions and felt the smaller scale was mostly down to a tighter budget. Despite this reception, the miniseries feels more like a fresh take than just another remake. It's less about divine fate and more about the tough, personal choices people make, a story not about miracles but real, flawed human beings.[21]

It's always tempting to create a sequel to a hugely successful story like *Ben-Hur: A Tale of the Christ*. In 2011, author Lois Scoten published an interesting take on the story called *Messala: The Return from Ruin*. This sequel explores a powerful idea: what if even someone like Messala, the villain, could find redemption?[22]

In Lew Wallace's original, Messala is portrayed as arrogant, cruel and ultimately destroyed by his own ambition. He doesn't go through any real change or show regret, so his story ends in shame. Scoten saw this as an opportunity to expand on the story of *Ben-Hur* by imagining how someone like Messala might confront his past and seek forgiveness.

A screen sequel without a religious message was produced as a 'direct to video' film in 2016, intended to piggyback on the publicity surrounding the MGM remake of *Ben-Hur* released in the same year. *Ben-Hur – Slave of Rome*, also known as *In the Name of Ben Hur*, was produced by the low-budget studio The Asylum.[23]

Set during the reign of Emperor Nero, the film follows Ben-Hur in later life, when he is seen battling Roman forces who are oppressing the local population in Lusitania, a Roman province roughly corresponding to modern-day Portugal.

In the film, there is a scene that references Ben-Hur helping early Christians in the Roman catacombs; a passing nod to the epilogue of Wallace's novel, where Ben-Hur uses his wealth to support the early Christian community, including founding a catacomb for their burials.

Chapter 18

Ben-Hur Reboot

The 2016 remake of *Ben-Hur* emerged amid a wave of Hollywood reboots that sought to modernize classic epics for contemporary audiences.[1] However, the project's origins were more personal and thematic, rooted in screenwriter Keith Clarke's search for a story centred on forgiveness.

Initially researching complex global conflicts such as the Israeli–Palestinian struggle and the unrest in Belfast, Clarke – already an accomplished screenwriter with numerous credits, including collaborating with legendary Australian director Peter Weir on the 2010 Second World War drama *The Way Back* – was struck by how often his findings centered on families and communities torn apart. This exploration eventually led him to the South African Truth and Reconciliation Commission, established after Apartheid to promote healing rather than retribution. Clarke was particularly moved by Nelson Mandela's unwavering determination to prevent civil war by fostering forgiveness instead of revenge.

Despite this inspiration, he still lacked the right vehicle for his story. That moment came unexpectedly one Easter, when he and his producer wife, Joni Levin, happened to re-watch the 1959 version of *Ben-Hur* on television.[2]

Inspired by the film, Clarke returned to Lew Wallace's 1880 novel for a fresh perspective. While it offered him plenty to consider, it also sparked a desire to raise the emotional stakes. He decided to reimagine Ben-Hur and Messala as adopted half-brothers, a change that would heighten the sense of betrayal at the story's core. Rather than concluding with Messala's disgrace and death, Clarke chose to emphasize forgiveness, envisioning an ending where Messala is reconciled with Ben-Hur and their adopted family.[3]

Meanwhile, MGM, fresh from emerging out of bankruptcy – thanks in part to the success of the *Bond* franchise and *The Hobbit* – was on the hunt for a new blockbuster. *Ben-Hur* had been a record-breaking hit for the studio in its early years, and executives felt the time was right to breathe new life into the story. They jumped at the opportunity to develop Clarke's script.

The package also included Clarke's wife as producer, alongside longtime friend and collaborator Sean Daniel. A veteran Hollywood producer who began his career at Universal Pictures, Daniel was best known for his work on *The Mummy* trilogy (1999–2008), making him a natural fit for another large-scale remake like *Ben-Hur*. He and Clarke had previously worked together on *The Mummy* franchise, further cementing the partnership.[4]

Interestingly, the project also included Paramount, who came on board to co-produce and distribute the film. This partnership allowed the studios to combine their strengths: MGM brought its rights to the original property, while Paramount contributed its distribution capabilities and marketing expertise. By joining forces, they aimed to revitalize a classic story for modern audiences while managing the financial risks associated with large-scale productions.[5]

Ironing out just who owned the rights to the original films proved complicated. MGM had made the 1925 and 1959 film versions, but the company had changed hands several times. One of its owners was media entrepreneur Ted Turner, who, when he sold the studio, retained their back catalogue of classic movies, including *Ben-Hur*. The film then formed part of the newly formed Turner Classic Movies in 1994.[6]

However, the book, originally published in 1880, was in the public domain so they could work around the original story.[7] Clarke's script and his focus on forgiveness formed the basis of the film's storyline, but the studio wanted more action to appeal to mainstream audiences. John Ridley, Oscar-winning screenwriter of *12 Years a Slave*, was brought in to refine the script.[8]

Ridley reworked the dialogue, made the story move faster and added emotions that felt more modern and relatable. Meanwhile, Daniel was scouting for a director who could capture the thrill and excitement of the story. He found Timur Bekmambetov, a Kazakh Russian filmmaker known for visually dynamic, action-heavy films and hailed as one of the most commercially successful Russian directors of the decade. In 2012 Bekmambetov, had worked with Tim Burton on the action horror film *Abraham Lincoln: Vampire Hunter*. Although his horror-action background seemed an odd fit, his experience in tech and action made him appealing.[9]

When Bekmambetov was first approached to direct a reimagining of one of cinema's most beloved classics, he hesitated. Daniel eventually convinced him to read Clarke's script, and that changed everything. Bekmambetov was struck by the power of the story and how its central theme of forgiveness felt more relevant than ever in today's world.[10]

MGM and Paramount were mindful of potential criticism regarding the portrayal of Christian elements in the remake of *Ben-Hur*. Paramount had already weathered considerable storm over biblical inaccuracies in their 2014 film *Noah*.[11]

To address this, MGM took deliberate steps to ensure the film's faith-based themes were handled with authenticity and respect. They enlisted Mark Burnett and Roma Downey to help produce the 2016 *Ben-Hur* remake due to their proven success in creating faith-based content that resonated with both religious and mainstream audiences. Burnett, a British-American television producer widely regarded as a pioneer in reality TV, had married Roma Downey, an Irish actress and producer, best known for her role as the angel Monica on the long-running TV series *Touched by an Angel*.[12]

The pair had joined forces to found LightWorkers Media, a company dedicated to creating inspirational and family-oriented programming.. Their previous projects, such as *The Bible* miniseries and *Son of God*, demonstrated their ability to craft compelling narratives with spiritual themes. Their involvement aimed to emphasize the story's themes of forgiveness and reconciliation, aligning with their mission to produce uplifting and inspirational content. Additionally, their production company had a track record of engaging faith communities, which MGM saw as valuable for promoting the film to a broader audience.[13]

With the production team in place, casting for the leading roles began in earnest. Tom Hiddleston, who had gained fame after starring in *Thor* and *The Avengers*, was initially considered for the lead role of Ben-Hur. However, Hiddleston was involved in multiple projects at the time and he decided not to pursue the role.[14]

It was then decided to focus on emerging talent for the key roles in the film. English actor Jack Huston, known for his role in *Boardwalk Empire*, was ultimately chosen to play Ben-Hur. His selection was influenced by his ability to bring depth and nuance to complex characters.[15] Toby Kebbell from *Fantastic Four*, another English actor, was cast as Messala, Ben-Hur's adoptive brother and eventual adversary.[16]

Morgan Freeman was cast as Sheikh Ilderim to add star power. The character of Ilderim was changed from that of a wealthy Arab to a Nubian, complete with impressive dreadlocks. Ilderim plays a much more important role in the film, serving as a catalyst for Ben-Hur's transformation. Unlike Wyler's version, where Ilderim was a secondary and slightly comic character, there is no humour in this update. The revamped character appealed to Morgan, who admitted in several interviews that he liked 'playing power'. He also said that he wasn't keen on the dreadlocks, which kept hitting him in the face.[17]

By elevating the importance of the role of Ilderim, both Clarke and Ridley downplayed the character of Quintus Arrius, the Roman tribune and commander of a Roman galley whom, in the novel and subsequent films, Ben-Hur saves and becomes pivotal in Ben-Hur's transformation from slave to wealthy Roman citizen. In this film, Arrius dies during the sea battle and Ben-Hur is pulled from the sea by Ilderim.

Israeli actress Gal Gadot from the *Fast & Furious* franchise was in the frame to play Ben-Hur's love interest, Esther, but had to withdraw due to scheduling difficulties. The role was then taken by Iranian-born Nazanin Boniadi, known for her part in the hit TV series *Homeland*. Boniadi was especially attracted to the role because in this version of the story, Esther is a strong character and, in many ways, an 'activist in her own time'.[18]

One striking and potentially controversial change in the 2016 version of the film was the figure of Christ, who was played by Brazilian actor Rodrigo Santoro, known for his role as Xerxes in *300* (2006) and its sequel *300: Rise of an Empire* (2014). Unlike the original films, Christ has a prominent role in this version. Paramount Pictures vice-chairman Rob Moore stated that Christ 'is going to be consistent with people's expectations', and that the 'expectations of the faithful will be honoured by this one'.[19]

Santoro said it was the most challenging character he had ever taken on, but he did receive a personal blessing from Pope Francis for his role as Christ.[20] The rest of the cast was made up of actors from America, Israel, Turkey, Denmark, Tunisia and Scotland.[21]

Filming began in Matera in Italy, later moving to Cinecittà Studios in Rome, the very same historic studio where the 1959 *Ben-Hur* had been filmed, and then on to Mexico. Like the 1925 and 1959 versions, the chariot race was the most complex scene, lasting ten minutes in the final cut. Horses were trained for months, and actors trained with stunt coordinators to perform close-up stunts. The training of horses and charioteers was overseen by Steve Dent, a seasoned horse master renowned for his work on major historical films. Dent supplied and trained eighty-six horses, preparing them over several months to race at speeds up to 40 miles per hour. To ensure the wellbeing of the animals, twelve horses were rotated for each four-horse chariot team, allowing for adequate rest periods.

Huston and Kebbell underwent more than three months of intensive chariot training to perform their own stunts. For safety during filming, chariots were often equipped with hidden professional drivers who controlled the horses while the actors focused on their performances.[22]

The production emphasized realism, with much of the chariot race filmed at full speed using practical effects. To capture dynamic action, the crew employed GoPro cameras mounted on chariots and utilized drones for aerial shots, minimizing reliance on CGI.[23]

Bekmambetov wanted the race to feel real and visceral, relying heavily on practical effects rather than CGI, almost like a car chase – gritty, fast and violent. Before he shot a single frame, he wanted to find out exactly what it felt like to drive a four-horse chariot in a race, so he asked the stunt co-ordinator to break the rules and let him have a go.

He described the experience as 'like being in a blender, hooves and dust flying in your face from four creatures you cannot really control. We used historically correct chariots, which are really shaky. There's no suspension. There's [*sic*] no brakes. It's like you're just flying above the track.'[24]

Once he understood what he was dealing with, Bekmambetov started preparing the scene. Unlike his predecessors, he didn't turn to classical paintings to inspire his action scenes. His inspiration came from YouTube videos. He modelled the chariot race on NASCAR, Formula 1 and street racing footage, collecting and selecting the most interesting accidents to build a library of real-life events that he used to plan out the action scenes using software.[25]

Initially, the team set their sights on filming the race at Rome's historic Circus Maximus, but Italy's cultural ministry refused, citing preservation concerns. Undeterred, they built their own full-scale arena, an astonishing 1,000ft long, on the backlot of Cinecittà World in Rome. Production designer Naomi Shohan drew on archaeological sources to recreate the ancient stadium with meticulous accuracy, constructing one-sixth of the massive structure as a practical set.[26]

Bekmambetov wanted real dust, real hooves pounding and real adrenaline. Even the stuntmen found the going tough. In one instance, a stuntman was thrown from his chariot and run over; fortunately, he walked away with only bruised ribs, thanks in part to hidden Kevlar protection under his Roman costume.[27]

The scene took forty-five days to shoot. The action was captured using a dynamic mix of high-speed cameras, drone footage and ground-level rigs to create an immersive, chaotic atmosphere. Bekmambetov and cinematographer Oliver Wood (*The Bourne Supremacy*) even placed GoPro cameras directly in the sand to capture jittery close-ups of horses, wheels, dust and drivers. Remarkably, these cameras were used not only for visuals but also to record sound, capturing the raw, visceral audio you'd expect from extreme sports documentaries. This approach added an extra layer of realism to the chariot race, pulling audiences deeper into the intensity of the scene.[28]

CGI was used minimally, mostly to extend the crowd and background, enhance dust and debris or ensure the safety of the actors and horses used in the race sequence. Previous versions of *Ben-Hur* had used concealed wires to trip the horses, but the 2016 movie deployed CGI to make it look like horses were stumbling to the ground without putting the creatures at risk. Bekmambetov said:

> 'When we see the horse jumping onto the steps of the coliseum and going into the crowd of people that was not really a horse. That shot came from video of a bull going astray. From the exact same camera angle, we just used the bull as a reference and then inserted a [digital] horse instead.'[29]

Unlike earlier versions of *Ben-Hur*, animal welfare was a top priority, and not just for the horses. Camels, goats, donkeys, sheep and even birds were carefully monitored, with trainers in costume by their sides throughout each scene. Other animals, like the rats scurrying through a shop and the seagull hovering above Ben-Hur's body after the shipwreck, were created entirely with CGI.[30]

The chariot race wasn't the only big action sequence in the movie. It also included the naval battle that has played a big part in nearly all dramatic versions of the story.

Instead of the sweeping spectacle of the 1959 version, Bekmambetov focused on Ben-Hur's experience below deck, capturing the chaos from the viewpoint of a chained galley slave. To achieve this, the production team built full-scale ship interiors on gimbals, mechanical platforms that mimicked the ship's movement. Actors physically rowed in real time, heightening the realism and intensity. Much of the surrounding battle – the sea, the ships, the destruction – was created with CGI, allowing for a broader depiction of the conflict while keeping the focus grounded in Ben-Hur's confined world.[31]

The camerawork reinforced this perspective, staying tight and handheld to emphasize the claustrophobia and brutality of the scene. Rather than showcasing grand strategy, the battle became a fight for survival. This modern approach intentionally diverged from the classic version, trading epic scale for emotional immediacy and using today's technology to plunge viewers into the heart of the action alongside Ben-Hur.[32]

With the shoot finally finished, the team return to the US. Post-production took over eighteen months, including the animation of thirty-two horses and eight chariots. Effects teams simulated muscle, skin and hair to an amazing level of detail.[33]

The film was initially set for release in February 2016 but was pushed back to August, which Paramount believed would offer better box office potential. The Summer Olympics were seen as a prime promotional opportunity. Marketing began with exclusive images and trailers in March 2016. The trailer amassed over 8 million views in its first week, which boded well for the success of the film.[34]

Yet despite the epic effort, *Ben-Hur* struggled at the box office. With a $100 million budget and high expectations, it grossed just $94 million globally, making it one of 2016's biggest flops and losing $47.8m for MGM. Analysts blamed weak marketing, lack of star power and lukewarm reviews.[35]

Certainly, the marketing strategy had only served to confuse the public. It was initially aimed at general audiences with a promise of action and spectacle, but the campaign changed course in its final weeks to court faith-based viewers, leaning heavily on the Christian credentials of producers Mark Burnett and Roma Downey, which alienated secular audiences and failed to resonate with younger moviegoers.[36]

Always essential to the success or failure of a film were the reviews, and these were scathing. The *Los Angeles Times*' Kenneth Turan dismissed the film as a '"dull and lethargic piece of work that had little reason to exist'. *Variety*'s Owen Gleiberman labelled it 'sludgy and plodding', lamenting that star Jack Huston paled in comparison to Heston. *The Observer*'s Wendy Ide described it as 'a thuddingly dull-witted remake of a biblical epic that wasn't exactly subtle to begin with', and the headline for *The Guardian*'s Peter Bradshaw review declared 'Chariots of Dire'. *The Hollywood Reporter*'s Todd McCarthy asked simply, 'what were they thinking?'.[37]

Interestingly, some reviewers suggested that the 'sword and sandal epic' which had once been a Hollywood staple had finally fallen out of fashion, a theory that would ultimately be disproved in 2024 with the box office success of *Gladiator II*.

Despite its scale, updated visuals and modern storytelling, the 2016 *Ben-Hur* struggled to connect with audiences and critics alike. This misfire stood in stark contrast to the enduring legacy of Lew Wallace's 1880 novel and the earlier, much-celebrated film adaptations. The 1925 silent epic had been a groundbreaking spectacle of its era, famous for its audacious stunts and breathtaking chariot race. Then came the 1959 version, a towering achievement in cinema that redefined epic filmmaking, swept eleven Academy Awards and became firmly entrenched as one of Hollywood's greatest triumphs.

By comparison, the 2016 film seemed to underscore a hard truth: some stories are so indelibly etched into the cultural imagination that attempts to reinvent them only serve as reminders of how masterfully they were told the first time.

Chapter 19

Advertising Across the Centuries: The Enduring Echo of *Ben-Hur*

From its sensational debut as a bestselling novel in 1880 to its multiple cinematic incarnations, *Ben-Hur* has not only captivated audiences with its epic storytelling but also helped shape the evolution of modern product advertising. As one of the earliest works of fiction to be marketed as a cultural phenomenon, *Ben-Hur* set a precedent for cross-promotional strategies that bridged literature, stage and screen.

Each new adaptation – from the 1925 silent film to the iconic 1959 epic and beyond – brought with it innovative advertising campaigns that blurred the line between entertainment and commerce.[1]

The 1880 publication of *Ben-Hur* couldn't have been better timed, coinciding with a revolution in how products and ideas were promoted in America. That same year, department store pioneer John Wanamaker hired John E. Powers – the nation's first full-time advertising copywriter – whose bold, plainspoken style nearly doubled Wanamaker's sales and proved just how potent the right words could be. Two years later, Procter & Gamble launched one of the country's first national advertising campaigns for Ivory Soap, branding it as 'the soap that floats'. The simple, memorable slogan was amplified by new advances in printing and design, which now allowed companies to broadcast their messages from coast to coast.[2]

Gustav A. Moebs was a prominent tobacco merchant in the late nineteenth century, also known for his innovative marketing strategies. In 1886, he introduced a line of cigars under the brand name 'Ben-Hur', capitalizing on the immense popularity of the novel. The cigar packaging featured imagery inspired by Alexander von Wagner's painting, depicting the lead charioteer with a team of all-white horses, a possible nod to themes of purity and heroism. The boxes bore the clever slogan 'Cigars Were What Wise Men

Smoked', subtly linking the product to the biblical Magi and infusing it with an air of tradition and sophistication.[3]

While Moebs' approach artfully connected the product to the novel's themes, other manufacturers were less concerned with such nuanced associations. They freely adopted the *Ben-Hur* name and imagery, often without any meaningful link to the original story.[4]

Around the same time, *Ben-Hur* began showing up in unexpected places. In 1891, a committee in Arizona used a sketch based on Wagner's famous painting of the chariot race to advertise a local event, one of the earliest known examples of the image being used to sell something. Then, in 1894, The Tribe of Ben-Hur was founded, offering life insurance and social support, and they also used the chariot from Wagner's painting as part of its logo, changing the horses from white to brown. *Ben-Hur* was swiftly moving beyond the page, becoming a familiar symbol in American life, something that could sell ideas, products and even community.[5]

By 1896, the influence of *Ben-Hur* had spread far beyond the pages of Lew Wallace's novel. The Central Cycle Manufacturing Company of Indianapolis introduced the *Ben-Hur* bicycle, while two-dozen steam and paddle boats also proudly took the name, along with trains, tapping into the novel's spirit of speed and adventure.[6]

New Lindell Mills of Fort Collins, Colorado, became the first food company to borrow the *Ben-Hur* name, branding their product *Ben-Hur Flour*. The choice had little to do with Lew Wallace's epic tale, but everything to do with the rise of American advertising and the evolution of the flour milling industry.

As *Ben-Hur* swept the nation and the world, the milling industry itself was undergoing profound change. Advances in processing techniques extended the shelf life of wheat flour, while the rapid expansion of the railroad network enabled producers to distribute their goods across unprecedented distances. But mass production created a new problem: how to sell ever-growing stockpiles of product. The answer came in the form of bold brand names and eye-catching imagery, marketing tools designed to grab the consumer's attention instantly and set one sack of flour apart from another.[7]

The chariot race, perhaps the most electrifying scene from *Ben-Hur*, proved perfect for the emerging world of visual advertising. It captured the excitement of the novel and, later, the stage adaptation, just as the rise of colour lithography made vibrant, mass-produced posters possible. By the early 1900s, companies such as The Royal Milling Company of Minneapolis, Minnesota, and Great Falls, Montana, were using bold, colourful posters both inside stores and plastered on town walls and fences. Few passers-by could ignore the thrilling sight of a chariot team thundering toward them.[8]

The iconic *Ben-Hur* imagery became a marketing mainstay for flour companies for decades, often paired with slogans evoking competition, quality and triumph: 'A Winning Product', 'Worthy of the Fame of a Famous Name', 'Wins the Race' and 'In the Race to Win Your Favor'. Soon, the *Ben-Hur* brand expanded beyond flour, gracing packaging for baking powder, coffee, tea, spices, fruit and veg, margarine, pudding, biscuits, chocolates and even whiskey and rye, firmly embedding itself in the American commercial landscape.[9]

It wasn't long before toiletry companies got in on the act. *Ben-Hur* soap began appearing in the US in the early decades of the twentieth century, alongside two different brands of *Ben-Hur* cutthroat razors. In 1904, The Andrew Jergens Company of Cincinnati developed a *Ben-Hur* line of toiletries'The decision to use the *Ben-Hur* name was a strategic marketing move, leveraging the existing popularity and cultural impact of the story to appeal to consumers looking for products that evoked a sense of adventure, opulence and historical romance. Another company, Brocard – a Russian perfumery – introduced their own version of *Ben-Hur* perfume in the early 1900s.[10]

The *Ben-Hur* collection was diverse, catering to various aspects of personal grooming and fragrance, including colognes, toilet waters, sachets, talcum powders, bath salts and bath oils, body lotions, cleansing creams and personal deodorants.[11]

The sense of speed, danger and heroic control embodied by *Ben-Hur* also translated perfectly into new forms of popular entertainment. Carousel rides, rollercoasters, chariot races and chariot displays all adopted the *Ben-Hur* name to evoke excitement and adventure. Even car manufacturers began using the *Ben-Hur* brand to suggest power and performance. Not to be outdone, mining and construction companies soon embraced the name and the iconic charioteer logo to promote strength, durability and reliability.[12]

One particularly creative example came from the Wire-Fence Company of Adrian, Michigan. They produced colourful posters featuring the Wagner charioteer, humorously suggesting what might have happened had one of their fences stood in Ben-Hur's way during his race, a clever demonstration of their product's strength and resilience.[13]

Both major film versions of *Ben-Hur* sparked an even greater explosion of merchandise. The 1925 silent epic was among the first Hollywood films to fully exploit the emerging techniques of advertising and film-related marketing. To promote the movie, MGM produced a range of printed materials, original posters, lobby cards and theatre programmes, all featuring dramatic imagery from the film. Today, these pieces have become highly sought-after collectibles.[14]

Photographic stills from the movie were widely distributed as well, showcasing key scenes and the film's stars, serving both as promotional tools and cherished souvenirs for fans. In a pioneering move for film marketing, MGM also partnered with outside companies to create tie-in merchandise. Jergens, for example, who had already used the *Ben-Hur* name for a line of toiletries, introduced a new *Ben-Hur* perfume. The fragrance became popular, endorsed by stars Carmel Myers, May McAvoy and Ramon Novarro in a 1926 issue of *Photoplay* magazine, where it was praised for its 'delicate' and 'exquisite' qualities.[15]

Advertising tie-ins stretched even further: Quaker Oats ran a campaign featuring a behind-the-scenes photo of the chariot race being filmed, urging readers that 'heads of great businesses are urging correct breakfast eating' to ensure the health and productivity of employees.[16]

A whole new wave of products began to benefit from the *Ben-Hur* brand, from Bell & Howell cameras to watches, clocks, jewellery, clothing and even Ramon Novarro dolls, capitalizing on the movie's star power and sweeping cultural impact.[17]

Even after the film had slipped from the cinema screens, some *Ben-Hur* established icons continued to flourish throughout the 1930s and 1940s, including Ben-Hur Coffee, Ben-Hur Manufacturing and Ben-Hur Hair Products. It was a name that was used to promote banking, real estate, fossil fuels, clothing and even horse racing alongside fraternal organizations.[18]

By the time MGM produced their 1959 epic version of the *Ben-Hur* story, the art of merchandising tie-ins had begun to be developed for popular TV shows and celebrities, but this kind of commercial application was still in its infancy within the film industry. The only studio that had really embraced this new marketing model was the Walt Disney Company.[19]

MGM would break new ground when, prior to the release of the film, the studio employed the services of a dedicated licensing agency to create and manage merchandising tie-ins. Gone were the days when any company could use the *Ben-Hur* imagery without first proving that their products were of top quality, and then paying MGM for the privilege of producing and selling them.[20]

This additional cost didn't deter companies from wanting to link in with the movie, and the market was soon flooded with *Ben-Hur* paraphernalia. People were able to buy *Ben-Hur* themed items 'for every room in the house and for every member of the family', as one studio press release put it.[21]

Toys included the inevitable helmets and swords, shields and scabbards, models of charioteers, painting-by-numbers sets, board games, model-kits and activity books, alongside massive and expensive play sets featuring a model of the amphitheatre with the imperial box and a selection of several dozen figures, including charioteers, gladiators and wild animals.[22]

Not quite such an obvious tie-in were the vast clothing and jewellery ranges that were licensed, everything from '*Ben-Hur* inspired' designer dresses and jewellery to baby grows and children's charm bracelets, with the inevitable T-shirts and caps in between.[23]

The film's score, composed by Miklós Rózsa, was released as a three-LP album, marking one of the earliest instances of a film score being made available to the public in its entirety.[24]

Interestingly, the 2016 *Ben-Hur* film arrived with extraordinarily little in the way of a major merchandising campaign, in sharp contrast to the merchandising juggernauts behind most modern blockbusters. This may have been due to the film's target audience: adults and fans of epic dramas, not the toy-buying demographic that typically drives sales of action figures, clothing lines and collectibles. As a result, most of the merchandising centred on literature, faith-based resources and religious discussion materials rather than mass-market products.

The cornerstone of the campaign was the rerelease of Lew Wallace's original 1880 novel, *Ben-Hur: A Tale of the Christ*, updated with a film-branded cover to capture renewed interest. In addition, there was a novelization of the film itself, adapted by Carol Wallace, a direct descendant of Lew Wallace, specifically marketed toward faith-based audiences. Publishers and producers recognized the story's deeply spiritual themes and leaned into that identity, producing special editions and discussion guides designed for churches and *Bible* study groups. Many Christian bookstores carried themed materials, including prayer guides and small-group discussion kits timed to the film's release.[25]

This restrained approach to merchandising was striking when compared with *Ben-Hur*'s long history as a cultural brand. As we have seen, in the decades after the novel's 1880 publication, the *Ben-Hur* name had appeared on everything from flour to bicycles, as manufacturers sought to capitalize on the novel's popularity and moral weight.

By contrast, the 2016 film avoided mass-market tie-ins in favour of materials that reflected its religious and spiritual themes. Rather than appearing on kitchen shelves or in department stores, its presence was felt in church pews and small-group *Bible* studies. This shift not only highlighted the evolving nature of movie merchandising but also underscored a larger truth: while *Ben-Hur* had once been a name used to sell everyday goods, in the modern era its resonance was strongest when tied back to the moral and faith-based themes that had defined it from the start.

The legacy of both the 1925 and 1959 *Ben-Hur* films continues to thrive through collectible memorabilia and modern reproductions. Vintage items such as the original *Ben-Hur* playset now sell for thousands of pounds on sites like eBay, while contemporary merchandise such as posters, T-shirts, mugs and other products featuring imagery from the films has been widely available through various retailers since the licences expired. These items appeal to both new fans and long-time collectors eager to celebrate the enduring impact of the franchise.[26]

Among the rarer and more valuable treasures from the 1925 film is a limited-edition bronze featuring Carmel Myers as Iras, dressed in the elaborate Egyptian gown and headdress designed by Romain de Tirtoff, better known as Erté. As noted earlier, Erté was brought to Hollywood by

Louis B. Mayer in 1925 to design costumes and sets for MGM productions, including *Ben-Hur*. His flamboyant designs for Myers as Iras became iconic, and his career would later extend to creating costumes for major theatrical productions in New York and the Folies Bergère in Paris. Erté's distinctive style, immortalized on the covers of *Harper's Bazaar magazine*, came to define the Art Deco era.

In 1990, at the remarkable age of 97, Erté collaborated with American sculptor Ira Bruce Reines to produce a bronze sculpture of Iras in her unforgettable costume. Limited to just 500 pieces – each signed by Erté and produced by Sevenarts Ltd in London – the sculptures have become highly sought-after collectors' items. Today, these bronzes routinely sell for thousands of pounds, a testament to the lasting allure of both Erté's artistry and the cultural weight of *Ben-Hur*.[27]

That enduring fascination is telling. Few works of popular entertainment have left such a broad and lasting imprint, spanning not just film and literature but also art, fashion and design. More than a century after Lew Wallace wrote his novel, *Ben-Hur* continues to inspire new generations of artists and collectors alike, proof that its influence reaches far beyond the screen and into the wider fabric of cultural history.

Chapter 20

A Fiction Forged in Antiquity: The Real World of *Ben-Hur*

'My God! Did I set all this in motion?' These were the astonished words of General Lew Wallace when he first witnessed *Ben-Hur* being brought to life on stage. More than a century later, the sentiment remains just as powerful.

Ben-Hur: A Tale of the Christ is a story that has evolved and expanded over the decades, influencing generations' perceptions of Roman, Jewish and early Christian history. Though audiences and scholars often criticize the *Ben-Hur* films, particularly the 1959 epic, for taking historical liberties, it's usually the directors or screenwriters who are blamed. But the roots of those inaccuracies trace back to Wallace himself.

Writing not as a trained historian but as a Civil War veteran and self-taught biblical enthusiast, Wallace fused scripture, classical sources and nineteenth-century Christian theology into a sweeping narrative. What emerged was less a work of strict historical fidelity than a richly wrought Victorian moral parable.

Let's explore some of the more unusual aspects of Wallace's vision, beginning with the story's opening scene. The novel and both the 1925 and 1959 film adaptations open with the arrival of the Magi or Three Wise Men and the birth of Jesus. But Wallace takes it a step further. Not only does he name the Magi – Balthasar, Melchior and Caspar – but he assigns them origins in Egypt, Greece and Hindustan and describes their philosophical backgrounds.

He weaves Balthasar into the main story by having him seek shelter from the avenging Herod with Sheik Ilderim. He becomes a central character in the narrative, serving as a spiritual mentor and guide for Ben-Hur, and in the novel he is also the father of enigmatic seductress Iras.

Balthasar and Iras appear in the 1925 film. In the 1959 version, Balthasar returns, this time alone, but his role is no less significant. He narrates key parts of the story, encourages Ben-Hur to seek out Jesus and witnesses the crucifixion alongside him.

Although Wallace has taken great liberties with the story of Balthasar, the identity and origin of the Magi has been a matter of speculation for centuries. The Gospel of Matthew is the only biblical account that mentions their visit. He refers to them simply as 'Magi', from the Greek *magos*, a term associated with the priestly and learned class of Persia. Matthew does not say how many there were, only that they brought three gifts: gold, frankincense and myrrh. It is from this list of gifts that the traditional number of three Magi was inferred.[1]

Nor does Matthew name them or describe exactly from where they came, only that they traveled 'from the East'. The theologian Tertullian, writing in the third century, described them as kings from Arabia, and a century later the Archbishop of Constantinople, John Chrysostom, placed them in Persia.[2]

In early Christian art, Roman catacomb frescoes from the third and fourth centuries sometimes depict two figures flanking the seated Virgin and Child, while others show as many as four.[3]

The names themselves first appear in an eighth-century Latin chronicle composed in Alexandria known as *Excerpta Latina Barbari*, a translation of a now-lost Greek text possibly dating back to the sixth century. In this early version, the Magi were called Bithisarea, Melchior and Gathaspa.[4]

A Syrian manuscript names the Magi as Hormizdah, King of Persia; Yazdegerd, King of Saba; and Perozadh, King of Sheba. Other traditions, however, differ. Syriac Christians named them Larvandad, Gushnasaph and Hormisdas. Ethiopian tradition calls them Hor, Karsudan and Basanater, while Armenian sources refer to them as Kagpha, Badadakharida and Badadilma.[5]

The eighth-century Irish manuscript *Collectanea et Flores* offers additional details about the appearance of the wise men. By this time, they were no longer depicted as Persian Magi but instead as figures embodying the three ages of life – youth, middle age and old age – and displaying distinct racial characteristics meant to represent Europe, Africa and Asia, the three known regions of the world.[6]

Around the same period, legendary Northumbrian monk the Venerable Bede wrote that the Three Wise Men could also signify the three sons of Noah, who, as tradition had it, re-peopled the globe and were the source of humanity's three basic racial groups.

Piggybacking on Bede's writings, an anonymous author known as the Pseudo-Bede expanded on the idea that the Magi were different ages and developed descriptions of them. According to this account, Melchior was an old man with white hair and a long beard, while Caspar was young and beardless and Balthasar was dark-skinned with a full beard.[7]

Some sources claim that the three Magi were martyred for their faith. Notably, in the 1270s, Marco Polo reported that he had been shown their tombs in Saveh, a city south of present-day Tehran.[8]

In the fourteenth century, *The Historia Trium Regum* (or 'History of the Three Kings') by John of Hildesheim, a German Carmelite friar, has a more detailed tale. He tells us the Magi were kings from the East, from the lands of Ind, Chaldea and Persia, and their names were Melchior, Balthasar and Gaspar.

After meeting the baby Jesus, they leave Jerusalem and, journeying together for many days, eventually come to a place called the Hill of Vaws, where they built a chapel. They agreed to meet once a year and ordained that the Hill of Vaws should be their place of burial. They all returned to the hill to die and were buried in the same tomb. Two centuries later, Saint Helena, the mother of the Emperor Constantine, journeyed to Ind and recovered the bodies of the three kings from their tomb. She put them into a single chest ornamented with great riches and brought the relics to Constantinople and the church of Hagia Sophia. In the fourth century, the relics were taken to Italy by Eustorgius I, the Bishop of Milan. Over 800 years later, in 1164, Holy Roman Emperor Frederick Barbarossa seized the relics from Milan and presented them to Rainald of Dassel, the Archbishop of Cologne. A grand shrine that was constructed to house them quickly became a major pilgrimage site, with Cologne Cathedral being built around it.[9]

In his autobiography, Wallace talks about his extensive research into the religious world of first-century Judea and Rome, and in many ways his descriptions are accurate. In Judea, people clung to their monotheistic Jewish faith while living under Roman rule, hoping for the arrival of a messiah to deliver them. Roman religion was polytheistic, with gods like Jupiter, Mars and Venus influencing every part of life. The Romans had inherited much of their mythology from the Greeks but adapted it to reflect Roman values and support the authority of the Empire. They were generally open to incorporating gods from other cultures, such as Isis from Egypt or Mithras from Persia, so long as those cults did not challenge Roman rule. This made the Empire religiously diverse, especially in the eastern provinces like Judea.[10]

Through the eyes of Ben-Hur, Wallace explores how these different beliefs clashed and connected, capturing the deep struggles and transformations of the era.

Judaism was one of the few religions officially recognized by Rome. Jews were allowed to practise their faith, avoid military service on the Sabbath and send tribute to the Temple in Jerusalem. Still, this tolerance had limits. Rome demanded loyalty above all, and emperor worship became a common practice, starting with Augustus. By the time of Jesus, emperors like Tiberius and Nero were expected to be honoured as divine, and refusing to participate could be seen as treason.[11]

In *Ben-Hur*, this conflict is shown through characters like Messala, who views Jewish customs with contempt and sees Rome as the ultimate power. His attitude reflects the larger Roman view that local religions were tolerated only if they could be absorbed or neutralized.[12]

Judea's status as a Roman province introduced a complicated dynamic between Roman law and Jewish religious autonomy. Roman governors such as Pontius Pilate often acted with disregard for Jewish customs. Tensions culminated in events such as Pilate's use of Temple funds for an aqueduct and the placement of imperial shields in Jerusalem, all acts interpreted as sacrilege by the Jewish population.[13]

Meanwhile, Jewish religious life in Judea was diverse and full of tension. Several sects vied for influence. These included the Pharisees, who emphasized strict adherence to the Torah – the first part of the Jewish Bible – and oral traditions and believed in the resurrection of the dead. The Sadducees supported traditional aristocratic rule and a priestly elite. They accepted only the written Torah and denied resurrection. The Essenes were a separatist group, who withdrew from mainstream society and awaited apocalyptic deliverance. They were thought to be the authors of the Dead Sea Scrolls, which reflect their apocalyptic expectations and rejection of Temple corruption. Then there were the Zealots, who advocated violent resistance to Roman occupation and yearned for a militant messiah to restore Israel. Their rebellion in 66CE led to the destruction of the Temple by a Roman army in 70CE.[14]

Wallace subtly captures these tensions in *Ben-Hur*. Ben-Hur's family, particularly his mother and sister, are portrayed as devout, law-abiding Jews, part of the aristocratic Sadducee sect. The Sadducees took literally the Old Testament's references to an 'eye for an eye'. This belief system explains Ben-Hur's lust for vengeance and his premeditated manoeuvre against Messala in the chariot race.[15] However, Ben-Hur would also become involved with the Zealots fighting against Roman oppression.

Messianic hope was a defining theme of first-century Jewish religion. Many believed that a promised anointed one, the messiah, would come to restore Israel. Some envisioned a warrior-king in the mould of David, while others – shaped by apocalyptic writings – looked for divine judgment and the arrival of a new heavenly kingdom. It was into this charged spiritual landscape that Jesus of Nazareth entered, a preacher whose proclamation of the Kingdom of God and works of healing drew devoted followers as well as fierce opposition. Wallace evokes this era of religious upheaval by weaving Jesus' appearances quietly yet powerfully into the fabric of his narrative.

Having established the rich religious and societal backdrop of first-century Judea, Wallace shifts to the personal drama at the heart of *Ben-Hur*. The story's catalyst comes in the form of a sudden, fateful accident, an incident that leads to Ben-Hur's wrongful arrest. It sets in motion the trials, betrayals and quests for vengeance that define his journey. This turning point not only propels the narrative forward, but also places Ben-Hur squarely within the turbulent world Wallace has so carefully constructed.

In the novel and the 1925 and 1959 films, this dramatic turning point occurs after a tile accidentally falls from Ben-Hur's balcony, spooking the horse of Valerius Gratus, the newly appointed governor of Judea, and causing him to be thrown. In the 2016 film adaptation, the plot diverges: Ben-Hur takes the blame for an assassination attempt on the governor, carried out by a young Zealot whom he had been sheltering.

However, in every version of the story, Ben-Hur is betrayed by Messala, arrested and condemned to serve as a galley slave, a brutal ordeal that forges him into a hardened survivor. This scenario, though compelling in a work of fiction, is historically implausible. By the first century CE, the Roman navy was manned primarily by professional, salaried sailors recruited from the provinces or drawn from the lower classes and non-citizen ranks. It was not standard practice to sentence aristocratic citizens to forced labour aboard naval galleys.

On a more practical level, Roman authorities typically avoided using slaves or convicts as rowers, both because of the technical skill required and the considerable risk of rebellion. Wallace's depiction of the horrors of the rowers chained to their benches for days on end, and the cinematic dramatizations it inspired, owe more to Romantic-era storytelling than to historical accuracy.[16]

In the novel and the 1925 and 1959 films, Ben-Hur rows aboard a Roman galley commanded by Admiral Quintus Arrius. The ship is attacked and destroyed by pirates. Wallace refers to these attackers as Macedonian pirates, though this, too, stretches the historical record. While Macedonia had indeed experienced a period of piracy – most notably around 348 BCE during the reign of Philip II, father of Alexander the Great – it became a Roman province in 148 BCE, so would not have been launching attacks on its own ships. The major piracy threat in the Mediterranean during the late Republic came not from Macedonia but from Cilicia, a coastal region in southern Anatolia. Even then, those pirates had been decisively defeated by Pompey the Great in 67–66 BCE. By the time Ben-Hur's story takes place, the Mediterranean had been free of organized pirate fleets for more than half a century.[17]

After the pirate attack, in both the book and the early films, Ben-Hur saves the life of Arrius, who is on the verge of suicide, believing his fleet has been lost. They are later rescued while adrift at sea. In gratitude, Arrius not only grants Ben-Hur his freedom but also adopts him as his son. The two return to Rome, where, in the novel and the 1959 film, they are honoured in a grand triumphal procession. Arrius receives a victory baton from Emperor Tiberius himself.

The 2016 film, however, discards this subplot entirely. In this version, Ben-Hur washes ashore and is taken in by the wealthy and enigmatic Sheik Ilderim, who becomes his mentor and sponsor in the chariot arena.

While the victory parade in the 1959 film is a cinematic spectacle, the parade would not have been an historical reality. After the reign of Augustus, full Triumphs – Rome's most prestigious military celebrations – were reserved exclusively for members of the imperial family. Commanders like Arrius might have been awarded an *ovatio ('ovation')*, a far more modest honour involving the sacrifice of a sheep and a brief public appearance accompanied by applause.[18] Furthermore, Emperor Tiberius would not have been available to bestow any honours in person. At the time Ben-Hur and Arrius would have returned to Rome, Tiberius was living in self-imposed exile on the island of Capri, gripped by paranoia and political isolation. He never returned to the capital.[19]

In the novel and the 1925 and 1959 films, Ben-Hur remains in Rome and trains as both a gladiator and charioteer, eventually gaining fame for his victories in the arena and circus. Historically, this too is problematic. No Roman or Jewish nobleman would have taken up such a profession. Charioteers, like gladiators, were typically slaves or freedmen and held the legal status of *infames*, a class of socially disgraced individuals that included actors, prostitutes and pimps. Being a charioteer would have stripped a citizen of many legal protections and barred them from holding public office. It would also have been regarded as a contrary to Jewish custom.[20]

That said, the allure of chariot racing was undeniable, and later emperors like Caligula and Nero broke with tradition, training as charioteers and even building their own racetracks in Rome. Despite the stigma, successful charioteers could earn immense wealth and enjoy widespread fame. Chariot races drew the biggest crowds both in Rome and across the Empire, and vast sums were wagered on who would win a race.[21]

Charioteers could achieve the kind of fame and fortune we associate with modern sports celebrities. Two real-life names have survived the centuries: Gaius Appuleius Diocles and Flavius Scorpus. Of the two, Scorpus' story is the more sensational and parallels Ben-Hur's rise from obscurity. Born a slave, Scorpus began racing as a teenager in the outer provinces of the Roman Empire. By the time he arrived at Rome's Circus Maximus in 90 CE, he was about 21 years old. Over the course of a decade, he is believed to have raced in 5,000–6,000 competitions. His skill and daring made him a superstar, amassing wealth that in today's terms has been estimated to rival modern billionaires. Some estimates suggest earnings equivalent to $15 billion. Tragically, his meteoric rise was cut short: Scorpus likely died mid-race around 95 CE, a victim of the very sport that had made him a legend.[22]

Gaius Appuleius Diocles' remarkable career as a charioteer in the second century CE is among the best documented in antiquity. Diocles began racing at the age of 18 and went on to compete in 4,257 four-horse races, winning 1,462 of them before retiring, relatively unscathed, twenty-four years later. It was an extraordinary achievement given the dangers of the sport. His total earnings amounted to nearly 36 million sesterces, an astronomical fortune that would have made him one of the wealthiest athletes in Roman history.[23]

We will return to the chariots again in a moment, but now let us turn to the next scene in the story Ben-Hur's return to Jerusalem and Antioch and the events leading up to the dramatic race that serves as the *defining moment in the story.* Now a respected Roman citizen, Ben-Hur returns to his hometown. There, he finds Simonides, a former servant of his father, who has safeguarded and grown the Hur family's wealth.

Ben-Hur soon discovers that Messala is in Antioch, preparing to compete in a prestigious chariot race. Determined to seek both justice and revenge, he allies himself with the wealthy Sheik Ilderim and agrees to drive the sheikh's powerful team of horses, setting the stage for their climactic confrontation.

There is no doubt that the chariot race is the highlight of *Ben-Hur.* In 1908, seeking to capitalize on the publicity surrounding the copyright case against Kalem Studios, Harper & Brothers even published an illustrated stand-alone book titled *The Chariot Race from Ben-Hur.*

In the novel, Wallace waxes lyrical about the design of Messala's chariot

> 'The wheels were very marvels of construction. Stout bands of burnished bronze reinforced the hubs, otherwise very light; the spokes were sections of ivory tusks, set in with the natural curve outward to perfect the dishing, considered important then as now; bronze tires held the fellies, which were of shining ebony. The axle, in keeping with the wheels, was tipped with heads of snarling tigers done in brass, and the bed was woven of willow wands gilded with gold.'[24]

This is a magnificent description, but of a parade chariot rather than a racing one. Roman chariots, which evolved from Etruscan designs, were much like the famous Monteleone chariot, discovered in Monteleone di Spoleto, Umbria, at the turn of the twentieth century and now housed in the Metropolitan Museum of Art in New York. Parade chariots typically featured a high front and enough space to accommodate a driver and an honoured passenger.[25]

The same grand style informed the chariot designs in the 1925 and 1959 films. Notably, the design on the front of Ben-Hur's chariot in the 1925 version depicting scenes from the life of Achilles, including Thetis presenting her son with a helmet and shield forged by the gods, is strikingly similar to the imagery on the Monteleone chariot. Since the museum acquired the chariot in 1903, it would have been readily available for the film's prop designers to study and emulate.[26]

In reality, Roman chariots were built for speed. Wheels were small and the chariots were light, made of wood and rawhide; the platform measured only about 1 metre from the rear axle to the front rail. The chariot driven by Ben-Hur in the 2016 film is the closest design to this. The British Museum has a miniature chariot dating from the first to second centuries CE that shows the design in more detail. The chariot was found in the Tiber River in the 1890s and is thought to have been made for a wealthy racing enthusiast. The body of the chariot is shown as being made of bent pieces of wood lashed together with a thong. The yoke pole is decorated with a ram's head terminal.[27]

Because Roman chariots were pulled by four horses, which made them trickier to control to gain leverage, the charioteer wrapped the reins around his waist, so he could use his body weight to control the horses. If they crashed, he had only seconds to cut himself free using a special knife, which was carried in the straps of his torso lacing. Interestingly, in both the 1925 and 1959 films Ben-Hur wears a knife, as does Messala in the 1925 film, but the reins remain firmly in their hands and not around their waists.[28]

Cinematic depictions of the drivers themselves often favour Hollywood fantasy over historical fact. Rather than revealing their bronzed bulging biceps as in the 1925 and 1959 movies, charioteers wore two layers of clothing, which included a long-sleeved shirt and short tunic worn over the shirt. Leather thongs would be wrapped around the upper body in a crisscross pattern, and there would also be a thick, rectangular belt, leather leggings with puttees, protectors around the thighs and a knife.

An essential part of the charioteer's clothing was a helmet (probably made of felt or leather), rounded or lozenge-shaped, with a thick brim (sometimes turned up at the back), secured by a chin strap. Ben-Hur in both the 1925 and 1959 films makes an attempt at wearing some sort of head covering, although in the 1959 version he appears to discard it before the race begins. In the 1925 film, Messala has overly theatrical sprouting wings decorating his helmet. No head covering is seen in the 2016 race, although Ben-Hur's clothing is the closest to accuracy.[29]

Another anachronistic anomaly appears in the 1959 film, with Charlton Heston wearing a Star of David on his charioteer tunic. The Star of David, composed of two overlaid equilateral triangles that form a six-pointed star, only became a distinctly Jewish symbol in the mid-fourteenth century, when Holy Roman Emperor Charles IV granted the Jews of Prague the right to carry a flag, and they chose the six-pointed star.[30]

Geographically, the films also diverge. The novel and the 1925 and 2016 films place the chariot race in the circus in Antioch, whereas the 1959 film locates it in Jerusalem. Antioch, now known as Antakya, is just north of the Syrian border, in the Hatay province of southern Turkey. It was the third-largest city in the Roman Empire, after Rome and Alexandria, and one of the most important cities in the eastern Mediterranean. It did indeed have a circus in the first century CE, whereas there had never been one in Jerusalem itself. Herod I had built a track outside the city, but it fell into disuse after his death in 4BCE.

In the book there are six teams entering the race, the 1925 film has nine chariots, as does the 1959 movie, and in 2016 there were eight, whereas a typical Roman race featured twelve chariots. In all three interpretations, the individual charioteers competing against each other represent a different ethnic group.

Wallace's description of the competitors in the novel is very precise.

- 'I. A four of Lysippus the Corinthian two grays, a bay, and a black; entered at Alexandria last year, and again at Corinth, where they were winners. Lysippus, driver. Color, yellow.

- ‘II. A four of Messala of Rome two white, two black; victors of the Circensian as exhibited in the Circus Maximus last year. Messala, driver. Colors, scarlet and gold.
- ‘III. A four of Cleanthes the Athenian three gray, one bay; winners at the Isthmian last year. Cleanthes, driver. Color, green.
- ‘IV. A four of Dieus the Byzantine two black, one gray, one bay; winners this year at Byzantium. Dieus, driver. Color, black.
- ‘V. A four of Admetus the Sidonian all grays. Thrice entered at Cesarea, and thrice victors. Admetus, driver. Color, blue.
- ‘VI. A four of Ilderim, sheik of the Desert. All bays; first race. Ben-Hur, a Jew, driver. Color, white.’[31]

The use of the term ‘*Byzantine*’ is another anachronism, inaccurate on two counts. First, the Byzantine Empire did not emerge until the fourth century CE, when Emperor Constantine moved the imperial capital from Rome to the former Greek colony of Byzantion, renaming it Constantinople. This city became the centre of the Eastern Roman Empire, whose inhabitants continued to call themselves Romans. Second, the word ‘*Byzantine*’ itself was not used at the time. It was coined much later, in the mid-sixteenth century, by German historian Hieronymus Wolf, who sought to distinguish the medieval, Greek-speaking empire from the classical, Latin-speaking Roman Empire.

However, what is even more relevant is that none of the competitors listed by Wallace would have been allowed to take part in a Roman chariot race. Roman races across the Empire did not allow individual entrants. Chariot racing was carefully organized and controlled. Charioteers were grouped into two levels of four factions. On top were the more prestigious Blues and Greens, and below them the Reds and Whites. These factions transcended geographic boundaries; every city with a major racetrack had all four. Each colour had a loyal fan base, and there was fierce rivalry. Charioteers may well have originated from all the different regions described by Wallace, but they would have still had to be accepted by an individual faction.[32]

As in the novel and the films, the beginning of the race was accompanied by a certain amount of pageantry, which is elaborately re-enacted in all three films. In the 1959 movie, the race is overseen by Pontius Pilate, governor of

Judea. He takes to the podium to announce the start of the race draped in Tyrian purple robes, a type of dress that would have been way above the 'pay grade' of a Roman governor. Tyrian purple dye was made from the mucus of several species of murex snail and was worth more than three times its weight in gold. It took more than 45kg of snails to produce a single gram of pure Tyrian purple extract. The most senior Roman magistrates were permitted to wear a white toga edged in Tyrian purple, but not the more sumptuous togas in solid Tyrian purple with gold thread edging.[33]

In another anachronism, Pilate drops a handkerchief to begin the race, a detail borrowed from the reign of Emperor Nero, who ruled between 54 and 68CE. According to legend, Nero once delayed the games with a long lunch and, in an impromptu gesture, tossed his napkin into the arena to start the show. The custom stuck, but would not have been known in Ben-Hur's era.[34]

While chariot racing was a central form of entertainment in Rome and throughout the Empire, the lethal tactics portrayed in all three film adaptations – including spiked wheels and deliberate mid-race attacks – were not representative of actual Roman races. Although the sport was undeniably dangerous, and accidents were inevitable during the heat of the moment, intentional acts of sabotage were officially prohibited and punishable. Roman races were highly organized public spectacles, overseen by magistrates such as the aediles, who were tasked with maintaining order, enforcing regulations and upholding the prestige of the Empire through the smooth execution of these events.[35]

A typical Roman race featured twelve chariots, with forty-eight horses lined up side by side at the starting gate. Tension ran high, and false starts, such as those portrayed in the 1959 film, were common. Once underway, the race resembled a chaotic stampede. Yet it was not unknown for some charioteers to strategically hold back, adding suspense but often provoking spectator unrest and calls for restarts. The problem became so widespread that Emperor Claudius introduced new rules to curb the excessive number of recalls.[36]

Understandably, such nuances, though historically accurate, were omitted from cinematic portrayals in favour of more dramatic storytelling.

Another element absent from the films is the vital presence of race assistants like the *sparsor*, who cooled the horses by dousing them with water, and the *hortator*, who rode nearby, guiding and encouraging the charioteer with tactical advice. In the 2016 film, Sheik Ilderim provided a broadly equivalent role, offering guidance from the sidelines.[37]

Once the race commenced in earnest, every charioteer's greatest fear was the *naufragium*, or 'shipwreck', a terrifying crash involving overturned chariots and tangled horses that could turn the track into a deadly obstacle course. These often stemmed from intentional moves, as competitors cut in front of one another, risking disastrous collisions. Charioteers, tied to their reins, faced the harrowing option of cutting themselves loose and fleeing on foot, at the risk of being trampled by another team.

Ironically, Wallace's novel has Ben-Hur commit just such a foul against Messala, using a calculated turn to smash his opponent's wheel and secure victory:

> 'They had not seen the cunning touch of the reins by which, turning a little to the left, he [Ben-Hur] caught Messala's wheel with the iron-shod point of his axle, and crushed it.'[38]

Across the Empire, a typical chariot race lasted about eight electrifying minutes, with teams reaching speeds of up to 45 miles per hour, an experience so breathtaking it drew enormous crowds. Wallace's own vivid, action-packed depiction captured that same energy, enthralling readers and performers alike and often earning thunderous applause during public readings.[39]

Remarkably, all three major film adaptations managed to capture the same sense of exhilaration. By coincidence, or perhaps as a deliberate nod to authenticity, both the 1925 and 1959 versions timed the climactic race at just over eight minutes, closely matching historical accounts. Even the 2016 adaptation, with its modern pacing and stylized approach, ran only two minutes longer. In doing so, the films bridged a century of storytelling, giving audiences past and present a visceral taste of one of ancient Rome's most spectacular and enduring entertainments and preserving the dramatic intensity that made Wallace's original depiction so unforgettable.

With the race over and Messala defeated, Ben-Hur goes in search of his mother and sister, Miriam and Tirzah, whom he has learnt are afflicted with leprosy and walled up in a prison. In the novel, Wallace's description of their condition is vivid and meant to stir horror, pity and a sense of injustice. He portrays Tirzah as 'a wasted figure, bent and shrunken, the flesh dried upon the bones, the eyes dull with despair', and describes Miriam's voice as 'thin and cracked, as if long unused'.[40] These images highlight their physical suffering and emphasize the spiritual and social isolation they face as lepers.

Wallace's vivid depiction of leprosy had a lasting impact on later adaptations of *Ben-Hur*. The 1925 silent film, the 1959 MGM epic and the 2016 remake all include scenes of Miriam and Tirzah as lepers, drawing heavily from Wallace's imagery. The 1959 film, in particular, uses stark lighting and costuming to evoke the same sense of isolation and horror found in the novel.

But how accurate is this view of leprosy and how did Wallace research the disease? It is very clear through Wallace's use of language that he has drawn the imagery from the *Bible*, in particular the Book of Leviticus, also known as the Third Book of Moses:

> 'Anyone with such a defiling disease must wear torn clothes, let their hair be unkempt, cover the lower part of their face and cry out, "Unclean! Unclean!" As long as they have the disease, they remain unclean. They must live alone; they must live outside the camp.'[41]

In fact, this passage relates to a variety of chronic skin diseases; the word 'leprosy' did not necessarily signify one single disease. In the ancient Greek texts attributed to Hippocrates, '*lepra*' described a range of different skin disorders.[42]

The description in Leviticus also reflects the ancient Israelite association of skin infections with ritual impurity and fear of contagion. It was an association that endured for centuries and was deeply embedded in Victorian religious consciousness.

To be fair to Wallace, it was not until 1873 that Norwegian physician Gerhard Henrik Armauer Hansen identified *Mycobacterium leprae* as the bacterium responsible for leprosy, and it was unlikely that the author would have been aware of this research. The disease, now more accurately known as Hansen's disease, can damage the nerves, respiratory tract, skin and eyes. This nerve damage often results in a loss of sensation, which in turn can lead to injuries and secondary infections that may cause the loss of fingers, toes or other extremities. True Hansen's disease progresses slowly and is not as grotesquely disfiguring or foul-smelling as Wallace suggests. Furthermore, it is far less contagious than his writing implies.[43]

Nevertheless, Wallace's description was consistent with nineteenth-century Western conceptions of leprosy. Missionary and colonial medical literature often portrayed the disease in sensational terms, focusing on its most advanced manifestations and reinforcing its perceived link to moral corruption and divine punishment.[44]

Furious and vengeful after discovering the plight of his family, it is at this point that Ben-Hur turns to the Zealots, becoming a local hero by killing a Roman soldier during a massacre of Jewish protesters. Galilean rebels begin to rally around him. Still searching for a greater purpose, he joins forces with Simonides and Ilderim to plan resistance to Roman rule. Wallace doesn't depict the Jewish–Roman War directly, but the threat of violence is always in the background.

Leaving the Zealots, Ben-Hur travels to Bethabara to hear John the Baptist preach. There, he recognizes Jesus as the man who once gave him water. Ben-Hur becomes a devoted follower, seeing Jesus as a spiritual leader rather than a military one. Ben-Hur's time with the Zealots shows how desperation for freedom can lead people to embrace violence. But Wallace's message is clear: true salvation doesn't come through swords, but through spiritual renewal.

Back in Jerusalem, Ben-Hur reunites with his mother and sister, who are healed by Jesus during his triumphal entry into the city. Now a follower of Christ, Ben-Hur witnesses Jesus' betrayal in Gethsemane. He tries to intervene but is too late. The next day, he watches in sorrow as Jesus is crucified. At the foot of the cross, Ben-Hur offers Jesus a final act of kindness, giving him watered-down wine on a sponge.[45]

Historically, however, all four Gospels agree that it was Roman soldiers who performed this gesture with what is described as 'vinegar'.[46] This was most likely *posca*, a cheap, sour wine diluted with water that soldiers commonly drank. Luke suggests the offer may have been made in mockery, while John emphasizes that it fulfilled the prophecy of Psalm 69:21: 'They gave me vinegar for my thirst.' By placing this moment in the hands of Ben-Hur,

Wallace transforms a brief, understated Gospel detail into a deeply personal encounter, linking his fictional hero directly to the suffering Christ.

As Ben-Hur's story draws toward its conclusion, Wallace heightens the drama by turning his hero's focus toward the plight of Christians suffering under the tyranny of the Emperor Nero. It is five years after the Crucifixion, and Ben-Hur and Esther are married and living in Misenum in Italy. They, along with Simonides and Malluch, have dedicated their wealth to supporting the early Christian Church in Antioch.

Upon hearing of the plight of the Christians in Rome, Ben-Hur searches for a way to help and Simonides proposes a daring and seemingly inspired solution:

> 'The Romans, even this Nero, hold two things sacred – I know of no others they so hold – they are the ashes of the dead and all places of burial. If you cannot build temples for the worship of the Lord above ground, then build them below the ground; and to keep them from profanation, carry to them the bodies of all who die in the faith.'[47]

Ben-Hur and Esther immediately set out for Rome to put Simonides' plan into action. With a flourish characteristic of his narrative style, Wallace signs off his epic by addressing his readers directly, linking Ben-Hur's fortune and legacy to the endurance of early Christianity:

> 'If any of my readers, visiting Rome, will make the short journey to the Catacomb of San Calixto, which is more ancient than that of San Sebastiano, he will see what became of the fortune of Ben-Hur, and give him thanks. Out of that vast tomb Christianity issued to supersede the Cæsars.'[48]

This stirring conclusion, though memorable, is not without historical issues. The Catacomb(s) of San Calixto (St Callistus) on the Appian Way date to the mid-second century CE, nearly 100 years after Nero's death in 68 CE. The oldest catacombs in Rome, they were named after the deacon Callixtus, who was appointed by Pope Zephyrinus in the early third century to oversee the cemetery, making it the official burial ground of the Roman Church. Far from being 'temples for the worship of the Lord', the catacombs were originally excavated out of the soft volcanic tufa outside the city walls to serve as communal burial grounds for Christians, Jews and even some pagans, in accordance with Roman law forbidding interment within the city.[49]

Archaeological evidence also makes it clear that the catacombs were never designed as places of formal worship or as secret refuges from persecution. Though occasional funeral banquets (*refrigeria*) and commemorative rites may have been held there, Christian liturgy was typically celebrated in private homes or, later, in purpose-built churches. Nor would the catacombs have been practical hiding places: they were dark, cramped, insanitary and well known to Roman authorities, as burial grounds were legal and clearly marked.[50]

By linking Ben-Hur's mission to the catacombs, Wallace was drawing upon a much older romantic image of Christians huddled underground, celebrating Mass by torchlight to avoid imperial troops. This evocative scene, though largely a fiction, had long been embedded in the narrative of Christian martyrdom and gained renewed popularity during the Victorian era. In *Ben-Hur*, Wallace gave this image one of its most vivid and enduring literary expressions.

It was a fittingly dramatic flourish to conclude a story that would not only capture the imagination of readers but also inspire countless reinterpretations across the arts, from paintings, magic lantern shows, *tableaux* and grand theatre productions to circus spectacles, stage musicals and – ultimately – some of the most iconic film adaptations in cinematic history.

Epilogue

The Race that Never Ended

From a quiet study in Crawfordsville, Indiana, to the dazzling lights of Hollywood and the shelves of grocers and department stores, *Ben-Hur* has travelled far beyond the imagination of its author. What began as Lew Wallace's deeply personal meditation on faith, redemption and justice became one of the most influential cultural forces of the modern era. The novel's spiritual core, rooted in the story of Christ and the transformation of one man's soul, resonated profoundly with readers, particularly in a rapidly industrializing America searching for moral clarity and inspiration.

Yet its impact would not end with the printed page. As *Ben-Hur* thundered into the twentieth century, it evolved into a multimedia and marketing phenomenon. The iconic chariot race became shorthand for excitement, power and triumph, lending itself to everything from flour sacks and bicycles to perfumes, rollercoasters and luxury toiletries. Its imagery, drawn from grand paintings and later film stills, leapt into posters, packaging and product design, making *Ben-Hur* a household name in ways Wallace could never have foreseen.

Cinema breathed new life into the story. The 1925 silent film set new standards for spectacle, while the 1959 MGM epic redefined the blockbuster with its grandeur, emotional weight and unforgettable score. These adaptations not only reignited interest in the story but also helped pioneer the very concept of film merchandising, bringing *Ben-Hur* into the lives of children and collectors alike through toys, games, costumes and keepsakes. The 2016 remake, though quieter in commercial scale, reaffirmed the story's spiritual dimensions, finding new audiences in religious and reflective communities.

In the end, *Ben-Hur* became more than a novel, a film or a brand. It became a symbol of enduring faith, cinematic ambition and the power of storytelling to transcend its own time. With each new generation, it raced forward anew, changing form but never losing the force of its original message. Even before

Wallace's novel reached readers, Alexander von Wagner's painting *The Chariot Race*, first exhibited in the 1870s, had already captured the public imagination with its sweeping, dramatic vision of ancient spectacle. Though not inspired by *Ben-Hur*, the painting's visual power was quickly folded into the story's identity, becoming an unofficial icon of the novel's most thrilling scene. Later, Ulpiano Checa's own depiction of the race, painted after the novel's release, added a new level of dynamic energy and cinematic movement. Together, these works provided the foundation for the bold visual language that would define *Ben-Hur* across posters, products and eventually film. The story was not just read, it was seen, worn, heard and held.

The legacy of *Ben-Hur* is not just that it was loved, but that it was lived, sold, celebrated and remembered. Across centuries and mediums, its wheels have never stopped turning. And somewhere, perhaps, Lew Wallace – soldier, diplomat and reluctant novelist – would have watched it all with awe, knowing that the tale he wrote for God and country had, in the end, spoken to the entire world.

Notes

Chapter 1

1. Manchester Art Gallery record: ArtUK – The Chariot Race.
2. Muybridge's obsession with motion made him one of the pioneers of early cinema. https://www.artnet.com/artists/eadweard-muybridge/.
3. The 1873 Vienna World Fair drew 7 million-plus visitors and featured technological and artistic marvels of the empire. The original painting may have been bought by one of Manchester Art Gallery's early benefactors, wealthy industrialist Henry Higgins, and donated to the gallery after his death.
4. *New York Art Journal*, 1877. The *New York Art Journal* was influential in shaping public and critical reception of artworks.
5. Florida Southern College's Art history professor, Dr Alex Rich, has identified the rediscovered canvas as either a reproduction or a fragment of Wagner's expanded work. In 2018, the canvas featured as the centrepiece of 'The Von Wagner Code' exhibition at the college's Ashley Gibson Barnett Museum of Art, https://agbmuseum.org/exhibitions/the-von-wagner-code.
6. https://museoulpianocheca.esy.es/.
7. I am grateful to the General Lew Wallace Study & Museum for providing a copy of this photograph.
8. Mainardi, Patricia, *The End of the Salon* (Cambridge Studies in New Art History and Criticism, 1994), p.95.
9. https://americanhistory.si.edu/collections/object/nmah_1002006.
10. Twyman, Michael, *Lithography 1800–1850* (Oxford University Press, 1970); Ivins, William M., *Prints and Visual Communication* (MIT Press, 1969), p.110; Castleman, Riva, *Prints of the Twentieth Century* (Thames & Hudson, 1988), p.39.
11. Mainardi, Patricia, *The End of the Salon* (1994), p.87.
12. Altick, Richard, *The Shows of London* (Harvard University Press, 1978), p.108.
13. Berger, John, *Ways of Seeing* (Penguin, 2008), p.23.

Chapter 2

1. McQueen, Kevin M., *The Amazing Mr. Wallace* (Indiana Historical Society Press, 2015); Morsberger, R.E. & Morsberger, K.M., *Lew Wallace: Militant Romantic* (McGraw-Hill Book Company, 1980), pp.297–312.
2. *Ibid.*; Morsberger & Morsberger, *Lew Wallace: Militant Romantic*, pp.3–7.
3. *Ibid.*; Stephens, Gail, *Shadow of Shiloh: Major General Lew Wallace in the Civil War* (Indiana Historical Society Press, 2010); Gugin, Linda C. & St Clair, James E. (eds), *The Governors of Indiana* (Indiana Historical Society Press, 2006), p.314.
4. *Ibid.*

5. Daniel, Larry J., *Shiloh: The Battle That Changed the Civil War* (Simon & Schuster, 1997); Morsberger & Morsberger, pp.79–115; Smith, Jean Edward, *Grant* (Simon & Schuster, 2001), pp.198–202.
6. *Ibid.*
7. *Ibid.*; Thomas, Benjamin P., *Abraham Lincoln: A Biography* (Alfred A. Knopf, 1952), p.287.
8. Morsberger & Morsberger, pp.221–42; Wallace, Lew, *The Fair God* (Houghton Mifflin, 1873).
9. Solomon, Jon, *Ben-Hur: The Original Blockbuster* (Edinburgh University Press, 2016), pp.46–59; Morsberger & Morsberger, pp.298–42.
10. Matthew 2:1–12 (NRSV / ESV / KJV / NIV); Solomon, *Ben-Hur: The Original Blockbuster*, pp.47–48; Wallace, Lew, *Lew Wallace: An Autobiography*, Vol. 2 (Harper & Brothers, 1906), p.833.
11. Wallace, *Lew Wallace: An Autobiography*, Vol. 2, p.833. This account appears to have evolved over time, and some historians believe Wallace romanticized the story to lend it a spiritual significance. However, there does seem to have been some element of truth, as had the encounter been a fabrication then it is likely Ingersoll himself would have challenged it. Solomon, *Ben-Hur: The Original Blockbuster*, pp.52–59.
12. McQueen, *The Amazing Mr. Wallace*; Solomon, pp.46–96.
13. Morsberger & Morsberger, *Lew Wallace: Militant Romantic*, pp.297–312; Solomon, Jon, *Fugitive Sources: Ben-Hur and the Popular Art Property* (RBM: A Journal of Rare Books, 2001); Solomon, *Ben-Hur: The Original Blockbuster*, pp.46–96.
14. Wallace, *Autobiography*; Morsberger & Morsberger, *Lew Wallace: Militant Romantic*, pp.297–312; Solomon, *Ben-Hur: The Original Blockbuster*, pp.52.
15. Wallace, *Autobiography*; Morsberger & Morsberger, *Lew Wallace: Militant Romantic*, pp.297–312. Descriptions of him writing his story under a beech tree in Crawfordsville are partly true, although they tend to ignore the fact that the bulk of Wallace's writing was executed at night after work or en route to appointments in his role as governor of New Mexico; Solomon, *Ben-Hur: The Original Blockbuster*, pp.46–96.
16. Horan, James D., *The Authentic Life of Billy the Kid* (Castle Books, 1955); Utley, Robert M., *Billy the Kid: A Short and Violent Life* (University of Nebraska Press, 1989), pp.212–15; Wallace, *Autobiography*.
17. Wallace, Letter to Susan Wallace, 1879. Indiana Historical Society Archives.
18. Morsberger & Morsberger, *Lew Wallace: Militant Romantic*, pp.297–312; McQueen, *The Amazing Mr. Wallace*; Solomon, *Ben-Hur: The Original Blockbuster*, pp.46–96.
19. Wallace, Lew, *Ben-Hur: A Tale of the Christ* (Harper & Brothers, 1880).
20. Solomon, *Ben-Hur: The Original Blockbuster*, pp.102–33.
21. *Ibid.*
22. Garfield, James, Letter to Lew Wallace, 1881. *Garfield Papers*, Library of Congress; Three months after writing the letter, Garfield was assassinated by Charles J. Guiteau, who believed he deserved a diplomatic post because of his (minimal) support for Garfield's election campaign.
23. The General Lew Wallace Study & Museum has faithfully preserved Wallace's personal memorabilia in the study that he designed and built in 1895 – on the same site where *Ben-Hur* was penned. https://www.ben-hur.com.
24. Solomon, *Ben-Hur: The Original Blockbuster*, pp.139–80.
25. *Ibid.*

26. Wallace, Lew, *The Prince of India or Why Constantinople* Fell (Harper & Brothers, 1893).
27. https://www.ben-hur.com/meet-lew-wallace/author.
28. Solomon, *Ben-Hur: The Original Blockbuster*, pp.52–59, 139–80.
29. *Ibid.*
30. Wallace, *Autobiography*.
31. Solomon, *Ben-Hur: The Original Blockbuster*, pp 52–59, 139–80.
32. *Ibid.*; Levine, Amy-Jill, *The Misunderstood Jew* (HarperOne, 2006).
33. Sears Catalogue, 1913. Wallace Memorial Edition, Sears Roebuck Archives. The Sears edition came in a cardboard box and paper cover depicting Checa's chariot race, with an advert to purchase a larger version ready for framing.
34. 'Tribe of Ben-Hur Fraternal Organization Records', Indiana State Library Archives. The Tribe of Ben-Hur was a fraternal benefit society providing life insurance, mutual aid and social fellowship, founded in 1894. It adopted the chariot from Wagner's painting as one of their logos, changing the colour of the horses from white to brown. Solomon, *Ben-Hur: The Original Blockbuster*, p.422.
35. John Philip Sousa wrote 'The Chariot Race' march in 1890, and in 1894 Edward Taylor Paull designed the sheet music using a five-colour chromolithographed composite of elements from both Checa and Wagner's paintings. Solomon, *Ben-Hur: The Original Blockbuster*, p.289.

Chapter 3

1. Bebbington, D.W., *Evangelicalism in Modern Britain: A History from the 1730s to the 1980s* (Unwin Hyman, 1989); https://www.puseyhouse.org.uk/info/the-oxford-movement.
2. Wigger, J.H., *Taking Heaven by Storm: Methodism and the Rise of Popular Christianity in America* (Oxford University Press, 2005); Miller, Randall M., Stout, Harry S. & Wilson, Charles R. (eds), *Religion & The American Civil War* (Oxford University Press, 1998), pp.113–14.
3. Bulwer-Lytton, Edward *Last Days of Pompeii* (Richard Bentley, 1834).
4. Wiseman, Nicholas *Fabiola: or The Church of the Catacombs* (Burns & Lambert, 1854).
5. Wallace, *Ben-Hur: A Tale of the Christ*.
6. Sienkiewicz, Henryk, *Quo Vadis: A Narrative of the Time of Nero* (trans. Jeremiah Curtin) (Little, Brown & Co, 1896).
7. https://pompeiiarchaeologicalpark.com/the-last-days-of-pompeii/#introduction; Beard, Mary, *Pompeii: The Life of a Roman Town* (Profile Books, 2008), p.212; Harris, Judith, Pompeii Awakened: A Story of Rediscovery (IB Tauris, 2007), p.164.
8. https://victorianweb.org/religion/catholicism/1.html.
9. Novels like *Fabiola* and *Ben-Hur* helped to promulgate the myth that the catacombs had been built to help Rome's early Christian community hide from those who persecuted them. Twentieth-century archaeology has shown that the catacombs were purely burial sites. Rutgers, Leonard V., *Subterranean Rome: In Search of the Roots of Christianity in the Catacombs of the Eternal City* (Peeters, 2000), p.6.
10. Wiseman, *Fabiola*, p.vii.
11. Rutgers, *Subterranean Rome*, p.6.
12. Sienkiewicz, *Quo Vadis: A Narrative of the Time of Nero*.
13. https://culture.pl/en/article/the-man-behind-quo-vadis.
14. Hopkin, J., 'Poland and Martyrdom: The Catholic Imagination in Sienkiewicz', *The Catholic Review*, 48(3), (2003), pp.212–26.

15. Nobel Prize Committee, 1905, 'Award Citation for Henryk Sienkiewicz (Stockholm: The Swedish Academy).

Chapter 4

1. Solomon, *Ben-Hur: The Original Blockbuster*, p.218; Hamilton, Kristie, *Ben-Hur and the Spectacle of Empire* (American Literary History, vol. 7, no. 3, 1995), pp.422–43; Morsberger & Morsberger, *Lew Wallace: Militant Romantic*, pp.220, 453, 455.
2. Solomon, *Ben-Hur: The Original Blockbuster*, p.218; Morsberger & Morsberger, *Lew Wallace: Militant Romantic*, pp.219–20.
3. Solomon, *Ben-Hur: The Original Blockbuster*, pp.218–19; Whitmore, William B., 'The Popular Reading and Recitation of Ben-Hur', *Indiana Magazine of History*, vol. 45, no. 3 (1949), pp.207–19.
4. Solomon, *Ben-Hur: The Original Blockbuster*, pp.167–72.
5. Dillenberger, Jane, *Visual Arts and Christianity in America: From the Colonial Period to the Present* (Crossroad Publishing, 1989).
6. Beacham, Richard C., *The Roman Theatre and Its Audience* (Harvard University Press, 1991).
7. Tydeman, William, *The Theatre in the Middle Ages: Western European Stage Conditions, c.800–1576* (Cambridge University Press, 1978).
8. Castle, Terry, *Masquerade and Civilization: The Carnivalesque in Eighteenth-Century English Culture and Fiction* (Stanford University Press, 1986), p.124.
9. https://www.courtauldian.com/single-post/the-attitudes-of-lady-hamilton.
10. Chapman, Mary, '"Living Pictures": Women and Tableaux Vivants in Nineteenth-Century American Fiction and Culture', *Wide Angle* 18.3 (Ohio University, 1996), pp.22–52.
11. Lewis, Robert M., 'Tableaux vivants: Parlor Theatricals in Victorian America', *Revue française d'études américaines*, No. 36, Les Lieux De La Vie Américaine (April 1988), pp.280–91.
12. Mainardi, Patricia, *The End of the Salon: Art and the State in the Early Third Republic* (Cambridge University Press, 1990).
13. Solomon, *Ben-Hur: The Original Blockbuster*, pp.220–29; Morsberger & Morsberger, *Lew Wallace: Militant Romantic*, p.454; Federal Copyright Records, Library of Congress, 'Selections from Ben-Hur Adapted for Readings with Tableaux', Registration No. A1887-239.
14. Solomon, *Ben-Hur: The Original Blockbuster*, pp.220–29; 'Art and Drama: The Ben-Hur Tableaux', *Boston Globe* (12 March 1888); 'Recitationists of Note', *Detroit Free Press* (7 April 1888).
15. Solomon, *Ben-Hur: The Original Blockbuster*, pp.220–29.
16. *Ibid.*; Wallace, Lew, Letter to Harper & Brothers (1888). Archives of the General Lew Wallace Study and Museum, Crawfordsville, IN.
17. Solomon, *Ben-Hur: The Original Blockbuster*, pp.229–61; Holsinger, Bruce, *Premodern Performance and the Postmodern Subject* (University of Chicago Press, 2005).
18. Solomon, *Ben-Hur: The Original Blockbuster*, pp.229–61.
19. *Ibid.*
20. *Ibid.*

Chapter 5

1. Mannoni, Laurent, *The Great Art of Light and Shadow: Archaeology of the Cinema*, trans. Richard Crangle (University of Exeter Press, 2000), pp.28–245.
2. *Ibid.*
3. *Ibid.*
4. https://www.magiclantern.org.uk/history.
5. Crangle, Richard, Van Dooren, Ine & Heard, Mervyn (eds), *Realms of Light: Uses and Perceptions of the Magic Lantern from the 17*th *to the 21*st *Century* (The Magic Lantern Society, 2005).
6. Solomon, *Ben-Hur: The Original Blockbuster*, pp.512–34.
7. *Ibid.*
8. Crangle, Van Dooren & Heard (eds), *Realms of Light.*
9. Solomon, *Ben-Hur: The Original Blockbuster*, pp.512–34.
10. The Magic Lantern 20.pdf.
11. Slide, Anthony. *Early American Cinema* (Scarecrow Press, 1994); 'The Stereopticon Illustrator of "Ben-Hur"', Library of Congress Registration (1896).
12. Solomon, *Ben-Hur: The Original Blockbuster*, pp.512–34.
13. *Ibid.*
14. The Magic Lantern 20.pdf.
15. Solomon, *Ben-Hur: The Original Blockbuster*, pp.512–34.
16. *Ibid.*; Gurlitz, Augustus T., 'Wallace v. Riley: A Landmark Case in Dramatic Copyright', *Columbia Law Review*, vol. 3, no. 2 (1896), pp.89–101; 'Riley Brothers. The Stereopticon Illustrator of "Ben-Hur": A Tale of the Christ', Library of Congress (1896); Holsinger, Bruce, 'The Visual Reproduction of Literature: Magic Lantern Shows and the Case of Ben-Hur', *Film History Journal*, vol. 13, no. 2 (2001), pp.123–35; Gurlitz, Augustus T., Letter to Walter Clark and Harper & Brothers (1896); The Magic Lantern 20.pdf.
17. *Ibid.*
18. *Ibid.*
19. *Ibid.*
20. *Ibid.*
21. Solomon, *Ben-Hur: The Original Blockbuster*, pp.512–34.

Chapter 6

1. Morsberger & Morsberger, *Lew Wallace: Militant Romantic*, pp.453–67; Solomon, *Ben-Hur: The Original Blockbuster*, pp.311–408.
2. https://www.vam.ac.uk › articles › the-story-of-theatre.
3. Booth, Michael R., *Theatre in the Victorian Age* (Cambridge University Press, 1991).
4. https://www.historytoday.com/miscellanies/britain-and-america%E2%80%99s-theatrical-war, Davis, Robert.
5. *Ibid.*
6. *Ibid.*
7. https://www.musicals101.com/index.html, John Kenrick.
8. https://www.gracegems.org/ATS/theater.htm.
9. Ryan, Barbara & Shamir, Milette (eds), *Bigger Than 'Ben-Hur': The Book, Its Adaptations, & Their Audiences* (Syracuse University Press, 2016), p.92.
10. Collins, Philip, *Dickens and the Drama* (Macmillan, 1963).
11. *Ibid.*

12. Ryan & Shamir (eds), *Bigger Than 'Ben-Hur'*, p.92.
13. Solomon, *Ben-Hur: The Original Blockbuster*, pp.311–408.
14. *Ibid.*
15. Morsberger & Morsberger, *Lew Wallace: Militant Romantic*, pp. 453–67; Solomon, *Ben-Hur: The Original Blockbuster*, pp.311–408.
16. Morsberger & Morsberger, *Lew Wallace: Militant Romantic*, pp.453–67; Hischak, Thomas S., *The Oxford Companion to the American Musical* (Oxford University Press, 2008), p.59; Solomon, *Ben-Hur: The Original Blockbuster*, pp.311–408.
17. https://www.ben-hur.com/william-farnum-ben-hur/.
18. Solomon, *Ben-Hur: The Original Blockbuster*, pp. 311–408.
19. Hewitt, Bernard, *The Renaissance Stage: Documents of Serlio* (Sabbattini & Furttenbach, University of Miami, 1958).
20. https://daily.jstor.org/diorama-quest-ce-que-cest/.
21. *Ibid.*
22. *Ibid.*
23. Oettermann, Stephan, *The Panorama: History of a Mass Medium* (Zone Books, 1997); https://www.vam.ac.uk › articles › the-story-of-theatre.
24. Solomon, *Ben-Hur: The Original Blockbuster*, pp.311–408; https://www.ben-hur.com/ben-hur-on-broadway/.
25. *Ibid.*
26. *Ibid.*
27. *Ibid.*
28. *Ibid.*
29. *Ibid.*
30. *Ibid.*
31. *Ibid.*
32. *Ibid.*; Hart, William S., *My Life East and West* (The Lakeside, 1994), p.153.
33. https://blogs.loc.gov/music/2013/07/ben-hur-and-music-to-race-chariots-by.
34. Hirsch, Foster, *The Boys from Syracuse: The Shuberts' Theatrical Empire* (Cooper Square Press, 1999), pp.38–39; Miller, Howard, 'In the Service of Christianity: Ben-Hur and the "Redemption" of the American Theater, 1899–1920', in Ryan, Barbara & Shamir, Milette (eds), *Bigger than Ben-Hur: The Book, Its Adaptations, & Their Audiences* (Syracuse University Press, 2016), pp.91–108; Solomon, *Ben-Hur: The Original Blockbuster*, pp.311–408.
35. Solomon, *Ben-Hur: The Original Blockbuster*, pp.338–39.
36. Collier, Constance, *Harlequinade* (Hutchinson, 1929), pp.175–76.
37. Solomon, *Ben-Hur: The Original Blockbuster*, pp.369–72.
38. *Ibid.*
39. *Ibid.*
40. Miller, 'In the Service of Christianity: Ben-Hur and the "Redemption" of the American Theater, 1899–1920', in Ryan & Shamir, *Bigger than Ben-Hur*, pp.91–108.
41. Gabler, Neal, *An Empire of Their Own: How the Jews Invented Hollywood* (Crown, 1988), p.42.
42. Ryan & Shamir, *Bigger Than Ben-Hur*, pp.91–108; Kenrick, John, *A History of the Musical Theatre* (Continuum International Publishing Group, 2008).
43. *Ibid.*
44. *Ibid.*
45. *Ibid.*

Chapter 7

1. Solnit, Rebecca, *Motion Studies: Time, Space and Eadweard Muybridge* (Bloomsbury, 2004); Mannoni, Laurent, *The Great Art of Light & Shadow* (University of Exeter Press, 2000), pp.304–19; Parkinson, David, *History of Film* (Thames & Hudson, 2012), p.13.
2. Mannoni, *The Great Art of Light & Shadow*, pp.320–63.
3. *Ibid.*
4. *Ibid.*
5. *Ibid.*
6. Parkinson, *History of Film*, pp.15, 16.
7. *Ibid.*
8. https://technica.inc/tech/dailytechnica-edison-film-kinetoscope.
9. Robinson, David, *From Peepshow to Palace: The Birth of American Film* (Columbia University Press, 1998); Mannoni, *The Great Art of Light & Shadow*, pp.387–416.
10. *Ibid.*
11. https://www.imdb.com/title/tt0132134/.
12. *Ibid.*
13. https://www.nytimes.com/athletic/2153332/2020/10/22/how-gentleman-jim-corbett-and-thomas-edison-gave-us-boxings-first-ppv/.
14. https://languageoflighting.com/history-of-lighting/this-is-the-day-thomas-edison-vitascope/.
15. *Ibid.*
16. *Ibid.*
17. https://en.wikipedia.org/wiki/The_Kiss_(1896_film).
18. Parkinson, *History of Film*, pp.16–17.
19. *Ibid.*
20. *Ibid.*
21. *Ibid.*
22. https://en.wikipedia.org/wiki/Georges Méliès.
23. Ibid; Parkinson, *History of Film*, p.18.
24. *Ibid.*
25. https://en.wikipedia.org/wiki/James_Williamson_(film_pioneer).
26. *Ibid.*
27. Musser, Charles, *Before the Nickelodeon: Edwin S. Porter and the Edison Manufacturing Company* (University of California Press, 1991). http://ark.cdlib.org/ark:/13030/ft3q2nb2gw/.
28. https://en.wikipedia.org/wiki Cecil Hepworth.
29. *Ibid*; https://en.wikipedia.org/wiki/Rescued_by_Rover.
30. https://en.wikipedia.org/wiki/Motion_Picture_Patents_Company.
31. *Ibid.*

Chapter 8

1. Solomon, *Ben-Hur: The Original Blockbuster*, pp.408–509.
2. Musser, Charles, *The Emergence of Cinema: The American Screen to 1907* (University of California Press, 1994), p.205.
3. Bowser, Eileen, *The Transformation of Cinema, 1907–1915* (University of California Press, 1990), p.20; Solomon, *Ben-Hur: The Original Blockbuster*, pp.534–52.

4. Crafton, Donald, *The Talkies: American Cinema's Transition to Sound, 1926–1931* (University of California Press, 1999), p.5; Solomon, *Ben-Hur: The Original Blockbuster*, pp.534–52.
5. Gauntier, Gene, *Blazing the Trail* (serialized in *Woman's Home Companion*, 1928).
6. Solomon, *Ben-Hur: The Original Blockbuster*, pp.534–52.
7. *Ibid.*
8. *Ibid.*
9. *Ibid.*
10. *Ibid.*
11. *Ibid.*
12. Slide, *Early American Cinema*, p.57; Solomon, *Ben-Hur: The Original Blockbuster*, pp.534–52.
13. Decherney, Peter, *Hollywood's Copyright Wars: From Edison to the Internet* (Columbia University Press, 2013), pp.45–54; Solomon, *Ben-Hur: The Original Blockbuster*, pp.534–52.
14. *Ibid.*
15. *Ibid.*
16. *Ibid.*
17. *Ibid.*
18. *Ibid.*; Kalem Co v Harper Brothers (222 U.S 55 (1911)).
19. Solomon, *Ben-Hur: The Original Blockbuster*, p.552.

Chapter 9

1. https://www.ben-hur.com/meet-lew-wallace/ben-hur/Ben-Hur, General Lew Wallace Study & Museum.
2. Slide, Anthony, *The Big V: A History of the Vitagraph Company* (Scarecrow Press, 1976).
3. https://betweenmovies.com/movie/the-life-of-moses-1909.
4. *Ibid.*
5. Schickel, Richard, *D.W. Griffith: An American Life* (Limelight Editions, 2004).
6. *Ibid.*
7. *Ibid.*
8. Schickel, *D.W. Griffith: An American Life*; Stokes, Melvyn. *D.W. Griffith's The Birth of a Nation: A History of the Most Controversial Motion Picture of All Time* (Oxford University Press, 2007).
9. *Ibid.*
10. Morsberger & Morsberger, *Lew Wallace: Militant Romantic*, p.470.
11. *Ibid.*, p.471.
12. Brownlow, Kevin, *The Parade's Gone By…* (Columbus Books, 1968), p.388.
13. Berg, A. Scott, *Goldwyn – A Biography* (Penguin Putnam Inc, Riverhead Books, 1989), pp.723–24.
14. Brownlow, *The Parade's Gone By…*, p.388.
15. Brunetta, Gian Pero, *The History of Italian Cinema: a Guide to Italian Film From its Origins to the Twenty-first Century* (2009), pp.15–67.
16. *Ibid.*
17. Stokes, *D.W. Griffith's The Birth of a Nation*.
18. *Ibid.*
19. *Ibid.*

20. Vieira, Mark A., *Cecil B. DeMille: The Art of the Hollywood Epic* (Running Press, 2014), pp.102–17.
21. *Ibid.*
22. *Ibid.*

Chapter 10

1. Beauchamp, Cari, *Without Lying Down: Frances Marion and the Powerful Women of Early Hollywood*, 1st ed. (University of California Press, 1997).
2. Brownlow, *The Parade's Gone By…*, p.390; Solomon, *Ben-Hur: The Original Blockbuster*, pp.571–77.
3. Solomon, *Ben-Hur: The Original Blockbuster*, p.571.
4. *Ibid.*, p.570.
5. *Ibid.*, pp.572–73.
6. *Ibid.*, p.573.
7. Brownlow, *The Parade's Gone By…*, p.391; Solomon, *Ben-Hur: The Original Blockbuster*, p.573.
8. https://www.britannica.com/biography/Francis-X-Bushman.
9. *Ibid.*
10. *Ibid.*
11. *Ibid.*
12. Brownlow, *The Parade's Gone By…*, p.390; Solomon, *Ben-Hur: The Original Blockbuster*, p.573.
13. Eyman, Scott, *Lion of Hollywood: The Life and Legend of Louis B. Mayer* (Simon & Schuster, 2005), p.100.
14. Solomon, *Ben-Hur: The Original Blockbuster*, p.574.
15. Brownlow, *The Parade's Gone By…*, p.391; https://www.imdb.com/title/tt0016641/trivia/?item=tr1861954.
16. Brownlow, *The Parade's Gone By…*, pp.393–94.
17. *Ibid.*, p.394.
18. *Ibid.*, p.449.
19. *Ibid.*
20. *Ibid.*
21. *Ibid.*
22. *Photoplay*, January 1925.
23. Brownlow, *The Parade's Gone By…*, pp.396–97.
24. Gutner, Howard, *MGM Style: Cedric Gibbons and the Art of the Golden Age of Hollywood* (Lyons Press, 2025), p.64.
25. Solomon, *Ben-Hur: The Original Blockbuster*, p.579; Brownlow, *The Parade's Gone By…*, p.402; Riley, Philip J. & Welch, Robert A. (eds), *The Wizard of MGM: Memoirs of A. Arnold Gillespie* (BearManor Media, 2012), pp.29–37.
26. *Ibid.* There are several differing accounts of what happened and how many had died. The true figure of any casualties has never been revealed.
27. Brownlow, *The Parade's Gone By…*, p.397.
28. *Ibid.*, p.403; Munn, Mike, *The Stories Behind the Scenes of the Great Film Epics* (Illustrated Publications, 1982), p.9.
29. Brownlow, *The Parade's Gone By…*, p.401.
30. *Ibid.*, p.399.

31. Eyman, *Lion of Hollywood*, p.104.
32. https://hollywoodessays.com/2017/09/18/there-would-be-no-greta-garbo-without-louis-b-mayer-sailing-to-italy-to-fix-the-epic-mess-that-was-ben-hur/.
33. DeCordova, Richard, *Picture Personalities: The Emergence of the Star System in America* (University of Illinois Press, 1990)
34. *Ibid.*
35. Barbas, Samantha, *Movie Crazy: Fans, Stars, and the Cult of Celebrity* (Palgrave Macmillan, 2001).
36. *Ibid.*
37. Solomon, *Ben-Hur: The Original Blockbuster*, pp.577–81.
38. *Ibid.*
39. *Ibid.*
40. *Ibid.*
41. *Ibid.*
42. *Ibid.*
43. *Ibid.*
44. *Ibid.*
45. *Ibid.*

Chapter 11

1. Brownlow, *The Parade's Gone By…*, p.405.
2. *Ibid.*
3. 'Theater Industry Gasps at Picture's Prodigal Expense/Ben Hur Film Staggers Imagination by Prodigal Outlay of Money, Time', *The Los Angeles Times* (4 October 1925), pp.19–20.
4. Eyman, *Lion of Hollywood*, p.107.
5. *Ibid.*, p.209; Howard, *MGM Style: Cedric Gibbons and the Art of the Golden Age of Hollywood*, pp.62–63.
6. Aquilina, Mike, *The World of Ben-Hur* (Sophia Institute Press, 2016), p.12.
7. Morsberger & Morsberger, *Lew Wallace: Militant Romantic*, p.476; Brownlow, *The Parade's Gone By…*, p.584.
8. Brownlow, The Parade's Gone By…, p.405.
9. Maeder, Edward (ed.), *Hollywood & History: Costume Design in Film* (Thames & Hudson, Los Angeles County Museum of Art, 1987), p.62; Personal correspondence with Manuel Carrera, Ph.D. *Accademia di Belle Arti di Carrara.*
10. https://www.motionpictures.org/2019/04/a-visit-to-theaterkunst-germanys-oldest-and-biggest-costume-design-house.
11. https://en.wikipedia.org/wiki/Harold_Grieve.
12. https://paperdollywood.com/index.php?main_page=page&id=28; Gutner, *MGM Style: Cedric Gibbons and the Art of the Golden Age of Hollywood*, pp.62–63.
13. https://ladailymirror.com/2022/02/28/mary-mallory-hollywood-heights-erte-and-the-movies-2/.
14. https://hickmet.com/products/erte-iras?srsltid=AfmBOooFXyeOGEIDVqlGMXisTLg9tAkCHbfAR93LubLpKBAeeZinpK-s.
15. Maeder, *Hollywood & History: Costume Design in Film*, p.62.
16. *Ibid.*
17. Brownlow, *The Parade's Gone By…*, p.405.

18. Morsberger & Morsberger, *Lew Wallace: Militant Romantic*, p.476; Hay, Peter, *MGM: When The Lion Roars* (Turner Publishing, 1991), p.28; https://recapretro.blogspot.com/2016/08/the-tale-is-in-telling.html.
19. Morsberger & Morsberger, *Lew Wallace: Militant Romantic*, p.476.
20. Madsen, Axel, *William Wyler: The Authorised Biography* (W.H. Allen, 1974), p.45.
21. Hay, *MGM: When The Lion Roars*, p.28; Brownlow, *The Parade's Gone By...*, p.408.
22. Morsberger & Morsberger, *Lew Wallace: Militant Romantic*, p.476; Brownlow, *The Parade's Gone By...*, p.408; The amount of the bonus varies from $100 to $5,000. It is possible that the initial bonus was $100 but later increased to $5,000 to further motivate the stunt performers.
23. Brownlow, *The Parade's Gone By...*, p.408; Solomon, *Ben-Hur: The Original Blockbuster*, p.585.
24. Eyman, *Lion of Hollywood*, p.108.
25. Hall, Sheldon & Neale, Stephen, *Epics, Spectacles, and Blockbusters: A Hollywood History* (Wayne State University Press, 2010), p.163.
26. Morsberger & Morsberger, *Lew Wallace: Militant Romantic*, p.477; According to *The Guinness Book of World Records* (2002), the chariot race was the most edited scene in cinema history. https://www.imdb.com/title/tt0016641/trivia/?item=tr1861954.
27. Brownlow, *The Parade's Gone By...*, p.408; Solomon, *Ben-Hur: The Original Blockbuster*, p.585.
28. https://en.wikipedia.org/wiki/Hays_Code.
29. Ibid.
30. https://www.imdb.com/title/tt0016641/parentalguide/; https://www.imdb.com/title/tt0016641/alternateversions/.
31. https://www.silentera.com/PSFL/data/B/BenHur1925.html.
32. The colour sequences were removed from the 1925 film and replaced with black and white footage when it was rereleased. These colour sequences were thought lost forever when they were found in the 1980s in a Czech film archive. The restoration of the 1925 film by Turner Broadcasting includes these colour sequences. https://www.ben-hur.com/ben-hur-1925-the-most-expensive-silent-film-ever-made.
33. Brownlow, *The Parade's Gone By...*, p.405.

Chapter 12

1. Fleming, E.J., *The Fixers: Eddie Mannix, Howard Strickling and the MGM Publicity Machine* (McFarland & Co, 2004).
2. Barbas, Samantha, *Movie Crazy: Fans, Stars, and the Cult of Celebrity* (Palgrave Macmillan, 2001); DeCordova, *Picture Personalities*.
3. *Ibid.*
4. *Ibid.*
5. *Ibid.*
6. Slide, Anthony, *Inside the Hollywood Fan Magazine: A History of Star Makers, Fabricators, and Gossip Mongers* (University Press of Mississippi, 2010).
7. Bernays, Edward, *Crystallizing Public Opinion*, https://gutenberg.org/cache/epub/61364/pg61364-images.html
8. *Ibid.*
9. Solomon, *Ben-Hur: The Original Blockbuster*, pp.596–617.
10. *Ibid.*

11. *The Daily Variety* (6 January 1926); https://goldenglobes.com/articles/restored-hfpa-ben-hur-tale-christ-1925.
12. Brownlow, *The Parade's Gone By…*, p.410.
13. Solomon, *Ben-Hur: The Original Blockbuster*, pp.596–617.
14. Gomery, Douglas, *The Hollywood Studio System* (BFI Cinema, 1986).
15. Hansen, Miriam, *Babel and Babylon: Spectatorship in American Silent Film* (Harvard University Press, 1991).
16. https://www.ben-hur.com/ben-hur-1925-the-most-expensive-silent-film-ever-made/.
17. Schatz, Thomas, *The Genius of the System: Hollywood Filmmaking in the Studio Era* (Henry Holt & Co, 1988), p.210.
18. Exhibitor's Trade Review (May–Aug 1925), https://archive.org/details/e00newy/page/n771/mode/2up?q=Ben-Hur.
19. Thompson, Kristen & Bordwell, David, *Film History: An Introduction* (3rd ed.) (McGraw-Hill, 2010).
20. Balio, Tino, *Grand Design: Hollywood as a Modern Business Enterprise, 1930–1939* (University of California Press, 1995).
21. Brownlow, *The Parade's Gone By…*, p.410.
22. Solomon, *Ben-Hur: The Original Blockbuster,* pp.617–21; Brownlow, *The Parade's Gone By…*, p.411.

Chapter 13

1. Eyman, *Lion of Hollywood*, p.110.
2. *Ibid.*, p.112.
3. Kemp, Philip (ed.), *Cinema: The Whole Story* (Thames & Hudson, 2011), pp.78–79.
4. Altman, Rick, *Silent Film Sound* (Columbia University Press, 2004).
5. Eyman, *Lion of Hollywood*, p.142.
6. *Ibid.*, pp.147–48.
7. *Ibid.*
8. Hay, *MGM: When The Lion Roars*, pp.68–90.
9. Eyman, *Lion of Hollywood*, p.148.
10. Docherty, Thomas, *Pre-Code Hollywood: Sex, Immorality, and Insurrection in American Cinema, 1930–1934* (Columbia University Press, 1999).
11. *Ibid.*
12. Vieira, Mark, *Irving Thalberg: Boy Wonder to Producer Prince* (University of California Press, 2009), p.252.
13. *Ibid.*
14. Wilson, Steve, *The Making of Gone with the Wind* (University of Texas Press, 2014).
15. *Ibid.*
16. Box Office Mojo (2024). All-Time Box Office Adjusted for Inflation.
17. Eyman, *Lion of Hollywood*, p.207.
18. https://indypendent.org/2023/08/hollywood-is-a-union-town-but-the-history-is-complicated/; https://www.latimes.com/archives/la-xpm-2000-jan-02-me-50000-story.html.
19. Eyman, *Lion of Hollywood*, pp.240–41.
20. Schatz, Thomas, *Boom and Bust: American Cinema in the 1940s* (University of California Press, 1997).
21. *Ibid.*

22. *Ibid.*
23. Ceplair, Larry, *The Inquisition in Hollywood: Politics in the Film Community 1930–1960* (Doubleday & Co, 1980), pp.75–78.
24. U.S. v. Paramount Pictures, Inc., 334 U.S. 131 (1948); Gomery, *The Hollywood Studio System*, 71.
25. Fleming, E.J., *The Fixers*, p.232.
26. Gomery, *The Hollywood Studio System*, p.71.

Chapter 14

1. Finke, Roger & Stark, Rodney, *The Churching of America, 1776–2005: Winners and Losers in Our Religious Economy* (Rutgers University Press, 2005): 'This Godless Communism' was an American propaganda comic feature that appeared in *Treasure Chest*, a biweekly, subscription-only comic book distributed in parochial schools across the US from 1946 to 1972.
2. Belton, John, *Widescreen Cinema* (Harvard University Press, 1992).
3. Lindvall, Terry & Quicke, Andrew, *Celluloid Sermons: The Emergence of the Christian Film Industry, 1930–1986* (NYU Press, 2011).
4. Wood, Robin, *Hollywood from Vietnam to Reagan* (Columbia University Press, 1986).
5. https://catalog.afi.com/Film/26090-SAMSON-ANDDELILAH?sid=62b0a901-160b-4824-bbcf-9eddfeedc69a&sr=0.16342735&cp=1&pos=0.
6. *Ibid.*
7. *Ibid.*
8. *Ibid.*
9. Ibid.
10. Solomon, Jon, *The Ancient World in Cinema* (Yale University Press, 2001), pp.216–17.
11. Ricci, Steven, *Cinema and Fascism: Italian Film and Society, 1922–1943* (University of California Press, 2008), p.69; https://en.wikipedia.org/wiki/Quo_Vadis_(1924_film)
12. Solomon, *The Ancient World in Cinema*, pp.81–82.
13. https://catalog.afi.com/Catalog/moviedetails/50257
14. *Ibid.*
15. *Ibid.*
16. *Ibid.*
17. Solomon, *The Ancient World in Cinema*, pp.216–17.
18. https://catalog.afi.com/Catalog/moviedetails/50257.
19. *Ibid.*
20. *Ibid.*
21. Richards, Jeffrey, *Hollywood's Ancient Worlds* (Continuum UK, 2008), pp.59–63.
22. *Ibid.*
23. *Ibid.*
24. Douglas, C. Lloyd, *The Robe* (1942).
25. Walker, J.M., 'Faith and Character in Lloyd Douglas's Fiction', *Studies in American Religious Literature*, 7(2) (1985), pp.113–29; Kozlovic, A., 'Film and Theology: The Robe and the Quest for Spiritual Meaning', *Theology Today*, 64(3) (2007), pp.350–60.
26. *Ibid.*
27. https://catalog.afi.com/Film/50996-THE-ROBE?sid=96df0476-556c-436f-b109-24239315c854&sr=6.5164757&cp=1&pos=0.
28. *Ibid.*

29. *Ibid.*
30. *Ibid.*
31. *Ibid.*
32. *Ibid.*
33. *Ibid.*
34. Richards, *Hollywood's Ancient Worlds*, p.69.
35. https://catalog.afi.com/Film/51179-DEMETRIUS-ANDTHEGLADIATORS?sid=05dbf8c3-579b-4b26-8ae2-41ec56cd79b3&sr=12.829758&cp=1&pos=0#
36. *Ibid.*
37. https://catalog.afi.com/Film/52028-THE-TENCOMMANDMENTS?sid=c9af78ef-dbcb-440c-8286-5af943a70436&sr=21.971237&cp=1&pos=0.
38. *Ibid.*
39. *Ibid.*
40. *Ibid.*
41. *Ibid.*
42. *Ibid.*
43. *Ibid.*
44. *Ibid.*

Chapter 15

1. https://en.wikipedia.org/wiki/Production_of_Ben-Hur_(1959_film); Hay, *MGM: When The Lion Roars*, p.319.
2. https://en.wikipedia.org/wiki/Production_of_Ben-Hur_(1959_film); *Ben-Hur* (1959) | 'The Making Of Ben-Hur | Behind The Scenes', https://www.youtube.com/watch?v=1UtPylOHoWE.
3. Hay, *MGM: When The Lion Roars*, p.318.
4. https://en.wikipedia.org/wiki/Production_of_Ben-Hur_(1959_film).
5. Madsen, *William Wyler: The Authorised Biography*, pp.336–37.
6. Solomon, *Ben-Hur: The Original Blockbuster*, p.731.
7. Madsen, *William Wyler: The Authorised Biography*, pp.338–39.
8. Morsberger & Morsberger, *Lew Wallace: Militant Romantic*, p. 480; https://catalog.afi.com/Film/52827-BEN-HUR.
8. Madsen, *William Wyler: The Authorised Biography*, pp.338–39.
9. Miller, Howard, 'The Charioteer and the Christ: Ben-Hur in America from the Gilded Age to the Culture Wars', *Indiana Magazine of History*, Vol. 104, No. 2, Lew Wallace (June 2008), pp.153–75.
10. https://en.wikipedia.org/wiki/Production_of_Ben-Hur_(1959_film).
11. https://en.wikipedia.org/wiki/Stephen_Boyd.
12. https://en.wikipedia.org/wiki/Production_of_Ben-Hur_(1959_film).
13. https://www.hollywoodreporter.com/news/general-news/claude-heater-dead-opera-singer-who-played-jesus-ben-hur-was-92-1297404/.
14. Madsen, *William Wyler: The Authorised Biography*, p.342.
15. Vidal, Gore, *Palimpsest: A Memoir* (Random House, 1995), pp.301–07; Solomon, *Ben-Hur: The Original Blockbuster*, pp.753–54.
16. https://www.karlowentunberg.com/ben-hur.
17. Freiman, Ray, *The Story of the Making of Ben-Hur: A Tale of Christ from MGM* (Random House Book, 1959).

18. *Ibid.*; Hay, *MGM: When The Lion Roars*, p.319.
19. *Ibid.*
20. Freiman, *The Story of the Making of Ben-Hur.*
21. *Ibid.*
22. *Ibid.*
23. *Ibid.*
24. *Ibid.*; Hay, *MGM: When The Lion Roars*, p.320.
25. *Ibid.*; https://en.wikipedia.org/wiki/Production_of_Ben-Hur_(1959_film).
26. https://en.wikipedia.org/wiki/Robert_Surtees_(cinematographer).
27. https://theasc.com/articles/flashback-ben-hur-1959.
28. *Ibid.* https://www.hollywoodreporter.com/news/general-news/claude-heater-dead-opera-singer-who-played-jesus-ben-hur-was-92-1297404/.

Chapter 16

1. https://en.wikipedia.org/wiki/Production_of_Ben-Hur_(1959_film).
2. Herman, Jan, *A Talent for Trouble: The Life of Hollywood's Most Acclaimed Director, William Wyler* (Da Capo Press,1997), p.403.
3. https://en.wikipedia.org/wiki/Production_of_Ben-Hur_(1959_film).
4. *Ibid.*
5. *Ibid.*
6. *Ibid.*
7. Model Ships in the Cinema, 2016, https://www.modelshipsinthecinema.com/2016/02/ben-hur-1959.html.
8. https://en.wikipedia.org/wiki/Production_of_Ben-Hur_(1959_film).
9. *Ibid.*
10. Riley & Welch (eds), *The Wizard of MGM: Memoirs of A. Arnold Gillespie*, p.121.
11. https://en.wikipedia.org/wiki/Production_of_Ben-Hur_(1959_film).
12. Solomon, *The Ancient World in the Cinema*, p.210.
13. *Ibid.*
14. Morsberger & Morsberger, *Lew Wallace: Militant Romantic*, p.483; Madsen, *William Wyler: The Authorised Biography*, p.344.
15. Seigel, Robert, *Ben-Hur The Making of an Epic*, https://www.blu-ray.com/news/?id=7408&utm.
16. *Ibid.*
17. https://en.wikipedia.org/wiki/Production_of_Ben-Hur_(1959_film).
18. Morsberger & Morsberger, *Lew Wallace: Militant Romantic*, p.483; Madsen, *William Wyler: The Authorised Biography*, p.482.
19. https://en.wikipedia.org/wiki/Production_of_Ben-Hur_(1959_film).
20. Solomon, *Ben-Hur: The Original Blockbuster*, p.766.
21. https://en.wikipedia.org/wiki/Production_of_Ben-Hur_(1959_film).
22. *Ibid.*
23. https://www.pololine.com/articles/the-horses-of-ben-hur-and-the-most-epic-scene-in-movie-history.
24. *Ibid.*
25. Morsberger & Morsberger, *Lew Wallace: Militant Romantic*, p.483.
26. *Ibid.*
27. Solomon, *Ben-Hur: The Original Blockbuster*, p.763.

28. *Ibid.*
29. Rothwell, Kenneth, *A History of Shakespeare on Screen: A Century of Film & Television* (Cambridge University Press, 2004), p.163.
30. Madsen, *William Wyler: The Authorised Biography*, p.351.
31. *Ibid.*
32. https://en.wikipedia.org/wiki/Production_of_Ben-Hur_(1959_film).
33. Morsberger & Morsberger, *Lew Wallace: Militant Romantic*, p.496.
34. Miller, 'The Charioteer and the Christ: Ben-Hur in America', *Indiana Magazine of History*, pp.153–75.
35. To avoid any unfavourable comparisons being made, MGM tried to suppress the 1925 version being screened at the same time the new version was released. They even went so far as to seize a collector's print and threaten to bring him up on charges. Ironically, the 1925 version was included as an extra in the 2005 four-disc DVD edition of the 1959 film.
36. https://en.wikipedia.org/wiki/Production_of_Ben-Hur_(1959_film).
37. *Ibid.*

Chapter 17

1. Solomon, *Ben-Hur: The Original Blockbuster*, pp.805–06; https://archives.shef.ac.uk/subjects/136?page=56&utm.
2. Solomon, *Ben-Hur: The Original Blockbuster*, pp.806–06.
3. *Ibid.*, pp.825–26.
4. Slide, Anthony, *Nitrate Won't Wait: A History of Film Preservation in the United States* (McFarland & Company, 2000).
5. 'The Survival of American Silent Feature Films: 1912–1929', by David Pierce, September 2013, The National Film Preservation Board, Library of Congress.
6. https://silentfilm.org/ben-hur-a-tale-of-the-christ- 1/#:~:text=In%201987%2C%20film%20historians%20Kevin,and%20two%2Dstrip%20Technicolor%20sequences.
7. https://www.kunc.org/2011-03-06/american-silent-films-repatriated-thanks-to-russia.
8. Library of Congress (2001). *Ben-Hur (1925) Restoration Project Report*, Washington, DC; https://catalog.afi.com/Catalog/moviedetails/2811.
9. Solomon, *Ben-Hur: The Original Blockbuster*, pp.846–47.
10. http://www.judahbenhur.com.
11. Solomon, *Ben-Hur: The Original Blockbuster*, pp.848–49; https://en.wikipedia.org/wiki/Ben_Hur_%282003_film%29.
12. Solomon, *Ben-Hur: The Original Blockbuster*, pp.851–52; https://fr.wikipedia.org/wiki/Ben-Hur_%28spectacle%2C_2006%29.
13. *Ibid.*
14. Solomon, *Ben-Hur: The Original Blockbuster*, pp.855–56.
15. https://www.independent.co.uk/arts-entertainment/theatre-dance/news/mad- genius-rides-in-to-resurrect-ben-hur-1789517.html.
16. *Ibid.*; https://www.spiegel.de/kultur/gesellschaft/ben-hur-als-live-spektakel-gott-wuerde-bravo-rufen-a-649887.html; https://news.pollstar.com/2010/02/02/ben-hur-goes-bust.
17. https://www.franz-abraham.com/.
18. https://en.wikipedia.org/wiki/Ben_Hur_(miniseries).
19. *Ibid.*
20. https://www.fxguide.com/fxfeatured/bigger_than_ben_hur.

21. https://en.wikipedia.org/wiki/Ben_Hur_(miniseries).
22. https://www.amazon.co.uk/Messala-Return-Ruin-Sequel-Ben-Hur-ebook/dp/B00TKTD6KS.
23. Wikipedia – Die freie Enzyklopädie.

Chapter 18

1. https://www.imdb.com/list/ls033805641/copy/.
2. https://deadline.com/2016/08/ben-hur-screenwriter-keith-clarke-on-the-making-of-1201802527/.
3. *Ibid.*
4. https://web.archive.org/web/20160316021210/http://deadline.com/2013/01/new-ben-hur-movie-remake-reboot-mgm-lew-wallace-novel-404155/.
5. https://variety.com/2014/film/news/paramount-joins-mgm-on-ben-hur-remake-exclusive-1201162065/.
6. Turner Classic Movies and MGM Catalog History. In 1996, Turner Broadcasting System merged with Time Warner, and in 2022 was absorbed by Warner Bros. Discovery. Turner Classic Movies (TCM) became part of Warner Bros. Discovery (WBD) in April 2022, following the merger of WarnerMedia (formerly Time Warner) with Discovery, Inc.
7. US Copyright Office: Public Domain Status of *Ben-Hur* (1880).
8. https://www.empireonline.com/movies/news/john-ridley-writing-new-ben-hur/.
9. https://www.hollywoodreporter.com/news/general-news/ben-hur-2016-ben-hur-916426/.
10. https://collider.com/timur-bekmambetov-ben-hur/.
11. https://www.hollywoodreporter.com/news/general-news/how-noah-overcame-christian-backlash-692424/.
12. https://www.pluggedin.com/blog/mark-burnett-roma-downey-talk-faith-film-ben-hur/.
13. *Ibid.*
14. https://www.theguardian.com/film/2014/aug/14/tom-hiddleston-ben-hur-remake-epic-film.
15. https://variety.com/2014/film/news/jack-huston-ben-hur-casting-1201281099.
16. https://variety.com/2014/film/news/toby-kebbell-ben-hur-messala-casting-1201308652/.
17. https://www.newyorker.com/magazine/2016/08/08/morgan-freemans-ben-hur.
18. https://www.refinery29.com/en-us/2016/08/120119/nazanin-boniadi-ben-hur-2016-interview.
19. https://archive.ph/20160619045415/http://mobile.nytimes.com/blogs/artsbeat/2015/06/25/paramount-promises-respectful-portrayal-of-jesus-in-ben-hur/?referer.
20. https://www.christiantoday.com/news/pope-francis-blesses-actor-playing-jesus-in-ben-hur-film.
21. https://en.wikipedia.org/wiki/Ben-Hur_(2016_film).
22. Behind the Lens: Jack Huston and Toby Kebbell Interview, https://behindthelensonline.net/site/interviews/jack-huston-toby-kebbell-round-and-round-the-spina-they-go-in-ben-hur/.
23. https://www.motionpictures.org/2016/08/youtube-inspired-director-used-gopro-cameras-capture-ben-hur-chariot-action/.
24. *Ibid.*
25. https://en.wikipedia.org/wiki/Ben-Hur_(2016_film).

26. https://www.theguardian.com/world/2015/mar/09/ben-hur-remake-banned-filming-rome-circus-maximus; https://en.wikipedia.org/wiki/Ben-Hur_(2016_film).
27. https://en.wikipedia.org/wiki/Ben-Hur_(2016_film).
28. https://www.motionpictures.org/2016/08/youtube-inspired-director-used-gopro-cameras-capture-ben-hur-chariot-action/.
29. *Ibid.*
30. https://humanehollywood.org/production/ben-hur/2016.
31. https://www.patheos.com/blogs/filmchat/2016/12/watch-making-sea-galley-sequence-ben-hur.htm.
32. *Ibid.*
33. https://www.technicolor.com/about/history/ben-hur-chariot-sequence-races-to-the-winners-circle-with-help-from-mr-x-mpc; https://www.youtube.com/watch?v=-pmSl5gWz1c.
34. https://en.wikipedia.org/wiki/Ben-Hur_(2016_film) has links to all major reviews of the film.
35. *Ibid.*
36. *Ibid.*
37. *Ibid.*

Chapter 19

1. Solomon, *Ben-Hur: The Original Blockbuster*, pp.408–509.
2. *Ibid.*, p.209.
3. *Ibid.*, pp.424–28.
4. *Ibid.*
5. *Ibid.*, pp.798–04.
6. https://commons.wikimedia.org/wiki/File:Steamer_%27Ben_Hur%27_on_Lake_McDonald,_Austin,_Tex_%286891833911%29.jpg; https://commons.wikimedia.org/wiki/File:Ben_Hur_Bicycle_%281896%29_%28ADVERT_413%29.jpeg.
7. https://www.thehenryford.org/collections-and-research/digital-collections/artifact/149699; Solomon, *Ben-Hur: The Original Blockbuster*, pp.428–40.
8. *Ibid.*
9. *Ibid.*
10. *Ibid.*, pp.446–48; https://cleopatrasboudoir.blogspot.com/2014/04/ben-hur-by-jergens-c1904.html.
11. *Ibid.*
12. Solomon, *Ben-Hur: The Original Blockbuster*, pp.475–88.
13. https://www.digitalcommonwealth.org/search/commonwealth:tm70nb20m.
14. https://www.ebay.com/shop/ben-hur-1925?_nkw=ben+hur+1925.
15. Solomon, *Ben-Hur: The Original Blockbuster*, pp.637–42; https://cleopatrasboudoir.blogspot.com/2014/04/ben-hur-by-jergens-c1904.html.
16. Solomon, *Ben-Hur: The Original Blockbuster*, pp.637–42.
17. *Ibid.*
18. *Ibid.*, pp.686–713.
19. *Ibid.*, pp.798–804.
20. *Ibid.*
21. *Ibid.*
22. *Ibid.*

23. *Ibid.*
24. https://en.wikipedia.org/wiki/Ben-Hur_(1959_film).
25. https://www.theatlantic.com/entertainment/archive/2016/08/why-hollywood-thought-remaking-ben-hur-was-a-good-idea/496868/.
26. https://www.etsy.com/uk/market/ben_hur; https://www.ebay.co.uk/sch/i.html?_nkw=Ben-Hur+&_sacat=1&_from=R40&_trksid=p2334524.m570.l1313&_odkw=Ben-Hur+merchandise&_osacat=1.
27. https://hickmet.com/products/erte-iras.

Chapter 20

1. The Gospel According to Matthew, Chapter 2, verses 1–12.
2. https://www.newadvent.org/fathers/0308.htm; Solomon, *Ben-Hur: The Original Blockbuster*, p.68.
3. Wilpert, Joseph, *Die Malereien der Katakomben Roms (Tafeln)* (Freiburg i.Br., 1903), plates 116 & 60.
4. https://www.attalus.org/translate/barbari.html#51B.
5. https://www.hymnsandcarolsofchristmas.com/Text/concerning_the_magi_and_their_na.htm.
6. Longenecker, Dwight, *Mystery of the Magi: The Quest to Identify the Three Wise Men* (Regnery History, 2017).
7. Trexler, Richard C., *The Journey of the Magi: Meanings in History of a Christian Story* (Princeton University Press, 1997), pp.38–39.
8. Latham, Ronald, *Marco Polo, The Travels* (Penguin Classics, 1958), pp.58–60.
9. https://reliquarian.com/2013/12/21/the-shrine-of-the-three-kings-grand-reliquary-of-the-magi.
10. Beard, Mary, North, John & Price, Simon, *Religions of Rome: Volume 1, A History* (Cambridge University Press, 1998).
11. Chadwick, Henry, *The Early Church* (Penguin Books, 1993), pp.24–25.
12. Beard *et al.*, *Religions of Rome: Volume 1, A History.*
13. Josephus, F. *The Jewish War*, trans. G.A. Williamson (Penguin Classics, 1981), 2, pp.175–77.
14. Janes, Dominic, *Romans & Christians* (Tempus, 2002), p.20; Horsley, Richard, A. (ed.), *Christian Origins* (Fortress Press, 2005), p.25; Goodman, Martin, *Rome and Jerusalem: The Clash of Ancient Civilizations* (Penguin, 2007), pp.20, 211–12.
15. Solomon, *Ben-Hur: The Original Blockbuster*, p.60.
16. Casson, Lionel, *The Ancient Mariners: Seafarers and Sea Fighters of the Mediterranean in Ancient Times* (Princeton University Press, 1991), pp.87, 188; James, Simon, 'The Roman Galley slaves: Ben-Hur and the birth of factoid', *Public Archaeology* 2 (1) (2001), pp.35–49.
17. Seager, Robin, *Pompey the Great: A Political Biography* (Wiley-Blackwell, 2002), pp. 47–48; Casson, Lionel, *The Ancient Mariners*, pp.177–83; Solomon, *Ben-Hur: The Original Blockbuster*, p.79.
18. https://en.wikipedia.org/wiki/Roman_triumph.
19. https://www.britannica.com/biography/Tiberius/Reign-as-emperor.
20. https://penelope.uchicago.edu/encyclopaedia_romana/circusmaximus/circusmaximus.html; Dodge, Hazel, *Spectacle in the Roman World* (Bristol Classical Press, 2011), p.22; Bell, Sinclair, 'Roman Chariot-Racing: Charioteers, Factions, Spectators', in Christesen,

Paul & Kyle, Donald J. (eds), *A Companion to Sport and Spectacle in Greek and Roman Antiquity* (Wiley Blackwell, 2013), p.496.

21. https://vroma.org/vromans/bmcmanus/charioteer.html.
22. https://vroma.org/vromans/bmcmanus/scorpus2.html.
23. Dodge, *Spectacle in the Roman World*, p.22; https://vroma.org/vromans/bmcmanus/charioteer.html; https://penelope.uchicago.edu/encyclopaedia_romana/circusmaximus/circusmaximus.html.
24. Wallace, *Ben-Hur: A Tale of the Christ*, p.214.
25. https://www.metmuseum.org/art/collection/search/247020.
26. The chariot was restored and reassembled in 2007. file:///C:/Users/gerip/Downloads/The_Etruscan_Chariot_from_Monteleone_di_Spoleto_The_Metropolitan_Museum_Journal_v_46_2011%20(3).pdf.
27. https://www.britishmuseum.org/collection/object/G_1894-1030-1.
28. Bell, Sinclair, 'The Costume of the Roman Charioteer – New Insights from a Statue Fragment in Hadrumentum (Sousse) and Related Sources', *Boreas*. Münstersche Beiträge zur Archäologie 41/42 (2018/2019) [2021], pp.73–87 + pls.
29. *Ibid.*
30. https://www.britannica.com/topic/Star-of-David.
31. Wallace, *Ben-Hur: A Tale of the Christ*, p.347, Chapter X.
32. The factions operated like a business, its racehorses were bred on private stud farms from as far afield as Spain and Cappadocia in Asia Minor, and a lot of time and money was invested in horse training, equipment and state-of-the-art chariots. The factions also competed for the services of the best charioteers, whose popular celebrity surpassed even that of modern sports heroes; https://www.vroma.org/vromans/bmcmanus/circus.html; https://penelope.uchicago.edu/encyclopaedia_romana/circusmaximus/circusmaximus.html; https://www.britannica.com/sports/chariot-racing.
33. St Clair, Kassia, *The Secret Lives of Colour* (John Murray Publishers, 2016), pp.162–64.
34. https://penelope.uchicago.edu/encyclopaedia_romana/circusmaximus/circusmaximus.html; Bell, 'Roman Chariot-Racing', in Christesen & Kyle (eds), *A Companion to Sport and Spectacle in Greek and Roman Antiquity*, p.495.
35. Fagan, Garrett G., *The Lure of the Arena: Social Psychology and the Crowd at the Roman Games* (Cambridge University Press, 2011).
36. https://penelope.uchicago.edu/encyclopaedia_romana/circusmaximus/circusmaximus.html.
37. Dodge, *Spectacle in the Roman World*, p.20.
38. Wallace, *Ben-Hur: A Tale of the Christ*, p.370.
39. https://penelope.uchicago.edu/encyclopaedia_romana/circusmaximus/circusmaximus.html.
40. Wallace, *Ben-Hur: A Tale of the Christ*, Book VI, ch. 1.
41. *Leviticus* 13–14, https://www.biblegateway.com/passage/?search=Leviticus%20 13-14&version=NIV.
42. https://www.historyextra.com/period/general-history/leprosy-history-disease-perception-treatment/.
43. Britton, Warwick J. *et al.*, 'Leprosy', *The Lancet*, Vol. 363, Issue 9416, pp.1209–19.
44. Edmond, Rod, *Leprosy and Empire: A Medical and Cultural History* (Cambridge University Press, 2006).
45. Wallace, *Ben-Hur: A Tale of the Christ*, p.410.

46. Matthew 27:48; Mark 15:36; Luke 23:36; John 19:29–30.
47. Wallace, *Ben-Hur: A Tale of the Christ*, p.416.
48. *Ibid.*
49. https://www.catacombesancallisto.it/en/le-origini-delle-catacombe.php.
50. Rutgers, V. *Subterranean Rome*, pp.5–8, 121–25; Lampe, Peter, *From Paul to Valentinus: Christians at Rome in the First Two Centuries* (T. & T. Clark International, 2003), pp.69, 381; Stevenson, James, *The Catacombs: Rediscovered Monuments of Early Christianity* (Thames & Hudson, 1978), p.7.

Bibliography

Altick, Richard Daniel, *The Shows of London* (Harvard University Press, 1978).

Altman, Rick, *Silent Film Sound* (Columbia University Press, 2004).

Aquilina, Mike, *The World of Ben-Hur* (Sophia Institute Press, 2016).

Balio, Tino, *Grand Design: Hollywood as a Modern Business Enterprise, 1930–1939* (University of California Press, 1995).

Barbas, Samantha, *Movie Crazy: Fans, Stars, and the Cult of Celebrity* (Palgrave Macmillan, 2001).

Beacham, Richard C., *The Roman Theatre and Its Audience* (Harvard University Press, 1991).

Beard, Mary, *Pompeii: The Life of a Roman Town* (Profile Books, 2008).

Beard, Mary, North, John & Price, Simon, *Religions of Rome: Volume 1, A History* (Cambridge University Press, 1998).

Beauchamp, Cari, *Without Lying Down: Frances Marion and the Powerful Women of Early Hollywood*, 1st edn (University of California Press, 1997).

Bebbington, D.W., *Evangelicalism in Modern Britain: A History from the 1730s to the 1980s* (Unwin Hyman, 1989).

Belton, John, *Widescreen Cinema* (Harvard University Press, 1992).

Berg, A. Scott, *Goldwyn: A Biography* (Riverhead Books, Penguin Putnam Inc., 1989).

Berger, John, *Ways of Seeing* (Penguin, 2008).

Booth, Michael R., *Theatre in the Victorian Age* (Cambridge University Press, 1991).

Bowser, Eileen, *The Transformation of Cinema, 1907–1915* (University of California Press, 1990).

Brown, Julie K., *The Gospel Stage: Christian Drama in America* (Cambridge University Press, 1994).

Brownlow, Kevin, *The Parade's Gone By…* (Columbus Books, 1968).

Brunetta, Gian Pero, *The History of Italian Cinema: a Guide to Italian Film From its Origins to the Twenty-first Century* (2009).

Bulwer-Lytton, Edward, *Last Days of Pompeii* (Richard Bentley, 1834).

Cameron, Alan, *Circus Factions: Blues and Greens at Rome and Byzantium* (Oxford, 1976).

Casson, Lionel, *The Ancient Mariners: Seafarers and Sea Fighters of the Mediterranean in Ancient Times* (Princeton University Press, 1991).

Castle, Terry, *Masquerade and Civilization: The Carnivalesque in Eighteenth-Century English Culture and Fiction* (Stanford University Press, 1986).

Castleman, Riva, *Prints of the Twentieth Century* (Thames & Hudson, 1988).

Ceplair, Larry, *The Inquisition in Hollywood: Politics in the Film Community 1930–1960* (Doubleday & Co, 1980).

Chadwick, Henry, *The Early Church* (Penguin Books, 1993).

Christesen, Paul & Kyle, Donald J. (eds), *A Companion to Sport and Spectacle in Greek and Roman Antiquity* (Wiley Blackwell, 2013).

Collier, Constance, *Harlequinade* (Hutchinson, 1929).

Collins, Philip, *Dickens and the Drama* (Macmillan, 1963).
Cook, D.A., *A History of Narrative Film* (3rd edn) (W.W. Norton & Company, 2000).
Crafton, Donald, *The Talkies: American Cinema's Transition to Sound, 1926–1931* (University of California Press, 1999).
Crangle, Richard, Van Dooren, Ine & Heard, Mervyn (eds), *Realms of Light: Uses and Perceptions of the Magic Lantern from the 17*th *to the 21*st *Century* (The Magic Lantern Society, 2005).
Daniel, Larry J., *Shiloh: The Battle That Changed the Civil War* (Simon & Schuster, 1997).
Decherney, Peter, *Hollywood's Copyright Wars: From Edison to the Internet* (Columbia University Press, 2013).
DeCordova, Richard, *Picture Personalities: The Emergence of the Star System in America* (University of Illinois Press, 1990).
Dillenberger, Jane, *Visual Arts and Christianity in America: From the Colonial Period to the Present* (Crossroad Publishing, 1989).
Docherty, Thomas, *Pre-Code Hollywood: Sex, Immorality, and Insurrection in American Cinema, 1930–1934* (Columbia University Press, 1999).
Dodge, Hazel, *Spectacle in the Roman World* (Bristol Classical Press, 2011).
Douglas, L.C., *The Robe* (Houghton Mifflin, 1942).
Dunning, John D., '"Good Stuff" Never Changes: John D. Dunning'. in Oldham, Gabriella (ed.), *First Cut: Conversations With Film Editors* (University of California Press, 1995).
Edmond, Rod, *Leprosy and Empire: A Medical and Cultural History* (Cambridge University Press, 2006).
Everson, William K., *American Silent Film* (Da Capo Press, 1998).
Eyman, Scott, *Lion of Hollywood: The Life and Legend of Louis B. Mayer* (Simon & Schuster, 2005).
Fagan, Garrett G., *The Lure of the Arena: Social Psychology and the Crowd at the Roman Games* (Cambridge University Press, 2011).
Finke, Roger & Stark, Rodney, *The Churching of America, 1776–2005: Winners and Losers in Our Religious Economy* (Rutgers University Press, 2005).
Fisher, James, *Historical Dictionary of American Theater: Beginnings* (Rowman & Littlefield, 2015).
Fleming, E.J., *The Fixers: Eddie Mannix, Howard Strickling and the MGM Publicity Machine* (McFarland & Co, 2004).
Freiman, Ray, *The Story of the Making of Ben-Hur: A Tale of the Christ, from Metro-Goldwyn-Mayer* (Random House, 1959).
Gabler, Neal, *An Empire of Their Own: How the Jews Invented Hollywood* (Crown, 1988).
Gomery, Douglas, *The Hollywood Studio System* (BFI Cinema, 1986).
Goodman, Martin, *Rome & Jerusalem: The Clash of Ancient Civilizations* (Penguin Books, 2008).
Gugin, Linda C. & St Clair, James E. (eds), *The Governors of Indiana* (Indiana Historical Society Press, 2006).
Gutner, Howard, *MGM Style: Cedric Gibbons and the Art of the Golden Age of Hollywood* (Lyons Press, 2025).
Hall, Sheldon & Neale, Stephen, *Epics, Spectacles, and Blockbusters: A Hollywood History* (Wayne State University Press, 2010).
Hansen, Miriam, *Babel and Babylon: Spectatorship in American Silent Film* (Harvard University Press, 1991).
Harris, Judith, *Pompeii Awakened: A Story of Rediscovery* (IB Tauris, 2007).

Hart, William S., *My Life East and West* (The Lakeside Press, 1994).
Hay, Peter, *MGM: When the Lion Roars* (Turner Publishing, 1991).
Hecht, Herman, *Pre-Cinema History: An Encyclopedia and Annotated Bibliography of the Moving Image before 1896* (Greenwood Press, 1999).
Herbert, Robert, *Impressionism: Art, Leisure, and Parisian Society* (Yale, 1988).
Herman, Jan, *A Talent for Trouble: The Life of Hollywood's Most Acclaimed Director, William Wyler* (Da Capo Press, 1997).
Hewitt, Bernard, *The Renaissance Stage: Documents of Serlio, Sabbattini & Furttenbach* (University of Miami, 1958).
Hirsch, Foster, *The Boys from Syracuse: The Shuberts' Theatrical Empire* (Cooper Square Press, 1999).
Hischak, Thomas S., *The Oxford Companion to the American Musical* (Oxford University Press, 2008).
Holsinger, Bruce, *Premodern Performance and the Postmodern Subject* (University of Chicago Press, 2005).
Horan, James D., *The Authentic Life of Billy the Kid* (Castle Books, 1955).
Horsley, Richard A. (eds), *Christian Origins* (Fortress Press, 2005).
Ivins, William M., *Prints and Visual Communication* (MIT Press, 1969).
Janes, Dominic, *Romans & Christians* (Tempus, 2002).
Josephus, Flavius, *The Jewish War*, trans. G.A. Williamson (Penguin Classics, 1981)
Kemp, Philip (eds), *Cinema: The Whole Story* (Thames & Hudson, 2011).
Kenrick, John, *A History of the Musical Theatre* (Continuum International Publishing Group, 2008).
Lampe, Peter, *From Paul to Valentinus: Christians at Rome in the First Two Centuries* (T. & T. Clark International, 2003).
Latham, Ronald (trans.), *Marco Polo, The Travels* (Penguin Classics, 1958).
Levine, Amy-Jill, *The Misunderstood Jew* (HarperOne, 2006).
Lindvall, Terry & Quicke, Andrew, *Celluloid Sermons: The Emergence of the Christian Film Industry, 1930–1986* (NYU Press, 2011).
Longenecker, Dwight, *Mystery of the Magi: The Quest to Identify the Three Wise Men* (Regnery History, 2017).
Macleod, Dianne Sachko, *Art and the Victorian Middle Class: Money and the Making of Cultural Identity* (Cambridge University Press, 1996).
Madsen, Axel, *William Wyler* (W.H. Allen, 1974).
Maeder, Edward (ed.), *Hollywood & History: Costume Design in Film* (Thames & Hudson, Los Angeles County Museum of Art, 1987).
Mainardi, Patricia, *The End of the Salon* (Cambridge Studies in New Art History and Criticism, 1994).
Mannoni, Laurent, *The Great Art of Light and Shadow: Archaeology of the Cinema* (University of Exeter Press, 2000).
Mayer, David, *Playing Out the Empire: Ben-Hur and Other Toga Plays and Films, 1883–1908. A Critical Anthology* (Clarendon Press, 1994).
McQueen, Kevin M., *The Amazing Mr. Wallace* (Indiana Historical Society Press, 2015).
MGM, *The Story of the Making of Ben-Hur: A Tale of the Christ* (Random House, 1959).
Miller, Gabriel, *William Wyler: The Life and Films of Hollywood's Most Celebrated Director* (University Press of Kentucky, 2013).
Miller, Howard, 'In the Service of Christianity: Ben-Hur and the "Redemption" of the American Theater, 1899–1920'. in *Bigger Than Ben-Hur: The Book, Its Adaptations, &*

Their Audiences, ed. Barbara Ryan and Milette Shamir (Syracuse University Press, 2016), pp.9–28.
Miller, Randall M., Stout, Harry S. & Wilson, Charles R. (eds), *Religion & The American Civil War* (Oxford University Press, 1998).
Morsberger, Robert E. & Katherine M., *Lew Wallace: Militant Romantic* (McGraw-Hill, 1980).
Munn, Mike, *The Stories Behind the Scenes of the Great Film Epics* (Illustrated Publications, 1982).
Musser, Charles, *Before the Nickelodeon: Edwin S. Porter and the Edison Manufacturing Company* (University of California Press, 1991).
Musser, Charles, *The Emergence of Cinema: The American Screen to 1907* (University of California Press, 1994).
Nead, Lynda, *Victorian Babylon: People, Streets and Images in Nineteenth-Century London* (Yale University Press, 2002).
Nochlin, Linda, *Women, Art, and Power* (Routledge, 2018).
Oettermann, Stephan, *The Panorama: History of a Mass Medium* (Zone Books, 1997).
Parkinson, David, *History of Film* (Thames & Hudson, 2012).
Ricci, Steven, *Cinema and Fascism: Italian Film and Society, 1922–1943* (University of California Press, 2008).
Richards, Jeffrey, *Hollywood's Ancient Worlds* (Continuum UK, 2008).
Riley, Philip J. & Welch, Robert A. (eds), *The Wizard of MGM: Memoirs of A. Arnold Gillespie* (BearManor Media, 2012).
Robinson, David, *From Peepshow to Palace: The Birth of American Film* (Columbia University Press, 1998).
Rothwell, Kenneth, *A History of Shakespeare on Screen: A Century of Film and Television* (Cambridge University Press, 2004).
Ruskin, John, *Modern Painters*, Vol. 3 (Project Gutenberg).
Rutgers, Leonard V., *Subterranean Rome: In Search of the Roots of Christianity in the Catacombs of the Eternal City* (Peeters, 2000).
Ryan, Barbara & Shamir, Milette (eds), *Bigger Than 'Ben-Hur': The Book, Its Adaptations, & Their Audiences* (Syracuse University Press, 2016).
St Clair, Kassia, *The Secret Lives of Colour* (John Murray Publishers, 2016).
Schatz, Thomas, *The Genius of the System: Hollywood Filmmaking in the Studio Era* (Henry Holt & Co, 2010).
Schatz, Thomas, *Boom and Bust: American Cinema in the 1940s* (University of California Press, 1997).
Schickel, Richard, *D.W. Griffith: An American Life* (Limelight Editions, 2004).
Seager, Robin, *Pompey the Great: A Political Biography* (Wiley-Blackwell, 2002).
Sherman, Daniel & Rogoff, Irit, *Museum Culture* (Routledge, 2017).
Sienkiewicz, H., *Quo Vadis: A Narrative of the Time of Nero*, trans. Jeremiah Curtin (Little, Brown & Co, 1896).
Silver, Kenneth, *Esprit de Corps* (Princeton University Press, 1992).
Slide, Anthony, *The Big V: A History of the Vitagraph Company* (Scarecrow Press, 1976).
Slide, Anthony, *Early American Cinema* (Scarecrow Press, 1994).
Slide, Anthony, *Nitrate Won't Wait: A History of Film Preservation in the United States* (McFarland & Company, 2000).
Smith, Jean Edward, *Grant* (Simon & Schuster, 2001).
Solnit, Rebecca, *Motion Studies: Time, Space and Eadweard Muybridge* (Bloomsbury, 2004).

Solomon, Aubrey, *Twentieth Century-Fox: A Corporate and Financial History* (Scarecrow Press, 1990).
Solomon, Jon, *Ben-Hur: The Original Blockbuster* (Edinburgh University Press, 2016).
Solomon, Jon, *The Ancient World in the Cinema* (Yale University Press, 2001).
Solomon, Jon, *Fugitive Sources: Ben-Hur and the Popular Art Property* (RBM: A Journal of Rare Books, 2001).
Stephens, Gail, *Shadow of Shiloh: Major General Lew Wallace in the Civil War* (Indiana Historical Society Press, 2010).
Stevenson, James, *The Catacombs: Rediscovered Monuments of Early Christianity* (Thames & Hudson, 1978).
Stokes, Melvyn *D.W. Griffith's The Birth of a Nation: A History of the Most Controversial Motion Picture of All Time* (Oxford University Press, 2007).
Thomas, Benjamin P., *Abraham Lincoln: A Biography* (Alfred A. Knopf, 1952).
Twyman, Michael, *Lithography 1800–1850* (Oxford University Press, 1970).
Tydeman, William, *The Theatre in the Middle Ages: Western European Stage Conditions, c.800–1576* (Cambridge University Press, 1978).
Trexler, Richard C., *The Journey of the Magi: Meanings in History of a Christian Story* (Princeton University Press, 1997).
Utley, Robert M., *Billy the Kid: A Short and Violent Life* (University of Nebraska Press, 1989).
Vidal, Gore, *Palimpsest: A Memoir* (Random House, 1995).
Vieira, Mark, *Irving Thalberg: Boy Wonder to Producer Prince* (University of California Press, 2009).
Vieira, Mark A., *Cecil B. DeMille: The Art of the Hollywood Epic* (Running Press, 2014).
Wallace, Lew, *Ben-Hur: A Tale of the Christ* (Harper & Brothers, 1880).
Wallace, Lew, *Lew Wallace: An Autobiography*, Vol. 2 (Harper & Brothers, 1906).
Wallace, Lew, *The Fair God* (Houghton Mifflin, 1873).
Wigger, J. H., *Taking Heaven by Storm: Methodism and the Rise of Popular Christianity in America* (Oxford University Press, 2005).
Wilpert, Joseph, *Die Malereien der Katakomben Roms (Tafeln)* (Freiburg i.Br., 1903).
Wilson, Steve, *The Making of Gone with the Wind* (University of Texas Press, 2014).
Wiseman, N.P., *Fabiola: or, The Church of the Catacombs* (Burns & Lambert, 1854).
Wood, Robin, *Hollywood from Vietnam to Reagan* (Columbia University Press, 1986).

Web Sources per chapter

Chapter 1

ArtUK – The Chariot Race
NICE Paintings – National Inventory of Continental European Paintings – VADS – Online resource for visual arts
https://www.artnet.com/artists/eadweard-muybridge
https://agbmuseum.org/exhibitions/the-von-wagner-code
https://museoulpianocheca.esy.es/
https://americanhistory.si.edu/collections/object/nmah_1002006

Chapter 2

https://www.ben-hur.com/meet-lew-wallace/author

Chapter 3
Unwin Hyman; https://www.puseyhouse.org.uk/info/the-oxford-movement
https://pompeiiarchaeologicalpark.com/the-last-days-of-pompeii/#introduction
https://victorianweb.org/religion/catholicism/1.html
https://culture.pl/en/article/the-man-behind-quo-vadis

Chapter 4
https://www.courtauldian.com/single-post/the-attitudes-of-lady-hamilton

Chapter 5
https://www.magiclantern.org.uk/history
The Magic Lantern 20.pdf

Chapter 6
https://www.vam.ac.uk/articles/the-story-of-theatre?srsltid=AfmBOopsU6t9x5bNfs_Yo26I_KNHoUxVK3SvevUj3XkrzfT2lUXGCwUo
https://www.gracegems.org/ATS/theater.htm
https://daily.jstor.org/diorama-quest-ce-que-cest/
https://www.ben-hur.com/ben-hur-on-broadway/
https://www.ben-hur.com/william-farnum-ben-hur/
https://blogs.loc.gov/music/2013/07/ben-hur-and-music-to-race-chariots-by

Chapter 7
https://technica.inc/tech/dailytechnica-edison-film-kinetoscope
https://www.imdb.com/title/tt0132134/
https://languageoflighting.com/history-of-lighting/this-is-the-day-thomas-edison-vitascope/
https://en.wikipedia.org/wiki/The_Kiss_(1896_film)
http://ark.cdlib.org/ark:/13030/ft3q2nb2gw/

Chapter 9
https://www.ben-hur.com/meet-lew-wallace/ben-hur/Ben-Hur
https://betweenmovies.com/movie/the-life-of-moses-1909

Chapter 10
https://www.britannica.com/biography/Francis-X-Bushman
https://www.imdb.com/title/tt0016641/trivia/?item=tr1861954.
https://hollywoodessays.com/2017/09/18/there-would-be-no-greta-garbo-without-louis-b-mayer-sailing-to-italy-to-fix-the-epic-mess-that-was-ben-hur/

Chapter 11
https://www.motionpictures.org/2019/04/a-visit-to-theaterkunst-germanys-oldest-and-biggest-costume-design-house
https://en.wikipedia.org/wiki/Harold_Grieve
https://paperdollywood.com/index.php?main_page=page&id=28;
https://hickmet.com/products/erte-iras?srsltid=AfmBOooFXyeOGEIDVqlGMXisTLg9tAkCHbfAR93LubLpKBAeeZinpK-s
https://recapretro.blogspot.com/2016/08/the-tale-is-in-telling.html
https://www.imdb.com/title/tt0016641/trivia/?item=tr1861954.

https://en.wikipedia.org/wiki/Hays_Code
https://www.silentera.com/PSFL/data/B/BenHur1925.html
https://www.ben-hur.com/ben-hur-1925-the-most-expensive-silent-film-ever-made

Chapter 12
https://gutenberg.org/cache/epub/61364/pg61364-images.html
https://goldenglobes.com/articles/restored-hfpa-ben-hur-tale-christ-1925
https://www.ben-hur.com/ben-hur-1925-the-most-expensive-silent-film-ever-made/
https://archive.org/details/e00newy/page/n771/mode/2up?q=Ben-Hur

Chapter 13
https://indypendent.org/2023/08/hollywood-is-a-union-town-but-the-history-is-complicated/
https://www.latimes.com/archives/la-xpm-2000-jan-02-me-50000-story.html

Chapter 14
https://catalog.afi.com/Film/26090-SAMSON-ANDDELILAH?sid=62b0a901-160b-4824-bbcf-9eddfeedc69a&sr=0.16342735&cp=1&pos=0
https://en.wikipedia.org/wiki/Quo_Vadis_(1924_film)
https://catalog.afi.com/Catalog/moviedetails/50257
https://catalog.afi.com/Film/50996-THE-ROBE?sid=96df0476-556c-436f-b109-24239315c854&sr=6.5164757&cp=1&pos=0
https://catalog.afi.com/Film/51179-DEMETRIUS-ANDTHEGLADIATORS?sid=05dbf8c3-579b-4b26-8ae2-41ec56cd79b3&sr=12.829758&cp=1&pos=0#
https://catalog.afi.com/Film/52028-THE-TENCOMMANDMENTS?sid=c9af78ef-dbcb-440c-8286-5af943a70436&sr=21.971237&cp=1&pos=0

Chapter 15
https://catalog.afi.com/Film/52827-BEN-HUR
https://en.wikipedia.org/wiki/Production_of_Ben-Hur_(1959_film)
https://en.wikipedia.org/wiki/Robert_Surtees_(cinematographer)
https://en.wikipedia.org/wiki/Stephen_Boyd
https://karlowentunberg.com/ben-hur
https://theasc.com/articles/flashback-ben-hur-1959

Chapter 16
https://en.wikipedia.org/wiki/Production_of_Ben-Hur_(1959_film)
https://www.modelshipsinthecinema.com/2016/02/ben-hur-1959.html
https://www.pololine.com/articles/the-horses-of-ben-hur-and-the-most-epic-scene-in-movie-history

Chapter 17
https://archives.shef.ac.uk/subjects/136?page=56&utm
https://catalog.afi.com/Catalog/moviedetails/2811
https://en.wikipedia.org/wiki/Ben_Hur_%282003_film%29
https://en.wikipedia.org/wiki/Ben_Hur_(miniseries)
https://fr.wikipedia.org/wiki/Ben-Hur_%28spectacle%2C_2006%29

https://www.amazon.co.uk/Messala-Return-Ruin-Sequel-Ben-Hur-ebook/dp/B00TKTD6KS
https://www.fxguide.com/fxfeatured/bigger_than_ben_hur
https://www.franz-abraham.com/
https://silentfilm.org/ben-hur-a-tale-of-the-christ-1/#:~:text=In%201987%2C%20film%20historians%20Kevin,and%20two%2Dstrip%20Technicolor%20sequences
https://www.kunc.org/2011-03-06/american-silent-films-repatriated-thanks-to-russia
https://de.wikipedia.org/wiki/Ben-Hur_%E2%80%93_Sklave_Roms.

Chapter 18
https://deadline.com/2016/08/ben-hur-screenwriter-keith-clarke-on-the-making-of-1201802527/
https://en.wikipedia.org/wiki/Ben-Hur_(2016_film)
https://humanehollywood.org/production/ben-hur/2016
https://www.imdb.com/list/ls033805641/copy/
https://www.patheos.com/blogs/filmchat/2016/12/watch-making-sea-galley-sequence-ben-hur.htm
https://www.technicolor.com/about/history/ben-hur-chariot-sequence-races-to-the-winners-circle-with-help-from-mr-x-mpc
https://web.archive.org/web/20160316021210/http://deadline.com/2013/01/new-ben-hur-movie-remake-reboot-mgm-lew-wallace-novel-404155/

Chapter 19
https://cleopatrasboudoir.blogspot.com/2014/04/ben-hur-by-jergens-c1904.html
https://commons.wikimedia.org/wiki/File:Steamer_%27Ben_Hur%27_on_Lake_McDonald,_Austin,_Tex_%2868918339l1%29.jpg
https://www.ebay.co.uk/sch/i.html?_nkw=BenHur+&_sacat=1&_from=R40&_trksid=p2334524.m570.l1313&_odkw=Ben-Hur+merchandise&_osacat=1
https://www.ebay.com/shop/ben-hur-1925?_nkw=ben+hur+1925
https://www.etsy.com/uk/market/ben_hur
https://www.thehenryford.org/collections-and-research/digital-collections/artifact/149699
https://www.digitalcommonwealth.org/search/commonwealth:tm70nb20m
https://en.wikipedia.org/wiki/Ben-Hur_(1959_film)
https://hickmet.com/products/erte-iras

Chapter 20
https://www.newadvent.org/fathers/0308.htm
https://www.attalus.org/translate/barbari.html#51B
https://www.hymnsandcarolsofchristmas.com/Text/concerning_the_magi_and_their_na.htm
https://reliquarian.com/2013/12/21/the-shrine-of-the-three-kings-grand-reliquary-of-the-magi
https://en.wikipedia.org/wiki/Roman_triumph
https://www.britannica.com/biography/Tiberius/Reign-as-emperor
https://penelope.uchicago.edu/encyclopaedia_romana/circusmaximus/circusmaximus.html
https://www.britannica.com/sports/chariot-racing
https://www.britannica.com/topic/Star-of-David
https://www.britishmuseum.org/collection/object/G_1894-1030-1
https://www.vroma.org/vromans/bmcmanus/circus.html

https://vroma.org/vromans/bmcmanus/scorpus2.html
https://www.metmuseum.org/art/collection/search/247020
https://www.britishmuseum.org/collection/object/G_1894-1030-1
https://www.biblegateway.com/passage/?search=Leviticus%2013-14&version=NIV
https://www.catacombesancallisto.it/en/le-origini-delle-catacombe.php

Archival and Legal Sources

Federal Copyright Records, Library of Congress, 'Selections from Ben-Hur Adapted for Readings with Tableaux', Registration No. A1887-239.

Garfield, James, Letter to Lew Wallace (1881), Garfield Papers, Library of Congress.

Gurlitz, Augustus T., 'Wallace v. Riley: A Landmark Case in Dramatic Copyright', *Columbia Law Review*, vol. 3, no. 2 (1896).

Gurlitz, Augustus T., Letter to Walter Clark and Harper & Brothers (1896), Archives of Clark & Cox Productions.

Kalem Co v Harper Brothers, 222 U.S 55 (1911).

Wallace, Lew, Letter to Harper & Brothers (1888), Archives of the General Lew Wallace Study and Museum, Crawfordsville, IN.

Wallace, Lew, 'Letter to Susan Wallace' (1879), Indiana Historical Society Archives.

Sears Catalogue (1913), Wallace Memorial Edition, Sears Roebuck Archives.

'Riley Brothers. The Stereopticon Illustrator of "Ben-Hur"', Library of Congress Registration (1896).

'Tribe of Ben-Hur Fraternal Organization Records', Indiana State Library Archives.

Nobel Prize Committee (1905), 'Award Citation for Henryk Sienkiewicz', Stockholm: The Swedish Academy.

US v. Paramount Pictures, Inc., 334 U.S. 131 (1948).

The Survival of American Silent Feature Films: 1912–1929 by David Pierce (September 2013), The National Film Preservation Board, Library of Congress.

Articles, Essays, and Journals

Bell, Sinclair, 'Roman Chariot-Racing: Charioteers, Factions, Spectators', in Christesen, Paul & Kyle, Donald J. (eds), *A Companion to Sport and Spectacle in Greek and Roman Antiquity* (Wiley Blackwell, 2013), p.495.

Bell, Sinclair, 'The Costume of the Roman Charioteer – New Insights from a Statue Fragment in Hadrumentum (Sousse) and Related Sources', *Boreas. Münstersche Beiträge zur Archäologie* 41/42 (2018/2019) [2021], pp.73–87 + pls.

Box Office Mojo (2024), All-Time Box Office Adjusted for Inflation.

Britton, Warwick J. *et al.*, 'Leprosy', *The Lancet*, vol. 363, Issue 9416, pp.1209–19.

Chapman, Mary, '"Living Pictures": Women and Tableaux Vivants in Nineteenth-Century American Fiction and Culture', *Wide Angle* 18.3 (1996), Ohio University.

Ellis, Samantha, 'The Miracle of Ben-Hur', *The Guardian* (8 October 2003), https://www.theguardian.com/stage/2003/oct/08/theatre.

Gauntier, Gene, *Blazing the Trail* (serialized in *Woman's Home Companion*, 1928).

Hamilton, Kristie, 'Ben-Hur and the Spectacle of Empire', *American Literary History* 7, no. 3 (1995), pp.422–45.

Holsinger, Bruce, 'The Visual Reproduction of Literature: Magic Lantern Shows and the Case of Ben-Hur', *Film History Journal*, vol. 13, no. 2 (2001).

Hopkin, J. 'Poland and Martyrdom: The Catholic Imagination in Sienkiewicz', *The Catholic Review*, 48(3) (2003), pp.212–26.

James, Simon, 'The Roman Galley Slaves: Ben-Hur and the Birth of a Factoid', *Public Archaeology* 2 (2001), pp.35–49.
Kozlovic, Anton K., 'Film and Theology: The Robe and the Quest for Spiritual Meaning', *Theology Today*, vol. 64, no. 3 (2007), pp.350–60.
Lewis, Robert M., 'Tableaux vivants: Parlor Theatricals in Victorian America', *Revue française d'études américaines*, No. 36, Les Lieux De La Vie Américaine (April 1988).
Miller, Howard, 'The Charioteer and the Christ: Ben-Hur in America from the Gilded Age to the Culture Wars', *Indiana Magazine of History* 104, no. 2 (June 2008), pp.153–75.
Monk, Claire, 'Tableaux Vivants and the Performance of Art', *New Theatre Quarterly* 6(24) (1990), pp.91–104.
Walker, J.M., 'Faith and Character in Lloyd Douglas's Fiction', *Studies in American Religious Literature*, vol. 7, no. 2 (1985).
Whitmore, William B., 'The Popular Reading and Recitation of Ben-Hur', *Indiana Magazine of History*, vol. 45, no. 3 (1949), pp.207–19.
file:///C:/Users/gerip/Downloads/The_Etruscan_Chariot_from_Monteleone_di_Spoleto_The_Metropolitan_Museum_Journal_v_46_2011%20(3).pdf.

Books, Magazines and Periodicals

Boston Globe (12 March 1888), 'Art and Drama: The Ben-Hur Tableaux'.
Detroit Free Press (7 April 1888), 'Recitationists of Note'.
Gauntier, Gene, 'Blazing the Trail' (ed. Gertrude B. Lane), *Woman's Home Companion* (October 1928), p.186. PDF copy in the Women Film Pioneers Project, Columbia University, https://www.ben-hur.com.
Hollywood Reporter, https://www.hollywoodreporter.com/news/general-news/claude-heater-dead-opera-singer-who-played-jesus-ben-hur-was-92-1297404/
Los Angeles Daily Mirror, https://ladailymirror.com/2022/02/28/mary-mallory-hollywood-heights-erte-and-the-movies-2/
New York Times, https://www.nytimes.com/athletic/2153332/2020/10/22/how-gentleman-jim-corbett-and-thomas-edison-gave-us-boxings-first-ppv/
Photoplay (25 January 1925).
Tablet Magazine, 'The Miracle of Ben-Hur', https://www.tabletmag.com/sections/arts-letters/articles/miracle-ben-hur.
The Art Journal (1875–1887), New Series, Vol. 3 (1877), pp.123–24. Published by Brooklyn Museum, https://www.jstor.org/stable/i20569000.
The Los Angeles Times, (4 October 1925), 'Theater Industry Gasps at Picture's Prodigal Expense/Ben Hur Film Staggers Imagination by Prodigal Outlay of Money, Time', pp.19–20.
The New Magic Lantern Journal, https://www.magiclantern.org.uk/new-magic-lantern-journal/pdfs/4008632a.pdf.
The New York Art Journal.
https://www.historyextra.com/period/general-history/leprosy-history-disease-perception-treatment/

Online news

https://archive.ph/20160619045415/http://mobile.nytimes.com/blogs/artsbeat/2015/06/25/paramount-promises-respectful-portrayal-of-jesus-in-ben-hur/?refererhttps://www.theatlantic.com/entertainment/archive/2016/08/why-hollywood-thought-remaking-ben-hur-was-a-good-idea/496868/

https://behindthelensonline.net/site/interviews/jack-huston-toby-kebbell-round-and-round-the-spina-they-go-in-ben-hur/
https://collider.com/timur-bekmambetov-ben-hur/
https://www.christianpost.com/news/ben-hur-2016-movie-film-outreach-church-screenings.html
https://www.christiantoday.com/news/pope-francis-blesses-actor-playing-jesus-in-ben-hur-film
https://www.empireonline.com/movies/news/john-ridley-writing-new-ben-hur/
https://www.guardian.com/film/2014/aug/14/tom-hiddleston-ben-hur-remake-epic-film
https://www.guardian.com/film/2016/sep/10/ben-hur-film-failure-2016-version
https://www.guardian.com/world/2015/mar/09/ben-hur-remake-banned-filming-rome-circus-maximus
https://www.hollywoodreporter.com/news/general-news/ben-hur-2016-ben-hur-916426/
https://www.hollywoodreporter.com/news/general-news/claude-heater-dead-opera-singer-who-played-jesus-ben-hur-was-92-1297404/
https://www.hollywoodreporter.com/news/general-news/how-noah-overcame-christian-backlash-692424/
https://humanehollywood.org/production/ben-hur/2016
https://www.independent.co.uk/arts-entertainment/theatre-dance/news/mad-genius-rides-in-to-resurrect-ben-hur-1789517.html
https://www.motionpictures.org/2016/08/youtube-inspired-director-used-gopro-cameras-capture-ben-hur-chariot-action/
https://www.newyorker.com/magazine/2016/08/08/morgan-freemans-ben-hur
https://news.pollstar.com/2010/02/02/ben-hur-goes-bust
https://www.patheos.com/blogs/filmchat/2016/12/watch-making-sea-galley-sequence-ben-hur.htm
https://www.pluggedin.com/blog/mark-burnett-roma-downey-talk-faith-film-ben-hur/
https://www.publishersweekly.com/pw/by-topic/industry-news/religion/article/71082-ben-hur-novelization-launches-faith-based-movie-tie-in.html
https://www.refinery29.com/en-us/2016/08/120119/nazanin-boniadi-ben-hur-2016-interview
https://www.spiegel.de/kultur/gesellschaft/ben-hur-als-live-spektakel-gott-wuerde-bravo-rufen-a-649887.html
https://www.technicolor.com/about/history/ben-hur-chariot-sequence-races-to-the-winners-circle-with-help-from-mr-x-mpc
https://variety.com/2014/film/news/jack-huston-ben-hur-casting-1201281099
https://variety.com/2014/film/news/paramount-joins-mgm-on-ben-hur-remake-exclusive-1201162065/
https://variety.com/2014/film/news/toby-kebbell-ben-hur-messala-casting-1201308652/
https://variety.com/2016/film/reviews/ben-hur-review-1201837567/
https://www.youtube.com/watch?v=-pmSl5gWz1c

Video

Ben-Hur (1959) | The Making Of Ben-Hur | Behind The Scenes, https://www.youtube.com/watch?v=1UtPylOHoWE
Seigel, Robert, *Ben-Hur: The Making of an Epic*, https://www.blu-ray.com/news/?id=7408&utm
https://www.youtube.com/watch?v=-pmSl5gWz1c